THE FILMS OF
Robert De Niro

THE FILMS OF
Robert De Niro

by DOUGLAS BRODE

A CITADEL PRESS BOOK

Published by Carol Publishing Group

Once again, for my mother and my father.

ACKNOWLEDGMENTS

With great thanks to my most helpful friends: Merci Sandberg-Wright, Mike Cidoni, Paul Willistein; everyone at Collector's Originals, Jerry Ohlinger's Movie Material Store, and Photofest; also, Warner Brothers, Paramount Pictures, MGM, Orion, Columbia, Savoy Pictures, TriStar, 20th Century-Fox, TriBeCa, Universal, United Artists, and Martin Scorsese.

A Citadel Press Book
Published by Carol Publishing Group
Citadel Press is a registered trademark of Carol Communications, Inc.
Editorial, sales and distribution, rights and permissions inquiries should be addressed to Carol Publishing Group, 120 Enterprise Avenue, Secaucus, N.J. 07094
In Canada: Canadian Manda Group, One Atlantic Avenue, Suite 105, Toronto, Ontario M6K 3E7

Carol Publishing Books may be purchased in bulk at special discounts for sales promotion, fund-raising, or educational purposes. Special editions can be created to specifications. For details, contact: Special Sales Department, Carol Publishing Group, 120 Enterprise Avenue, Secaucus, N.J. 07094

Designed by A. Christopher Simon

Manufactured in the United States of America

10 9 8 7 6 5 4 3 2 1

Library of Congress Cataloging-in-Publication Data

Brode, Douglas, 1943–
        The films of Robert De Niro / Douglas Brode.—Updated.
              p.   m.
        "A Citadel Press Book."
        ISBN 0-8065-1779-4 (pbk.)
        1. De Niro, Robert—Criticism and interpretation.   I. Title.
PN2287.D37B76 1996
791.43'028'092—dc20   96-36130
                                                                                           CIP

CONTENTS

Introduction

"You talkin' to me?"

Certainly, it's one of the most famous lines in contemporary American movies; doubtless among the best-remembered bits of screen dialogue from the seventies, uttered by Robert De Niro in *Taxi Driver*. His Travis Bickle rates as a remarkably unique human being, yet also an effectively universal symbol for the walking wounded who have, since the culture shocks of the late sixties, inhabited the mean streets of our major metropolises (along with our movie screens) in ever-increasing numbers. Travis was not De Niro's first great role, nor was it his last; and while *Taxi Driver* does not qualify as a perfectly realized work, it cannot be dismissed as the kind of cinematic wasteland most contemporary movie heroes inhabit. Still, Travis remains, some twenty years later, the single part with which De Niro is most often associated: lost and lonely, dark and dangerous, an invisible man who suddenly turns violent, finally forcing everyone to take notice that he exists.

Of that part, Robert De Niro has spoken with uncharacteristic eloquence. "I got this image of Travis as a crab," he explained several years ago. "I just had that image of him. . . . You know how a crab sort of walks sideways and has a gawky, awkward movement? Crabs are very straightforward, but straightforward to them is going to the left and to the right. They turn sideways, that's the way they're built." He is speaking of crabs and characters; he is also speaking, at least by implication, about himself. There are no modern screen performances that qualify as more "straightforward" than those De Niro has paraded before us. Still, there is Bobby the man to be dealt with, and he clearly prefers to flash that weird, wild, wonderfully macabre (if occasionally maniacal) grin as he turns first one way, then the other, avoiding contact at all costs, while he slips away sideways—sideways to us, though doubtless straightforward to him. There's a clear-cut agenda going on in his head that we can never guess, and he will never articulate. It's

1

MEN OF THE STREET: Throughout his career, De Niro has played disenfranchised contemporary characters, defined and dwarfed by their big city environments. Note the similarity in scene (despite the extreme difference in personality and genre) of his antiheroes in *Taxi Driver* and *Midnight Run*.

the motor of his every move, seemingly erratic though potentially understandable if we could ever somehow share the special way he sees things.

A Robert De Niro performance is forever etched in your memory; in person, Robert De Niro is something else; elusive and undefinable.

"I think your grandmother gave you the book I wrote about the sixties for Christmas one year," the slightly apprehensive author mentions as he and De Niro momentarily huddle following a late 1991 Manhattan press conference for Universal's then-upcoming release *Cape Fear*. Though the two have not spoken since United

Artists' similar press junket for *New York, New York* some fifteen years earlier, the author lives in the same upstate area numerous De Niro relatives call home.

"Yeah, yeah, I think maybe . . . ," he says, trying to remember, or perhaps marking time while a dozen more important things fly through his mind like bats bounding off the wall of a cave.

"I also did the *Films of* books on Hoffman, Nicholson, and Woody Allen," the author continues, treading lightly while clearly building up to something here.

"Yeah, yeah," De Niro mumbles, managing an enthusiastic smile, apparently not yet aware of what's coming. He thinks maybe he has seen them in the windows of bookstores, maybe he's even read one or two along the way.

"Guess who's next?" the author asks abruptly.

There's no verbal reply; only a moment of surprise, along with what looks like trepidation as De Niro at last briefly focuses his eyes on the person he's speaking to. Then, his eyebrows raise anxiously; the author nods toward him; De Niro pulls back slightly, as if apprehen-

sive, or fearful of attack. He could kiss you or he could kill you now, at least if he's remotely like some of those characters he plays. With him, as with them, there's no way of guessing what's about to come next. The sensation is scary—and scintillating.

"That okay?" the author asks softly.

De Niro considers for a moment. Then with wide, generous eyes, he nods his head affirmatively, while shrugging as if to say, "It doesn't really matter, anyway. What matters is the work. You treat the work fairly in your book, we got no problems. You don't, I'll survive." Leastways, that's what the author assumes De Niro means by the look. You can't be sure, though—not with De Niro. But by then, he's already gone, moved by some inner sense of panic or priority to dash off hurriedly. It's as if De Niro spends his whole life like Edmond O'Brien in *D.O.A.*, living under the threat of some ticking clock only he can see and hear.

Like so many of the characters he has played, Robert De Niro is a product of New York's mean streets. Born

on August 17, 1943, he spent his early years on the funky avenues of Greenwich Village and the tough turf of Little Italy, the former serving as the basis for his artistic inclinations, the latter an introduction to the alienation and rough realism he would so often portray on-screen. "Bobby Milk" is what the urban rednecks of the Lower East Side called him, owing to De Niro's pallid complexion, frail build, and reticent manner; while other kids carried switchblades, he was the outsider whose nose was always buried in the pages of one of those paperback books he carried everywhere.

If he learned about life on the street, he discovered art in his home. Robert senior was a critically acclaimed abstract expressionist, working in varied mediums that included painting and poetry. Mrs. De Niro painted, too (she sold one to the Museum of Modern Art), and also edited an avant-garde literary magazine, *The Experimental Review*. For a while, the family lived on Bleecker Street, in the heart of the Village's bohemian culture during the mid-to-late 1950s. It appeared then as if Bobby would grow up in the center of an urban art colony; his father, a contemporary of Jackson Pollock's, had like him been introduced to the art world in Peggy Guggenheim's premier postwar gallery, The Art of This Century. The era of Kerouac and Ginsberg, this was a time of wine and cheese parties during which beatnik poetry would be read aloud, often to the tune of a solitary guitar or the primitive beat of bongo drums.

But his parents broke up when he was two; he moved with his mother to West Fourteenth Street, where she supported them through the more mundane, practical pursuit of a typing and offset-printing business. Initially, young Bobby expressed interest in painting and music, but by the age of ten was certain he wanted to act. School chums who visited his house still recall the numerous costumes hanging in his closets, which allowed young De Niro, when alone, to briefly become a series of characters he created for himself. At that time, he won his first role—the cowardly lion in a production of *The Wizard of Oz* at P.S. 41. During the following years, he maintained a dual life, alternating his time between membership in a rough street gang and studying at the New School for Social Research. By the time he was in high school, majoring in art and music, he'd completely succumbed to the freedom of the streets and the lure of the boards. At age sixteen, Bobby quit school to work as a professional actor, having auditioned for and received a part in a touring company's rendition of Chekhov's *The Bear*.

In short order, he then appeared in such Off-Broadway works as *One Night Stands of a Noisy Passenger* by Shelley Winters, *Schubert's Last Serenade* by Julie Bovasso, and *Glamour* by Jackie Curtis. In that last one, he played five roles. Actress Sally Kirkland recalls being so

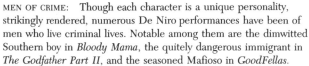

MEN OF CRIME: Though each character is a unique personality, strikingly rendered, numerous De Niro performances have been of men who live criminal lives. Notable among them are the dimwitted Southern boy in *Bloody Mama*, the quietly dangerous immigrant in *The Godfather Part II*, and the seasoned Mafioso in *GoodFellas*.

impressed by how vivid each of the individual roles was realized, as well as how adept De Niro was at leaping from one to the other, that she ran backstage afterward, gushing, "Do you know that you are going to be [an] incredible star?" With that show, Bobby also earned his first critical accolades, the *Village Voice* noting that De Niro "made clean, distinct character statements in a series of parts which many actors would have fused into a general mush."

Acting lessons with such prestigious teachers as Lee Strasberg and Stella Adler confirmed that the young De Niro had quickly become an accepted part of New York's serious-theater scene. But movie stardom of the Hollywood variety still seemed unlikely. De Niro's timing, however, could not have been better, for this was in the early sixties, precisely that moment of transition when Universal closed down its training school for young starlets, Warner Brothers stopped offering long-term

4

that the four individual photographs did not appear to be of the same person.

Most of his competitors were dreaming of becoming movie stars; De Niro became a movie star by dreaming of being a character actor. Years later, director John Hancock would, in a similar vein, comment, "He reminds me of Alec Guinness, submerging himself completely in a role. Guinness isn't a personality actor; he's a character actor who [also happens to have emerged as a] star—and that's Bobby. But [Bobby] has an eroticism Guinness never had," which is why he qualifies as full-blown superstar as well as actor.

It was Hancock who gave De Niro his first lead in a mainstream movie (*Bang the Drum Slowly*), though he'd already worked in a Roger Corman exploitation flick (*Bloody Mama*) and an ambitious comedy flop (*The Gang That Couldn't Shoot Straight*). But the first significant meeting with the director who would virtually change De Niro's life, as they formed an actor/filmmaker partnership that would define movie icons for the next two decades, was all but accidental. Martin Scorsese was best known for the documentary *Elvis on Tour* and was planning a tightly budgeted, autobiographical film when he accepted an invitation to film

MEN OF THE CLOTH: Though he tends to be remembered for his street people and criminal characterizations, another recurring figure in De Niro's films has been the spoiled priest. In *True Confessions*, Des has been true to the letter but not the spirit of Catholicism; in *We're No Angels*, the disguised convict Ned is true to the spirit of Catholicism if not the letter of religious law.

contracts, and MGM auctioned off everything on their back lot including Judy Garland's ruby slippers from *The Wizard of Oz*. Suddenly, a new type of filmmaking—a cross between the B-budget independents of the Roger Corman variety and the socially conscious avant-garde experiments—was about to hit the mainstream. The critically acclaimed *Putney Swope* and financially successful *Easy Rider*, in 1969, would force Hollywood to sit up and take notice of a changing of the guard, though in truth the counterculture films had begun creeping into the mainstream a year earlier.

De Niro appeared in several inexpensive pictures: *Greetings*, *The Wedding Party*, and *Hi, Mom!*—all for Brian De Palma. At that point, Bobby—like every other aspiring performer—had a photograph made up for his agent to use in trying to win him commercials and more significant roles. But whereas most performers opted for eight-by-ten "head shots"—posed pictures calculated to make them look as much as possible like traditional movie stars—De Niro instead insisted on a composite featuring a quartet of shots in which he wore so much makeups and was so distinctly locked into separate roles,

critic Jay Cocks's Manhattan home for dinner and, upon arriving, sensed that he recalled one of the other guests from his boyhood.

"I know you," Scorsese said.

"I don't know you," De Niro replied.

"Didn't you used to hang around Hester Street?" Scorsese persisted. De Niro admitted that he had. "And Kenmare Street?" Guilty as charged. Before long, they realized that while the two had never been friends, they'd constantly drifted past one another in their boyhoods.

Scorsese was about to cast *Mean Streets*. Though no one, himself included, could know it at the time, this would be a watershed film not only in his career but also in movie history. Marty was searching for someone with a street-savvy quality to play the semicrazed Johnny Boy; the role went to Robert De Niro. It's a cliché, of course, but as they say—the rest is history. Or, at least, movie history.

The unknowability of De Niro has been noted by numerous journalists. In 1989, *Playboy* commented that "De Niro is almost as famous for his silence as for his movie roles. He has thrown a Garbo-like cloak of mystery around himself, leaving gossip columnists a diet of hearsay. He apparently looks on interviews as a form of torture." The magazine's own interviewer, Lawrence Grobel, noted with exhaustion: "After a period of seven months—waiting for him to arrive late and knowing that he would leave early—I began to understand that it wasn't just me he was juggling around; it was his life. Every day, weekends included, De Niro lives a moment-to-moment existence, balancing his time among his children, his friends, his associates, his lovers, and himself. Like mercury, he slips right through your fingers; you can't grasp him, can't hold on to him. Try to shake his hand and it's limp. Try to look him in the eyes and they're darting around. Corner him and he sidesteps you. Ask him about his childhood, his parents, his interracial marriage, and he's ducking out the door. Robert De Niro, it finally occurred to me, is the real-life White Rabbit, always on the move, always checking his watch, always late for every important date."

Of course, it's nothing new for an actor/star to be wary of the press. But De Niro is considered elusive even among his collaborators. "Terrific onstage," one actor who worked with him often in the early days but now prefers to remain anonymous recalls, "but very quiet backstage." Another performer agrees: "A very private person, not given to small talk." Roland Joffe, director of *The Mission*, smiled when he said, "De Niro, the man? There is an area of Bobby that I didn't get to know. He is very guarded, although I found him warm and person-

able. But I think it is very sane of Bob to hold back a part of himself in a working relationship . . . you have to feel that there is a part of you where a director's sticky fingers haven't pried. It's important for a performer to keep a sense of himself. You give up a lot as an actor, and Bob especially gives an enormous amount to the films he's in. So he most definitely needs his privacy. He has earned it."

Sometimes, former costars—especially females—allow us insight in their observations of such a charismatic male. Shelley Winters, who claims to have discovered De Niro, says, "Bobby will never talk about what made him the way he is, but I suspect he must have been a lonely kid, that somewhere along the line he was brutalized." Liza Minnelli, who played his brutalized wife in *New York, New York*, insists that the De Niro impact is based on "his complexity—you're never sure what he's going to do next. There's intensity and mystery. His eyes look out, but they also look in."

The two world-class American directors of our time that De Niro has worked with relate to him in extremely different ways. Martin Scorsese, who grew up in the same neighborhoods as De Niro and has directed the actor more times than any other filmmaker, insists that a shared vision is basic to their collaboration when he comments, "We see things the same way; we both have the sense of being outsiders." But Francis Ford Coppola—who immensely admires Bobby's talent, yet feels less comfortable with it than does Scorsese—has called De Niro "a strange, dark figure," adding, "I don't know from where he's looking at me. The only thing we agree on is I like him. But I don't know if Bobby likes himself."

Whether or not he does like himself, De Niro has been honing his chameleonlike skills since before he was a big star. Longtime friend and onetime fellow Off-Broadway actor Sally Kirkland recalls, "I always remember Bobby, in the early days, going to auditions with a portfolio of pictures of himself in various disguises, to prove to the casting directors he wasn't just an ethnic." He proved that early on and has, in his film and occasional live-theater roles, chosen projects in large part based on the "stretch" demanded of him, always desiring to be someone different up there on-screen, to conceal far more of himself than he reveals of the individual he's momentarily bringing to full-bodied life. Critics have duly noted this, their reviews ringing out with ecstatic words of praise for his breadth, as well as his depth, as an actor. In 1975, *Time* marveled: "Lean, with lanky brown hair and narrow, green-brown eyes, a pallid face by turns near-handsome and homely, he has the protective coloration of a chameleon." Reporter Paul Gardner, visiting the set of *The Deer Hunter*, was

MEN OF CHRIST: Though De Niro turned down Martin Scorsese's offer to play Jesus in *The Last Temptation of Christ*, he has in fact often played characters who, like Jesus, are crucified in numerous other films for that director. Note the similarly outstretched arms of the realistically portrayed but ultimately allegorical men in *Raging Bull* and *The King of Comedy*.

stunned to note that the Oscar winner "wandered in and out of the Holiday Inn with complete anonymity. Nothing about his features or size or voice suggests that he takes extraordinary possession of a camera. De Niro undergoes a chilling metamorphosis with each part, but offscreen he remains a nondescript face. . . . He could be a Village punkster or a college student. He could be anybody."

De Niro has rarely relied much on makeup to alter his appearance, *Raging Bull*'s partial facial reconstruction being the exception rather than the rule. Yet he is clearly a different person in each film, and none of those finely wrought parts correlates precisely to him. He is part chameleon, taking on the qualities of the world he temporarily enters, part invisible man, disappearing into the character. Once, while visiting family in Syracuse,

through the character, and it made him exciting to watch." But even as De Niro impressed others by trying a wide variety of character roles, from the inarticulate blue-collar worker in *Stanley and Iris* to the quietly handsome, highly educated yuppie in *Falling in Love,* Kael found herself recoiling: "He started turning himself into repugnant, flesh effigies of soulless characters." In 1983, she complained about his "disfiguring" himself in such films as *Raging Bull* and *King of Comedy:* "If De Niro . . . has removed himself from comparison with other handsome young actors, it's not because what he does now is more than acting. It's less; it's anti-acting." Admittedly, great actors of the past enjoyed "disfiguring" themselves to a degree, whether it was Lon Chaney (Sr.) earning himself a reputation as the Man of a Thousand Faces, including his Quasimodo in *Hunchback of Notre Dame,* or Charles Laughton trying on as many challenging roles (including Quasimodo) a generation later. Elegantly handsome Laurence Olivier likewise played a frightful hunchback in his adaptation of Shakespeare's *Richard III,* obviously taking great relish in burrowing deep into the dastardly character.

Yet that, for Kael, was the point: we were aware of the pleasure Olivier took in delivering the performance, as

MEN OF MONEY: Though the public may vividly remember the downtrodden heroes of films like *Taxi Driver* and *The Deer Hunter,* De Niro has also played men who acquire and are corrupted by great wealth. Des perfects his golf game in *True Confessions,* while Noodles toasts his newfound success in *Once Upon a Time in America.*

New York, De Niro visited the state fair and walked around the midway in a manner no other movie star could have. People assumed that this bearded guy in the windbreaker bore an uncanny resemblance to Robert De Niro in *The Deer Hunter*—was, in fact, the very kind of walking-wounded type De Niro had played so strikingly in that film. In another context entirely, one journalist wrote: "We wouldn't recognize him in the street because, in a sense, he is all around us."

This "disappearing act" performed by Hollywood's anonymous actor won De Niro considerable acclaim early on, though there were those who eventually objected to the absoluteness with which Bobby obliterated himself on-screen. In particular, the always intriguing, often irksome Pauline Kael—now retired from her post with *The New Yorker*—took objection. Originally, Kael—a major supporter of De Niro's work—praised the "bravura" in his early performances, those edgy, offbeat roles he did for Brian De Palma (*Hi, Mom!*), Scorsese (*Mean Streets*), and Coppola (*The Godfather II*): "You could feel the actor's excitement shining

he allowed something of himself to be recognizable, if only barely, under all that makeup. Though he never stooped to anything so obvious as winking at the audience, there was nonetheless a sense that only 99 percent of what we saw was Richard, the other 1 percent offering a faint touch of the great actor playing the misanthropic crookback king. "A great actor merges his soul with that of his characters—or, at least, gives us the illusion that he does," Kael continued, suggesting that Bobby fell short of true greatness: "De Niro in disguise denies his characters a soul. It's not merely that he hollows himself out and becomes Jake La Motta, or Des the priest in *True Confessions*, or Rupert Pupkin (in *King of Comedy*)—he makes them hollow, too, and merges with the characters' emptiness."

A fascinating point, like every point she makes. Not one, though, that many fans of modern cinema would agree with. De Niro continues to be widely regarded as the single greatest American film actor now working, Kael's complaints aside. Perhaps, though, her argument can be modified slightly, a germ of truth in her commentary acknowledged, though transformed into something more positive. Is it really a problem that so many of De

Niro's characterizations lack soul, or has he achieved such incredible status in large part by offering, in his rogues' gallery of characterizations, a reflection of a society that has seemingly lost its soul? Perhaps, beginning in the midsixties—the very time that Bobby began working as an actor—T. S. Eliot's prediction that modern life would turn into a wasteland has at last come true. De Niro is not only our most skilled actor, then, but also our most representative screen icon, in that his characters, however diverse they at first seem, actually embody Eliot's concept of contemporary existence: the hollow man.

Is Kael correct, then, in insisting De Niro fails to show us enough of himself, that being the element which keeps him from qualifying as a true genius-actor, or is that possibly the key to his genius? By denying us some aspect of the people he plays, Robert De Niro reminds us of his own ongoing search for himself, as well as our own. Centuries ago, Aristotle wrote that true tragedy comes when the audience experiences pity and fear simultaneously: pity for the character we watch, fear that he represents our own fate. If that is true, then De Niro's acting—including his comedic roles—is tragic in nature.

who the man is, and why he has provided us with the fascinating if eclectic array of characters—Bickle, Rupert Pupkin, Vito Corleone, Jake La Motta, Michael Vronsky—who have become basic staples of American film lore, all but defining urban alienation in the closing decades of the twentieth century.

So here are three such stories, which may strike the reader as nothing more than intriguing incidents from the life of Robert De Niro. On the other hand, they may provide some insight into the man behind the masks.

1. Shelley Winters, an early supporter who gave him a role in a play she wrote herself, vividly recalls a moment involving the prestardom Robert De Niro. In New York, Winters threw a Thanksgiving party for all the young actors who had become her "theatrical waifs, my babies." De Niro arrived early, his face beaming with pride at the thought of the pretty actress who would shortly arrive as his date. It was clear he had a huge crush on the girl, but as the holiday afternoon wore on, people arriving and leaving, the girl did not make an appearance. The

MEN OF DOUBT: Many of De Niro's most remarkable characterizations—including those in Martin Scorsese films—have cast him as insecure, troubled men who strike out violently at the world around them. They include Travis Bickle in *Taxi Driver* and Jimmy Doyle in *New York, New York*.

One reason De Niro avoids interviews is his fear that he'll be unable to express himself effectively in words. Director Ulu Grosbard (*True Confessions, Falling in Love*) admits this is true, but cautions it's wrong and unfair to assume that this proves that De Niro is not terribly sharp-witted. Grosbard observes: "De Niro is not as articulate [as certain other actors]—an example that intelligence and verbal facility don't [necessarily] go hand in hand." De Niro is every bit as bright as those actors who ramble on in words, sounding highly intelligent; his intelligence is merely of a more primal order, expressed in physical gesture and voice intonations—all brilliantly chosen, all right-on every single time—rather than through choice of words.

So De Niro loathes interviews and, when he on rare occasion actually puts himself through the horror of doing them, says little that's valuable. How, then, do we learn something of him, get a handle on what he's all about? Sometimes, an anecdote from a person's life can provide the key that unlocks a complex personality for us. In the case of a major talent, whose impressive body of work makes us want to understand and appreciate the personality behind the creations, an investigation of such moments proves useful. With Robert De Niro, such interpretation is perhaps the only way to get a sense of

MEN OF ALIENATION: More often than not, the De Niro character is a man who stands alone, removed from the normal flow of human life, so filmmakers have purposefully framed him in long shots that convey the sense of alienation. This theme runs through films (and characterizations) as different from one another as *Bang the Drum Slowly* and *The Godfather Part II.*

congregation sat down to dinner, De Niro with an empty space beside him, something he and the other partygoers tried their best to ignore. Just as dessert was being served, the girl rushed in, making lame, casual excuses for not arriving sooner, assuming the air of a striking beauty whose looks allow her to get away with such irresponsible behavior. Winters knew, from Bobby's eyes, how deeply hurt he was.

What impressed her most, though, was that he didn't say a thing to the girl, didn't even reveal his anger through body language. Today, Winters vividly recalls that after a while, he excused himself, went into Shelley's bedroom, and alone, pounded his fist against the headboard until his hand bled. After that, De Niro refused to speak to the girl ever again. Hence, a basis in reality for those characters (especially in such Scorsese films as *Taxi Driver* and *Raging Bull*) consumed by a violence they long repress, then suddenly, frightfully unleash.

2. If De Niro is known as a meticulous researcher who learns everything possible about not only his role but also

the world in which that character lives ("I want to earn the right to play a character," he has said in defense of his self-imposed homework), he is legendary for his refusal to rush into an interpretation of his character, allowing it to evolve slowly over a considerable period of time. Bovasso, the late playwright whose avant-garde piece *Serenade* was performed in 1973 at the Manhattan Theatre Club, remembered the rehearsal period as a time when the supposedly brilliant young actor appeared ready to destroy her delicate work with a bizarre bit of business. As Alfred, a construction worker who falls in love with a Radcliffe undergraduate, De Niro—clearly unable to get a full grasp on his character—asked Bovasso if she'd mind his doing one scene while eating breadsticks.

Though nervous about the idea, she consented, then realized in dismay that no one in the audience would be able to hear a word of her dialogue. Distraught, she watched the dress rehearsal, fearing the worst, only to see De Niro play the scene without the breadsticks, every line coming out not only audibly but also emotionally just right. When, with trepidation, Bovasso asked about the missing breadsticks, De Niro—somewhat surprised she'd even bothered to bring them up—shrugged and said, "I don't need them anymore."

Years later, Bernardo Bertolucci—who cast De Niro against type as a weak aristocrat in his epic *1900*—claimed, on reflection, that "the first few days were a nightmare. But I told myself that what I had felt about Bob when I met him was so strong I couldn't have been wrong. I began to try and help him build confidence, and slowly a fantastic [character] emerged. The fact is that with Bob, you mustn't judge by the first few days." So here, we have in a nutshell the essence of De Niro's acting approach.

3. Paul Schrader, who wrote *Taxi Driver*, recalls that, during planning of the film, Bobby admitted he had himself come up with an idea for a similar script seven years earlier. In it, he saw himself as playing a would-be assassin who wanders into the United Nations building and, at random, picks a foreign ambassador out of the crowd, then stalks and kills the man. Struck by the similarities between their two stories, Schrader insisted on interpreting De Niro's concept according to Freudian dream-symbolism, asking the actor to try to guess what the gun actually represented, why the setting had been the U.N.

When De Niro shrugged and shook his head, Schrader insisted that the gun represented the actor's talent, ready to go off, a loaded gun that people were at that point still unaware of, but which would eventually have to be fired. When that happened, the entire world would be forced to sit up and take notice. That is De Niro, the anonymous man of hidden genius, searching for success and exploding into the popular imagination.

As early as 1977, *Newsweek* noted: "Aside from his great talent, [his] protean quality is what distinguishes De Niro from other outstanding actors of his generation like Al Pacino . . . and Dustin Hoffman. It's not just the personal rhythm of good acting that De Niro gives you. He gives you the shock of becoming, of a metamorphosis that can be thrilling, moving, or frightening." Those very qualities immediately established Bobby as our greatest screen actor, on the level of a Guinness or Olivier. Or, in American movies, such performers as Chaney and Paul Muni, all but unrecognizable from one picture to the next.

Bobby, in a rare moment of unguarded articulation and psychological self-examination, explained the appeal of doing such a disappearing act back in 1975: "To totally submerge into another character and experience life through him, without having to risk the real-life consequences—well, it's a cheap way to do things you would never dare to do yourself." Acting, then, is a way to cheat death, at least in a manner of speaking; if it's true that once is not enough, an actor lives a thousand lives before he dies.

However, those very qualities might have seemed likely to rule De Niro out as an icon, a popular symbol of his time, the modern equivalent of, say, James Dean in the 1950s, who in *East of Eden*, *Rebel Without a Cause*, and *Giant* represented and reflected the very audience that came to see him. In *The Graduate*, Hoffman had temporarily taken on just such an aura for the youthful audience of the late 1960s, though he shied away from such pop symbolism, searching for roles (such as *Midnight Cowboy*) that were highly specific characterizations rather than roles that, like his Benjamin Braddock, would appear as symbolic of his generation. Fascinatingly enough, then, it was De Niro who came to best represent his times—not, ironically, by playing the same character again and again, but rather by following in the footsteps of mighty Marlon (the actor he'd replaced in *The Godfather II*, thereby creating an unavoidable point of comparison). Brando had played a youth symbol only once (*The Wild One*), afterward insisting on the most diverse series of scripts (casting him as everything from an Oriental to Napoleon) he could lay his hands on.

Likewise, De Niro did play a symbol of today's disenfranchised youth in *Taxi Driver*, but then burrowed into as many other roles as he could find. Ironically enough, by trying to avoid typecasting as an audience surrogate, De Niro—like Brando—only took on an ever-greater aspect of that, since their respective complicated eras called for a screen hero who likewise was

MEN IN RELATIONSHIPS:
However lonely he may
be, the De Niro character
attempts to forge
relationships, often finding
himself in an awkward
situation as he relates to a
close friend and a young
woman at the same time.
This theme runs through
films as disparate as *Bang
the Drum Slowly* and
Jacknife.

A DIRECTOR'S ACTOR: De Niro has forged strong relationships with directors he admires, those being the ones willing to offer him full collaboration. Pictured: **A.** Martin Scorsese *(Taxi Driver)*, **B.** Michael Cimino *(The Deer Hunter)*, **C.** Brian De Palma *(The Untouchables)*, **D.** Penny Marshall *(Awakenings)*, **E.** David Jones *(Jacknife)*, and **F.** Martin Ritt *(Stanley and Iris)*.

A

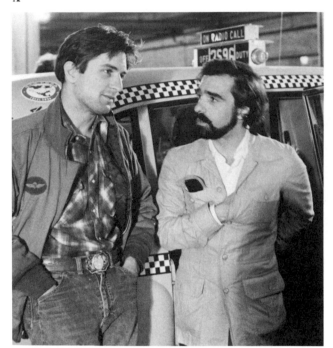

B

14

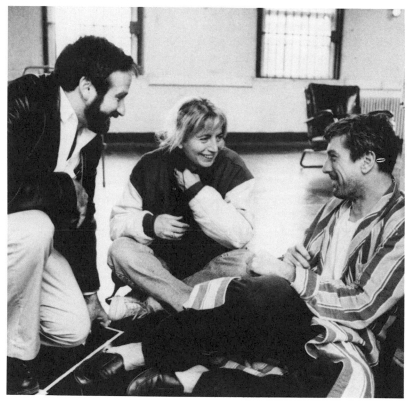

D

C

E

F

15

confused about his identity. That same early *Newsweek* profile picked up on this aspect of De Niro's appeal: "As Brando did in the postwar decades, De Niro seems to embody the conflicting, questing energies of his generation, the generation coming to young maturity in the fragmented seventies." This helped to define the power of *Taxi Driver*, and why such an artistically uneven film could exert such immense impact, arriving on theater screens when it did. *Newsweek* continued: "All great acting has an ethical dimension, and De Niro always suggests positive energy that has been perverted. Even his poor, crazy, shaven-skulled Travis Bickle, aiming his vigilante guns at pimps and politicos, expresses a diseased gallantry that's a tragic part of an era in which you can't always tell the saints from the swine."

Similarly, Molly Haskell noted early on that De Niro "came ashore in the same 'new wave' that flushed up unglamorous types like Pacino and Hoffman and made them stars. But they begin to look like pussycats next to De Niro, much the way the Beatles, once so alarming to the middle class, came to look like choirboys in the wake of their punk-rock and acid-rock successors." Dustin was scruffy/cuddly, while Pacino radiated sexiness and stoicism. Most fascinating was "De Niro—mysterious, inaccessible, more menacing than either, but with a degree of irony to the menace, an overlay of awareness . . . his natural tendency has been to go against the grain, to play unsympathetic roles without apology or concession. . . . De Niro is one of those rare stars—Brando and Bette Davis were others—who can play unsympathetic roles and get away with it. . . . The power of these performers goes beyond everyday star charisma into something like hypnosis, a quality of fierce will and bravura they fling at us, chaining us to their purposes and making their most monstrous deeds acceptable. But beneath the dare we perceive some unexpressed quality—call it intelligence or soul—to which we give our trust. De Niro will test this relationship as no other star has ever done." Haskell's words proved prophetic.

Once, De Niro described in great detail his love of the Walter Huston performance in *The Treasure of the Sierra Madre;* but when the listener brought up Bogart's equally acclaimed performance in that film, De Niro grew uncomfortable, not wanting to knock another actor but making clear he was not a great fan of Bogey's work. Though not necessarily speaking of Bogart per se, he commented, "There's nothing more offensive to me than watching an actor act with his ego. Some of the old movie stars were terrific, but they romanticized. People chase illusions and these illusions are created by movies. I want to make things concrete and real and to break down the illusion. There's nothing more ironic or strange or contradictory than life itself. What I try to do

is make things as clear and authentic as possible." Though De Niro's version of the old Bogart vehicle *We're No Angels* may have been a flop, it's worth comparing Bogart's performance with De Niro's in light of the above comment, noticing how romanticized Bogart's vision of the escaped criminal is, compared to De Niro's more realistic portrayal. Ultimately, the key to understanding De Niro's work is his emphasis on substance over style: "I don't want people years from now to say, 'Remember De Niro? He had real style.' I want to do things that will last because they have substance and quality, not some affectation or [technique], because that's all bullshit."

Robert De Niro married the beautiful black actress Diahnne Abbott in 1976 and subsequently adopted her then eight-year-old daughter from a previous marriage. They had a son, Raphael, in 1977—named after the luxury hotel in France where he was conceived. Finally, De Niro moved out of his $75-a-month apartment in New York and began taking on some of the trappings of a superstar. However, things did not always go smoothly. He was fired from *Bogart Slept Here* by director Mike Nichols, who could not deal with the actor's complicated approach. The Neil Simon script was, in a slightly different form, eventually shot under the title *The Goodbye Girl* and won an Oscar for Richard Dreyfuss, who played what was to have been the De Niro part. But De Niro had already won a Best Supporting Actor Oscar for *The Godfather, Part II* and would pick up the Best Actor statuette in 1981 for *Raging Bull*.

De Niro even returned on occasion to appear in plays he felt were substantial in nature, including the 1986 production of *Cuba and His Teddy Bear*. He also apparently understood that films are business, as well as art, choosing to do some clearly commercial ventures, such as *Midnight Run*, one of his rare box-office smashes.

The notion of living a series of alternative lives through a career as an actor was rendered crystal clear when De Niro spoke of his role in *Raging Bull:* "I wanted to play a fighter—just like a child wants to be somebody else," such as a cowboy or fireman, and dresses up in that role, then—in his child's imagination—becomes that person, at least for a while. Because of his meticulousness, De Niro must gradually ease into a character—and into a specific scene. Jerry Lewis, who acted with him in *The King of Comedy*, recalls that De Niro is anything but a "first-take" actor: "Take one, [and] Bobby's getting oriented. By ten, you're watching magic, and in take fifteen, you're seeing genius." Likewise: "He's incapable

A MAN WHO DOES HIS
HOMEWORK: In addition to his
own natural talents, De Niro
creates authentic portraits of
people by learning all he can
about their milieu; He hung
out with jazz musicians for *New
York, New York*, boxed with
Jake LaMotta for *Raging Bull*,
and walked the streets with
costar Jodie Foster and director
Martin Scorsese for *Taxi
Driver*.

of making a fake movie," Meryl Streep noted on the set of *Falling in Love*, "so when there was something wrong with the writing, he just couldn't [play] it. Then, everyone would realize that the scene was wrong [as written], and we'd fix it. He's infallible, like a compass." Once he's "found" the character, his lock is complete. For De Niro is the total Method actor, literally disappearing into his roles and living them out entirely.

Liza Minnelli, De Niro's costar in *New York, New York,* noted that he seemingly has no interest in or time for the big-star syndrome, stating, "He never expects a car, or any of that. He's not into the star trip." However, an actor playing a minor role in that film observed, "Bobby hogs Marty [Scorsese] on the set, [and] Marty gives Bobby anything he wants. What Bobby wants is constant attention—constant talk about his character." If he is clearly not on a big-star trip, he certainly is on a great-actor trip. De Niro may be uninterested in the spoils of commercial success—the cars, the yachts, the sycophants, etc.—but he is hungry for something else, starved even.

"He hates to break character," Jon Cutler, De Niro's sometimes stand-in, has said, "even [when he goes home at] night or on weekends. It's spooky." For the purpose of contrast, recall that famous line attributed to the master of "technique" acting, Sir Laurence Olivier. "The key to acting," he once said, perhaps half-jokingly, "is sincerity—once you learn to fake that, the rest is easy."

THE WINNER: De Niro won his first Oscar in 1975 for his supporting role in *The Godfather Part II*, then won again in 1981 as Best Actor for *Raging Bull*; Sissy Spacek won Best Actress that year for her work in *Coal Miner's Daughter*.

Then, there's De Niro: "I just can't fake acting. I know movies are an illusion, and maybe the first rule is to fake it—but not for me." Then, he adds intriguingly and revealingly, "I'm too curious. I want the experience." That of course calls for the endless research, sometimes lasting years, that he heartily leaps into. Director Elia Kazan noted De Niro's total commitment when, after completing *The Last Tycoon*, the filmmaker was happily surprised by a phone call from Bobby: "He's the only actor I've ever known who called me on the Friday night after we finished shooting, wanting to know if we could get together the next day to work on the character some more."

Despite the apparent objectivity of his approach, there is nonetheless something subjective and personal about his work. Again and again, De Niro has chosen roles that allow him to deal with aspects of himself: the Catholic religion and his Italian heritage, the difficulty of maintaining male-female relationships as opposed to the longevity of male-bonding friendships, the repression of violence and the frightful consequences of its being unleashed, alienation and loneliness of a contemporary order, the sense of a single person living dual lives in alternate worlds he inhabits . . . all have occurred to character after seemingly varied character in film after apparently differing film. While the central character may be articulate or idiotic, and the world he lives in our shared, modern world or a period-piece re-creation of history, those diverse people he has played so perfectly share a surprising number of character traits.

As far apart as the soft-spoken, sophisticated Monroe Stahr in *The Last Tycoon* and the abusive tyrant Jake La Motta in *Raging Bull* may be, both men are obsessed with success, the need to prove themselves by making vast sums of money in their chosen professions, as if to prove to the world—and themselves—that they are worthy. More significant still, the seemingly opposite men are both hopeless romantics, yearning after an impossibly perfect dream girl, falling in love with the fantasy of her rather than the reality, crushed when the real women cannot live up to their idealistic expectations of her.

With a lesser actor, this might be written off as mere coincidence. When we're dealing with a performer as in demand as De Niro, the single actor to whom most scripts are sent first, then it becomes a case of employing the films to make (however unconsciously) a personal statement. De Niro has had it both ways: delivering an emotional autobiography to us in his work, though doing so in such a disguised way that without extremely close examination, we would never notice the consistency of concerns, so varied and diverse are the surfaces.

When Bobby began working for such filmmakers as De Palma, Scorsese, and Coppola in the late 1960s, they were considered the movie brats—young filmmakers begging for the chance to break into the Hollywood Establishment. In short order, they did just that, their early shoestring-budget films giving way to major-league productions as they eased out the older filmmakers and became the contemporary top-of-the-line directors. Likewise, the youthful stars—Pacino, Hoffman, etc.—quickly adjusted to the fact that they were no longer the alienated outsiders, but the new elite of Hollywood. Only De Niro held out. Though his name was always above the title, he seemed to stand away from the machinery of moviemaking, still seeing himself as an outsider, a loner, an actor who showed up and did remarkable work, then faded back into the woodwork.

That all changed, almost overnight, beginning in 1988, when a forty-five-year-old De Niro at last assumed the kind of control of his career his contemporaries had, in the absence of a strong studio system, seized for themselves some time earlier. A film like *Taxi Driver* probably couldn't get made in the late eighties—not with former agents and corporate types in "creative" (a virtual contradiction in terms) control of the movie business, now funded by foreign money. The artistic, experimental, original side of moviemaking was diminishing, replaced by packaging deals and high concept, in which a film got made only if it could be summarized, over a three-martini lunch, in a single, clever-sounding sentence. For a movie such as *Twins*, the poster was designed before the script was written, while the film would not have been made if the stars had not been willing to do it. Suddenly, most movies were synthetic products, all style and no substance, lacking the edgy excitement De Niro demands from a project.

There was nothing to do but return to the East Coast—and try to drag the movie business, or least a part of it, back there with him. So De Niro became a film producer, forming TriBeCa Productions, of which he would be president, locating the business in an eight-story, eighty-three-year-old, red-brick building—the converted Martinson Coffee factory—at Greenwich and Franklin Streets, located near the Hudson River, where he could not only house his own company but also rent out space to gifted independent filmmakers. There would even be a restaurant, the TriBeCa Bar and Grill, which he opened with such filmmaking friends as Sean Penn, Bill Murray, and Mikhail Baryshnikov as fellow investors. Now divorced from Abbott after a dozen years of marriage and dating Toukie Smith, the more mature Robert De Niro personally supervised not only the creation of the restaurant, but also the renovation of the building (of which he owned 50 percent), insisting on a balance between what was best about the original structure (all the industrial details, such as old factory pipes, now painted forest green but not removed, or the giant coffee scales in his office, spruced up but left essentially intact) and what was necessary for the new wave of work (a state-of-the-art seventy-seat screening room, designed by filmmaker George Lucas's production company). Which meant that De Niro's building mirrored his approach to Hollywood: hang on to what was best about the past, but modify it for the present, thereby preparing for the future.

Clearly, De Niro would rather have spent his time working at his acting craft, but that was no longer an option. Even Scorsese, De Palma, and Coppola had a harder time putting together an intriguing, original production in light of the anticreative packaging policies in effect. In order to remain true to one's vision, it was necessary to incorporate—and produce the films that you were eager to work on. Hollywood could no longer be trusted to do that as it had back in the 1970s.

De Niro reflected all this when he stated, "I never had the full responsibility for a film before and never wanted it. But now I do. Ultimately, it's to have control." In quiet ways, though, he has always exerted more control over the films he has appeared in than perhaps even he knows, as close examination of the films themselves will reveal.

THE FILMS

You are cordially invited to attend "The Wedding Party" for Josephine and Charlie

The Wedding Party

Starring JILL CLAYBURGH
ROBERT DeNIRO
A Film by WILFORD LEACH
CYNTHIA MUNROE
BRIAN DE PALMA

When *The Wedding Party* was released theatrically in the early 1970s (by Ajay Film Co.) and on videocassette (from VidAmerica) several years later, the advertising exploited the fact that both De Niro and Jill Clayburgh had become major stars since the time when that 1966 film was shot on a shoestring budget.

AN INAUSPICIOUS DEBUT:

Brian De Palma, then a young teacher of filmmaking, chose the unknown stage actor De Niro despite the fact that Bobby completely flubbed his official "reading."

The Wedding Party

(1963/1969)

Powell Productions Plus/An Ondine Presentation
An Ajay Film Company release

CAST:

Jill Clayburgh (*Josephine the Bride*); Charles Pfluger (*Charlie the Groom*); Valda Satterfield (*Mrs. Fish*); Raymond McNally (*Mr. Fish*); John Braswell (*Reverend Oldfield*); Judy Thomas (*Celeste the Organist*); Sue Anne Converse (*Nanny*); John Quinn (*Baker*); Robert De Nero [*sic*] (*Cecil*); William Finley (*Alistair*); Jennifer Salt (*Phoebe*).

CREDITS:

Produced, directed, written, and edited by Cynthia Munroe, Brian De Palma, and Wilford Leach; photography, Peter Powell; music, John Herbert McDowell; sound, Henry Felt, Betsy Powell, and Jim Swan; running time, 90 minutes.

Though shot in late 1963 by Brian De Palma, in collaboration with fellow Sarah Lawrence College student Cynthia Munroe and faculty member Wilford Leach, *The Wedding Party* never received official theatrical distribution at that time. Hollywood's A movies still dominated the market (recall, this was the era of *The Sound of Music*), while the notion of B pictures still conjured images of Vincent Price in some Roger Corman thriller. Yet in the aftermath of the Kennedy assassination and the moral, political, and cultural confusion that set in, there was clearly room for something more.

Viewing *The Wedding Party* in 1969 was a strange experience, as theaters were then glutted with movies (including De Palma's own) about the unique situation of American youth surviving the hippie counterculture era. Though marketed as just such a film, *The Wedding Party* in fact concerned itself with the more idealistic Kennedy-era youth of the early sixties. While five years may not seem such an immense gap in time, Alvin

Josephine Fish (Jill Clayburgh) makes it down the aisle, despite the fact that all the grand plans for her wedding appear to be collapsing around her.

Josephine allows Charlie (Charles Pfluger) to steal a quick kiss; De Palma's fascination with voyeurism is in evidence early on, in terms of this camera placement.

Toffler had already coined the phrase *future shock.* Social values and popular culture were changing so rapidly that it became all but impossible to adjust to the latest style or attitude before it was already gone, replaced by something else.

Too bad, perhaps, that the movie was not withheld from release for several more years. In 1973, with the hippie era already waning, movies set in the year 1963 proved to be the vogue: *American Graffiti, The Lords of Flatbush,* and best of all Martin Scorsese's *Mean Streets* starring Robert De Niro set the tone of the early 1970s film experience by examining young people in the last days of American innocence. *The Wedding Party,* with its similar socially oblivious characters, would certainly have had a greater shot at commercial success if released then, exploiting the nostalgia craze. It had little chance when in competition with the radical movies of 1969, in part because it did not deliver what the dishonest advertising promised, in part because it was not, in truth, a particularly strong example of student filmmaking.

The *Variety* review succinctly summed up the film's problems: "The assumption that young [read college] filmmakers have a special advantage in treating youth-oriented themes is proven erroneous by *The Wedding Party.* . . . [The] Trio [of De Palma, Munroe, and Leach] wrote, produced, directed, and edited the comedy, an arrangement that may account for the film's constantly shifting point of view. . . . This mildly amusing film occasionally hits a mark that will evoke a response from a general audience, but only very occasionally. . . . Much of the film has a frenzied pace employing crosscut editing and fast motion in a manner that produces an erratic, unsettling quality. One suspects the various techniques were used either to cover an absence of content or that the techniques were deemed more fundamental than substance."

At the time of the filming, De Niro, then little more than a teenager, heard about the call for actors willing to work for practically nothing and eagerly went after a role. As soon as the audition was over, he sensed that he had blown it; reading a few scraps of a script was not his best means of showing what he could do. So instead of leaving, Bobby then asked to improvise for De Palma, leaping into a free-flying interpretation of the old leftist classic from the 1930s, *Waiting for Lefty.* "He came on," De Palma later recalled, "like Broderick Crawford—reading a speech to the cabbies in the union hall. He was simply great." Great enough that the youthful filmmakers sensed this was potentially an important young actor they might help start on the road toward stardom. No one knew for sure which role De Niro would play; everyone agreed that he would be in the picture, at a total payment of $50 for his services.

De Palma's own students
and friends played the parts
of various wedding guests.

The story (using that term loosely, for this is little more than a series of vignettes, varying drastically in tone and quality) takes place on a Long Island estate, where Charlie (Charles Pfluger) and his two friends, Baker (John Quinn) and Cecil (De Niro, billed in the credits as "De Nero"), arrive for the ceremony. Though the bride, Josephine (Jill Clayburgh, another future star making her film debut), is gorgeous and rich, Charlie isn't sure whether he's happy with the idea of marrying into money, then being expected to live according to this family's standards, especially since he and his pals had planned to experience many more adventures before settling down. While at college, they talked endlessly about all the bohemian experiences they'd have together; now, they must—like all young people—come to grips with whether those were realistic projections or only adolescent fantasies.

The improvisational quality of the scenes suggests De Palma and his colleagues (imitating the films of John Cassavetes, halfway between commercial cinema and the Underground) provided their actors with only a minimal amount of dialogue, explaining to them where the scene had to go, what key lines needed to be said, then allowing the performers to create the sequences on the spot, working as true collaborators in the piece. The ad-lib quality does not, however, lead to the desired sense of authenticity so much as an awkwardness, a

Jill Clayburgh, early in her career.

25

feeling that no one was really in control (in a Cassavetes film such as *Shadows*, *Faces*, or *Husbands*, it's always clear the director was first among equals). "Each scene is only loosely connected with what went before it," *Variety* reported, "and direction of the dialogue is sacrificed for a certain spontaneity that is seldom forthcoming."

To be fair, several reviewers were positive, perhaps hoping to encourage and support promising filmmakers working on a shoestring. The New York *Daily News* reported that the film "has style, charm, and humor galore. It's a pleasure to see!" The *New York Times* claimed that *The Wedding Party* was "like a dipper of spring water . . . something fresh and funny." Gene Shalit hailed it as "one of the most charming, gayest, most frothy and inventive pictures in a long time . . . this wedding takes the cake." However, most De Palma/De Niro buffs who catch it today will agree with Leonard Maltin's capsule commentary in his *Movie and Video Guide:* "Talky, corny, boring comic oddity."

It's worth noting that in 1965, Leo R. Dratfield and his Pathe Contemporary Films (a McGraw-Hill subsidiary) offered to buy the rights and distribute 35mm theatrical prints, saturating the art-house circuit and college market, but would only do so if a New York theatrical screening could be arranged. It did not matter whether the film made money, only that the critics would be forced to review it; there would invariably be some strong words of support that could be used to hype subsequent engagements. But the producers had to put up the costs of a Manhattan booking, including a "house guarantee" and all advertising and publicity expenses—something they could little afford. The better part of two decades later, in 1982, Troma Films—the New York film company best known for self-consciously schlocky productions such as *The Toxic Avenger*—obtained worldwide theatrical and ancillary rights (including cable TV and home videocassette) to *The Wedding Party*, in large part owing to the ongoing marquee value of De Palma and De Niro. It's worth mentioning that, in their promotional materials for this "pickup," they chose to spell De Niro's name correctly while allowing him second billing to Clayburgh, implying that Bobby was the film's focal male character.

In his supporting role, De Niro was rarely singled out for his work by the critics. However, *Variety* did note that "the cast includes professional actors combined with Sarah Lawrence workshop students, with only Valda Satterfield as the bride's mother, Robert De Nero as one of the groom's friends, and Judy Thomas as the organist Celeste making any impression." De Niro biographer Keith McKay would, in retrospect, comment, "De Niro played his role like a third stooge, or a Ringo Starr." *The Wedding Party* may have been an inauspicious debut, but it was, after all, a beginning.

Greetings

(aka *The Three Musketeers*)

(1968)

A Sigma III Release of a West End Film

CAST:

Jonathan Warden (*Paul Shaw*); Robert De Niro (*Jon Rubin*); Gerritt Graham (*Lloyd Clay*); Megan McCormick (*Marina*); Ashley Oliver (*Bronx Secretary*); Cynthia Peltz (*Divorcée*); Ruth Alda (*Linda*); Mona Feit (*Mystic Date*); Carol Patton (*The Blonde*); Allen Garfield (*Smut Peddler*); Sara-Jo Edlin (*Nymphomaniac*); Roz Kelly (*Photographer*); Ray Tuttle (*TV Correspondent*); Tisa Chiang (*Vietnamese Girl*).

CREDITS:

Director, Brian De Palma; producer, Charles Hirsch; screenplay, De Palma and Hirsch; photography, Robert Fiore; editor, Brian De Palma; music, The Children of Paradise; running time, 88 minutes; rating: X (later adjusted to R).

One of the first significant movies to be created by America's new breed of filmmakers during the late 1960s was *Greetings*. Charles Hirsch, then in his early twenties, conceived the idea. Hirsch had found employment with Universal Pictures as a "talent director," sent out to discover young filmmakers in New York who might be brought into the stodgy company as new blood, able to connect with young potential moviegoers who read *Rolling Stone* rather than *Reader's Digest,* who wanted films fashioned for them rather than their fathers' generation. In Manhattan, Hirsch met Brian De Palma, already the auteur of both *The Wedding Party* and a little tongue-in-cheek thriller called *Murder à la Mod.* The two hit it off and, in their spare time, began sharing interests—De Palma's intense, almost obsessive fascinations with voyeurism and filmmaking, Hirsch's similarly compulsive concern with computer dating and Kennedy-assassination conspiracy theories. Before long, the two were pouring their ideas into a script, the first

Robert De Niro as Jon Rubin.

A paranoid sense of conspiracy runs through the film, making it an effective time-capsule for the era during which it was made.

draft of which featured a single hero. The idea was to find one actor able to represent their values much as Jean-Pierre Leaud had for their idol, French New Wave writer-director François Truffaut, in *The 400 Blows* and its sequels.

Certainly, De Niro—who had impressed De Palma immensely while shooting *The Wedding Party* at Sarah Lawrence—was a strong contender. The collaborators decided, however, that as talented as Bobby might be, they would do better by splitting that single character into a trio of heroes, each representing one aspect of their concerns. The screenplay completed, they handed it over to Hirsch's employers. But Universal passed on *Greetings*—the company was not ready yet to try anything quite so daring—at which point Hirsch and De Palma raised money from friends and relatives, eventually shooting the film for a grand total of $43,000 (this was a time when a major Hollywood movie cost about $5 million) during a thirteen-day period while Hirsch was on his paid vacation. Though not a runaway success in the theaters, the movie easily made back its investment plus a handsome profit. This marked the beginning of the end for studio-controlled projects, though just the beginning for the new Hollywood. Sensing the enormity of the revolution his modest movie had helped kick off, Hirsch said at the time, "Things have started to change—*Greetings, Faces,* and *Chafed Elbows* showed people in the business that there is a financial potential in movies of this kind—films which say what they want to say." Indeed, columnist Deac Rossell went so far as to write: "Regardless of individual reactions or critical approbation, *Greetings* and *Faces* may be the most important films of the last decade for America's confused movie industry." Though it would not be until 1969, with the advent of *Easy Rider,* that the underground completely broke through to mainstream moviemaking, the process had clearly begun, and De Niro was in on the ground level.

The film was shot entirely on location in New York, in notably déclassé—at times, even grimy—streets and apartments. What the movie lacked in careful craftsmanship, it made up for in exuberance and energy—ironic, considering that De Palma would shortly be perceived as the filmmaker most emphatically reviving the old movie formulas he had, in 1969, helped at least temporarily to bury. But he—and his youthful star, Robert De Niro—made their first notable impact with this ensemble comedy. Not without controversy, though; for anyone who has grown up with the rating system in place, it's sobering to recall that up until late 1967, there was little if any need for one, so homogenized was the standard Hollywood product. By early 1968, the MPAA's code (which initially featured G, M,

Jon is seduced by an older woman (Cynthia Peltz); the film is suffused with a young-against-old mentality.

R, and X designations) was deemed necessary, owing to the major changes occurring in popular entertainment. At that time, the X rating stood not for hard-core pornography (this was a full three years before the advent of *Deep Throat*) but rather for any film (however serious) containing what were then considered adults-only elements of sex, violence, and language. *Midnight Cowboy*, which won the Oscar as Best Picture of the Year for 1969, was originally rated X, as was the earlier *Greetings*—only the fifth film submitted to the ratings board to be so stigmatized. Also, for trivia fans, it's worth noting that *Greetings* marked the first time ever that an MPAA rating was appealed, though Leonard Gruenberg of Sigma III productions did eventually withdraw this request before the final hearing could take place.

The title derived from the opening sentence of that officious letter every young male dreaded receiving in 1968–69. But the movie was not (like Arthur Penn's *Alice's Restaurant*) primarily about the antiwar resistance movement. Employing the draft as a framing device (one of the heroes receives his notice at the beginning and must deal with it before the end), *Greetings* swiftly moved on to the other Hirsch/De Palma

concerns. Most of the film's running time is given over to observing the boys trying to pick up girls—that oldest of male hobbies as it was just then being adjusted to the post-sexual-revolution, post-"pill" realities. The three youthful antiheroes of the piece were what social observers were just then beginning to call "hippies." Interestingly enough, that term was so new at the time of *Greetings*' release that many reviewers (including *Variety*'s) incorrectly referred to them as "beatniks," a holdover from the late 1950s nonconformists.

During the final days of LBJ's presidency, the trio dart about—occasionally viewed together, more often off on their own particular adventures. Paul (Jonathan Warden) is concerned with pretty women, now supposedly liberated and no longer uptight about romance, espousing "free love" as part of their Age of Aquarius lifestyle, though incongruously more difficult to comprehend than they previously were in the plastic era of the early sixties. Lloyd (Gerritt Graham) obsessively searches for a satisfying JFK assassination theory, leading him to a virtual state of paranoia in which he suspects practically everyone. And Jon (De Niro) harbors a compulsion to film people while they are unaware, transforming their private lives into public programs through his Peeping Tom activities. (Clearly, he represents De Palma in the film.) But voyeurism and conspiracy theories must temporarily take a backseat when Paul receives his induction notice, his two buddies then coaching him on how to best go about failing the physical examination: faking that he's a homosexual or a right-wing extremist; exhausting himself so completely that he's a physical wreck by the testing time.

The movie owes much to François Truffaut, Jean-Luc Godard, and other members of the French New Wave, who, a decade earlier, rebelled against the stodgy state of commercial French cinema by "freeing" the camera. Their films, such as *Jules and Jim* and *Breathless,* may have been seen by relatively few Americans in their art-house bookings, but were devoured by impressionable upcoming filmmakers such as De Palma, who dreamed of creating an American counterpart. Therefore, De Palma felt free to employ any film device or technique, suddenly throwing in title cards to precede some action or utilizing films within the film, allowing his characters to speak in asides to the audience one moment or shifting into double exposure a second later, speeding up the action or slowing it down. The resultant film was a hodgepodge, a virtual patchwork quilt of cinematic techniques, some of which worked in context, others seeming grotesquely out of place.

But at a time when mainstream movies had become dull, predictable, and empty, it was a delight to see such wild, outrageous stuff—helping us understand some of the raves from supportive youthful critics of the time. Their reviews, when read closely, reveal that their enthusiasm grows not just from an appreciation of the film but from a desire to encourage such maverick moviemakers. The ultrahip *Boston After Dark* was typical: "*Greetings* is a contemporary farce, tickling current issues with an exaggerated celluloid finger. Its loose construction breathes spontaneity and youth. . . . *Greetings*' comedy is not the mannered vision of scriptwriters huddling in the corridors of some vast movie studio." Even the Silver Bear award at the Berlin Film Festival seemed more a political statement than a comment on the quality of the moviemaking, the judges citing "its lighthearted nonconformity and the immaculate teamwork of its actors and director." In fact, watching *Greetings* was like witnessing a series of college comedy skits performed in blackout fashion and commited to film; but in the year 1969, the ordinarily dismissive term *sophomoric* was often intended as praise.

On the other hand, any reviewer who attempted to deal with *Greetings* in the manner of a traditional Hollywood vehicle was in the same position as a music critic of that time analyzing Rod Stewart from the value system previously applied to Perry Como; the film would be found wanting, so sloppy was its execution; the narrative elements don't always hang together; the sound recording is not what it should be; the overall tone of the film changes jarringly from one sequence to the next. One of those unappreciative and/or uncomprehending reviews was written by James Powers of the *Hollywood Reporter.* Filing his notice from Berlin, he churlishly commented: "Some of this is fairly amusing and might be very amusing if the various sequences were developed, but nothing is. It is all done with a casualness verging on chaos, so no joke is ever fully explored or pointed. . . . *Greetings* was obviously made on a minimum budget, so perhaps it was money that handicapped them. It seems, rather, to have been a deliberate style: an attempt to film a 'happening,' improvisational and sketchy." The condescending tone suggests a disdain for the very same elements that *BAD*'s reviewer obviously admired.

Then there were reviewers who refused to take sides, opting for a balanced approach that still seems fair today. In particular, the *Variety* review, with its sincere attempt at on-the-spot evenhandedness: "Granted that *Greetings* has its sluggish sequences (such as protracted opening in which Warden is coached to cop out at his army physical), but these misses are forgivable. Much of the production has an intense freshness." In a similar vein, *Time* noted that "*Greetings*' vitality and weakness are both due to [De Palma's] inability to concentrate on any subject for more than a moment." Perhaps most fascinating of all was the approach taken by *Boxoffice,* which uncritically but realistically considered the commerciality of the film's approach: "*Greetings* is so in tune with the frustrations and desires of today's 18–29 year old audience, so relevant, topical . . . that, properly sold, it could emerge as a substantial [financial] success."

A few critics attempted serious consideration of why the film, not without merit, seemed limited in impact. Michael Ross of the *Los Angeles Herald-Examiner* complained that "De Palma never shows the over-thirty audience what it's like to be young and aware in sixties America. . . . His Swiftian glimpse of contemporary life is directed (solely) at a 'now' audience." John Walker of *Films and Filming* complained that rather than study truly idealistic youth, De Palma had concentrated on self-interested pseudos: "They worry about how to dodge the draft without breaking the law (and thereby getting in serious trouble) rather than how to stop the war." Critic Michael Bliss noted, beneath the obvious peace-and-love shenanigans, the film's "subtext of violence," which would shortly hit the surface of films by both director De Palma and star De Niro. One such moment—a macabre combining of the film's sexual and violent interests—occurs when Lloyd, having just seduced a woman, immediately begins spilling out his

A smut peddler (Allen Garfield) interests Jon in this line of work . . .

. . . causing Jon to try his luck with a nymphomaniac (Sara-Jo Edlin) . . .

. . . at which point he lives out the fantasies of the free-love generation.

conspiracy theories. On her naked body—still writhing with postcoital bliss—he then draws diagrams to prove that Kennedy was hit by more than one bullet.

Just as telling is the fact that De Niro's Jon—throughout seen filming sex scenes—is, at the very end, being filmed himself, though not in one of those pornographic pictures he loves, but rather in pornography of a very different order. He is in Vietnam, caught by a TV news camera on a battlefield with death all around him—looking prophetically like the later heroes of *The Deer Hunter* and *Jacknife*. For Jon, sex has given way to violence, and his role has been inverted—the subject of a film rather than the creator of it. The look on his face—stunned, bemused, acceptant, angry—is priceless, and an indication of the richness and depth De Niro could convey in a mere moment of screen time.

Few critics commented specifically on his performance; more often, the actors were praised as an ensemble. Michael Ross of the *Los Angeles Herald-Examiner* noted that "the actors, especially the three leading men, are all fine comics in this existential clown show." Kevin Thomas of the *Los Angeles Times* praised the work by Warden, Graham, and De Niro in a peculiar if intriguing way: "All three of these fellows are good-looking, talented, and ingratiating." Ingratiating is one trait that has seldom been attributed to Bobby; in fact, his character here, less accessible than those played by either of his costars, would appear even more iconoclastic in the soon-to-be-released sequel.

In true antiwar fashion, the boys pretend to be Nazi sympathizers in hopes this may cause them to be rejected for the draft.

De Niro 'n the hood.

Waiting for news about who is to be drafted.

VENGEANCE, ITALIAN STYLE:

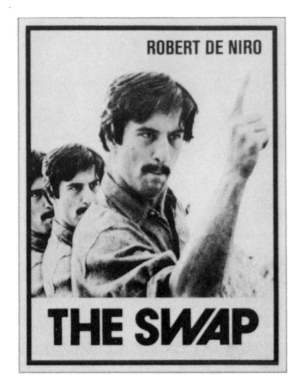

The Swap

(aka *Sam's Song*)

(1969/1971/1980/1983)

Cannon Releasing Corporation

CAST (*Sam's Song*):

Robert De Niro (*Sam*); Jered Mickey (*Andrew*); Jennifer Warren (*Erica*); Terrayne Crawford (*Carol*); Martin Kelley (*Mitch*); Phyllis Black (*Marge*); Viva (*Girl With Hourglass*).

CAST (*The Swap*):

Anthony Charnotta (*Vito*); Sybil Danning (*Erica*); James Brown (*Detective*); Lisa Blount (*Porno Star*); also, Sam Anderson, John Medici, Tony Brande, Matt Green, Alvin Hammer, Jack Slater.

CREDITS (*Sam's Song*):

Director, Jordan Leondopoules; producer, Christopher C. Dewey; photography, Alex Phillips, Jr.; editor, Arline Garson; music, Gershon Kingsley; running time, 120 minutes; rating: R.

When this 1969 film was released in the eighties, distributors made certain that De Niro was prominently featured in all advertising—however misleading that may have been.

Breathtaking Sybil Danning as the femme fatale in the new footage that was added in order to turn a pretentious arthouse-circuit film into a murder mystery.

CREDITS (*The Swap*):

Written and directed by John Broderick (Johnny Shade); running time, 90 minutes; rating: R.

Less has been written about this picture than any of the other early De Niro efforts. The little-seen movie, originally called *Sam's Song*, was shot in 1969, then received an aborted release in 1971. One of the late hippie-era movies (having more in common with Dennis Hopper's disastrously self-indulgent *The Last Movie* of 1971 than his socially conscious, highly impactful *Easy Rider* of 1969), the film concerns a young, idealistic moviemaker (De Niro) who takes off for a weekend at a posh estate owned by corrupt people who are toying with the notion of financing his films, Sam then finds himself sucked into the mind and bed games they play.

Sam's Song looked like an ambitious if unsuccessful attempt to create an American combination of *Last Year at Marienbad* and *La Dolce Vita*. The slow-moving two-hour picture was, at the time, considered all but unreleasable. However, when De Niro achieved major stardom, someone at Cannon Films recalled that this clinker still sat in a vault somewhere, located and dusted it off, releasing *Sam's Song* in December 1980. Vincent Canby of the *New York Times* didn't even bother to offer a full review, insisting that *Sam's Song* "looks like the souvenir of the late sixties and early seventies that it is—a movie made sincerely and independently by young people enchanted by the films of Michelangelo Antonioni, Claude Chabrol, and Claude Lelouch."

Canby's relatively kind words were not repeated by those who deigned to review *The Swap* three years later. Since even the now-formidable De Niro name had failed to win *Sam's Song* an audience, another filmmaker—John Broderick—was brought in to create an entirely new thriller plot, employing some of the De Niro footage for flashbacks. *The Swap* ran only ninety minutes, released by Vestron Home Video, hyped by the following tag line: "He's tough. He's cool. He's murder on women . . . and they're death on him." Actually, that's a fair description of the character played by Anthony Charnotta in the newly shot footage; De Niro's Sam is intellectual and withdrawn. At any rate, the film has been widely dismissed, even by De Niro, who has expressed embarrassment over the exploitation of his name during the 1983 release. Peter Cargin, of *Continental Film and Video Review*, described it as "something of a mess."

Yet the film, while certainly no masterpiece, is certainly far more fascinating than its reputation would suggest. Broderick did an intriguing, if uneven, job of creating an entirely new film around pre-existing footage. *The Swap* is of particular interest to De Niro buffs, since many of the themes that would emerge in his later work are notably present here, while his characterization is an embryonic incarnation of personality traits that would later appear in roles as diverse as Travis Bickle and Rupert Pupkin. The opening sequence (1969 footage) is especially strong: an image of Sam, wandering the mean streets of Manhattan, glimpsed from a series of odd angles as the neon lights and harsh cityscape reflect in puddles of water, presenting a dreamlike, off-kilter quality. Sam is the alienated loner, trudging through the crowd but unnoticed by those around him.

Sam wanders into his editing room, immediately beginning an elaborate rolling up of his sleeves, this action seemingly a necessary ritual, as psychological as it is physical. He will repeat it throughout the movie—before sex as well as before work—until it transforms into something more than just a bit of business. Part of De Niro's acting approach is based on discovering such little "keys," which have great import to him. They add an interesting texture to what might otherwise have been clichéd characters, allowing Bobby to realize the person fully rather than merely suggest him.

In the following sequence, Sam reads a note from "Nick" about additions and deletions to a film in progress, then edits a graphic sex scene. This is effectively intercut with images of black-gloved hands, menacingly fingering film cans in the next room; Sam is hit from behind and falls over. A title then informs us it is ten years later; in a prison cell, smoking cigarettes, Sam's brother Vito awaits release. His pal Joey picks him up in a truck, insisting that a home-cooked Italian meal is waiting. First, though, Vito insists on going to the cemetery where his entire family is buried. Vito is obsessed with seeing the grave of his younger brother, killed (the police wrote it off as an unsolved robbery-related death, though Vito still suspects murder) while Vito was in prison for criminal activities. When Vito vows revenge ("I'll find whoever did this to you, kill them with my bare hands!"), he introduces the theme of vengeance, Italian style, which will run through considerably loftier De Niro vehicles to come: *Mean Streets, The Godfather, Part II*, and *GoodFellas.*

The film then takes on a film-noir quality when Vito learns an attractive, mysterious woman has been leaving flowers on his brother's grave every Thursday morning for the last ten years. Vito will be waiting for her next time; meanwhile, he visits the priest who helped raise him and Sam and is told that "the old gang is gone, the neighborhood has changed." The priest also hands Vito a thousand dollars, his meagre inheritance, plus a large cardboard box filled with cans of fading film stock Sam had left with the priest shortly before his death. We sense what neither of them grasp yet: this is what those black-gloved hands were searching for the night of the murder. In the meantime, though, Vito—warned not to seek vengeance by the priest—insists, "I was supposed to look out for Sammy," expressing the Italian street ethic that calls out for a bloody vendetta. The concerned priest expresses the other side of the Italian ethos, the Catholic conscience: "Do, and you'll condemn your soul to everlasting hell." Vito, like the hero of so many later, greater Scorsese and Coppola films De Niro would appear in, finds himself trapped between two mutually exclusive value systems. It is the unique trap of the Italian American male.

Vito next visits the Erica Moore office, confronting the attractive literary agent (played in the new footage by

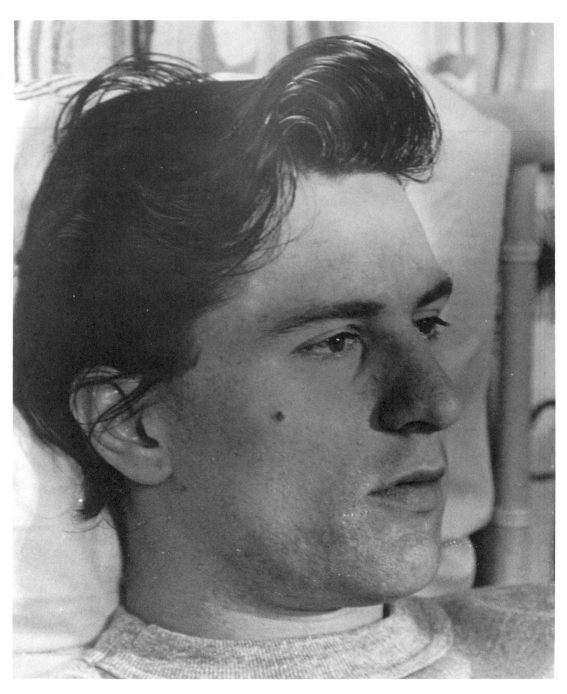

Handsome young Robert De Niro, at the time he prepared to play Sammy.

Sybil Danning) with the fact that a letter he received in prison—mailed just before Sam's death, though arriving just after it—mentioned that she was with Sam the weekend before he died. "Could you tell me what his last three days were like?" Vito requests. Erica recalls how she, her then-husband Andrew, and Sam drove together to Long Island. In the 1969 footage, Erica (played here by Jennifer Warren, then billing herself as Jennifer De Boer) and the men are seen at the estate. While the business-oriented film people mix on the elaborate grounds, Sam is glimpsed alone upstairs, reading a serious critical analysis of cinema by Andre Bazin, peering out the window at the fun and games. Sam is with them, but not of them. Here, De Niro's Sam incarnates the young hopefuls who made the original 1969 *Sam's Song* film—as well as De Palma, Coppola, Scorsese, and the other young maverick filmmakers Bobby was then working with, all hungry to get Hollywood to bankroll their offbeat projects but hoping to do so without surrendering their integrity, so important to youth in those heady hippie-era days. He holds his "serious" film-as-art book tight to him, as if it were a Bible, for courage. He knows that to walk downstairs is to surrender to the seductively superficial commercial side of film, "the business." The simple choice of whether to remain in the room or to join the crowd is a moral decision De Niro's director friends were already facing in real life. Understandably, then, Sam slowly, methodically rolls up his sleeves before working up the courage to go down and join the others.

However, from the moment Sam descends, he ceases to function as a symbol of De Niro's favorite young directors, becoming a projection of Bobby himself by embodying the De Niro approach to acting as life. The first thing Sam spots is an empty wheelchair, which piques his curiosity. Without hesitation, Sam slips into it, learns how to manipulate himself around the pool and the partygoers while seated. He then experiments with passing himself off as a cripple. When he meets Carol, a beautiful miniskirted blonde, he convinces her he's an invalid. The idea of a relationship being formed as a man plays a role for a woman—acting and in the process turning life into theater—will be the basis for Travis's relationship with Betsy in *Taxi Driver*. "It's a war wound," Sam informs Carol, his voice basically convincing—though with just the slightest undertone of irony to make her wonder if he really is what he says. "Which war?" she asks, partly taken in, partly incredulous. Sam continues to improvise a character, allowing her to fall in love with the person he is performing, both for her benefit and his own perverse amusement. Later, they hop into the now-deserted pool (shades of *La Dolce Vita*'s Trevi fountain sequence), and the final image of the wheelchair on the bottom is striking, even memorable. Later, when Sam makes love to Carol back in his room, he follows their sexual bout with an impersonation of a stud-type character from an Italian film: "How'd you like it, baby?" he asks with a ridiculously overstated accent. Their afternoon affair is an imitation of something each has seen in some foreign film; he acknowledges with his gag that rather than living spontaneously, they are attempting to measure up to the way life looks in the movies.

The next day, everyone goes yachting, and it's clear that Erica is jealous of Carol, in part because she's winning away the affections of best friend Sam, in part because Carol's also having an affair with Erica's husband, Andrew. First Sam, then Andrew, make love to the amoral Carol in the downstairs stateroom. Erica angrily insists a passing boat be hailed so she can return to shore, and Sam dutifully accompanies her. "The next morning, he went to work," Erica tells Vito, "and I never saw him again." Her story sounds sincere, though she becomes

visibly distraught when Vito mentions the box of film he has received—presumably, the same film that the mysterious black-gloved intruder was after ten years earlier.

Though Erica warns Vito against revenge, he insists on "blood for blood—an old Italian tradition," a precursor of the Charlie–Johnny Boy friendship in *Mean Streets*. "These are modern times," Erica warns him, though the interest here—as in so many of the better films to follow—is in the way Italian-American male characters cling to a code from the past, much to the chagrin of the uncomprehending modern women in their lives.

On Thursday, Vito visits the cemetery, confronting the pretty young woman who has been regularly leaving flowers. Vito is distraught to learn that Vivien Buck was—at age thirteen—an "actress" in the porno flicks Sam made out of financial necessity. The young man who cherished Bazin and wanted—but feared—moving into commercial movies also paid his dues (as did so many of the real-life budding filmmakers) laboring in the industry's seediest subpocket. Lieutenant Benson (James Brown, not "the hardest-working man in show business" but the veteran white actor of TV's *Rin-Tin-Tin*) from homicide pays Vito regular visits, insisting Vito ought to back off from his private investigation; if he can't, then he should call the policeman if anything turns up. Vito also learns Andrew Moore is running for governor. After someone attempts to kill Vito and make it look like an accident (he's saved only by the intervention of Vivien), Vito visits Andrew at his spectacular mountain-view home—noticing Andrew's now grayhaired but still beautiful second wife, Carol.

Vito asks Andrew about the much-discussed weekend, and as he relates his version of the story, *The Swap* takes on aspects of both *Citizen Kane* and *Rashomon*—not in an aesthetic league with either, certainly, but at least suggesting that filmmaker Broderick attempted to do something more than merely supply filler, as most critics have heretofore suggested. Broderick employs a fascinatingly cinematic approach to the flashbacks. Much of the original 1969 footage we see next is identical to what appeared on-screen earlier, when Erica was reminiscing. However, her voice-over for this footage was notably different—in tone and emphasis—than the voice-over Andrew now offers, implying that what is visually repeated on-screen is objective truth, while the different interpretations we simultaneously hear are the selective subjective truths of the narrators. Here, we again see Andrew and Sam, Erica and Carol, all going on board the yacht together, doing the same things they did earlier. However, in his narration, Andrew never once mentions the presence of Carol. Since she is now his respectable wife, he cannot openly admit the amoral circumstances under which he met her during more free-living and free-loving times.

Later, Carol shows up at Vito's place and seduces him, after reminiscing about Sam: "He loved making films—couldn't leave it alone!" Vito wakes up alone, realizing Carol was there to find the box everyone wants. But it has been placed in the hands of Joey (that notion of intense loyalty between Italian-American men who are at best distantly related but treat one another like brothers is another recurring theme in De Niro films), and the two decide to visit the film-developing lab indicated on the label. The people there attempt to prepare the old, worn film for screening, while the manager shows Vito contracts Sam supposedly signed—dated two days after his death.

Carol and Erica are both killed in confrontations with Vito, as *The Swap* becomes more melodramatic by the minute. From them, Vito learns bizarre, contradictory variations on why Sam had to be silenced: because he had porno-flick footage of each woman (and Andrew) taken in the late sixties, while the three were under the influence of drugs, later regretting the wildness. In one interpretation, the seemingly innocent Sam was killed not just because he had the footage but because he was using it to blackmail his way into the legitimate film industry. It's fascinating to note, from our perspective, that in an age when a seemingly conservative Supreme Court nominee had to withdraw after it was disclosed that, in the early seventies, he casually smoked pot with students, the implied theme of *The Swap* is legitimate. This is a movie about corrupt, conservative leaders of the then-emerging Reagan era trying to eliminate any evidence of their swinging lifestyles in the supposedly liberated sixties.

Then, Vito watches footage of Sam taken just before his death; what we see on-screen is the most fascinating thing in the entire movie. "The place reminds me of a scene in a French movie I saw once," Sam says of the Long Island estate, clearly recalling the last shot in Fellini's 1960 film *La Dolce Vita,* also set seaside as a young man of wavering integrity must decide whether or not to wholeheartedly surrender to the superficially seductive lifestyle around him. What Vito (and we) then see on-screen is De Niro's Sam darting about the beach, gazing into the camera like an educated, intellectualized, articulate precursor of Travis Bickle: pretending to fire a gun at someone. The camera cuts to the man being shot, and it is Sam himself. There are several repeated variations of this image, and it is a lingering one—the notion of the character trapped, at once a victimizer and the victim, ultimately bearing the brunt of his own pent-up violence. The two sides of Sam—like the two sides of so many other remarkable De Niro characterizations—are at odds with one another; if he is destroyed, it is more by his own hand than anyone else's.

The final sequence, in which Vito exacts revenge on Andrew and, wounded, drives away with an adoring Vivien, is conventional, overplayed, and unconvincing, as is much that happens in the second half of *The Swap*. This is certainly not a fine film of its era, such as *Greetings*, nor is it even as fascinating a failure as *The Wedding Party*. Yet *The Swap* is far more intriguing than anyone has yet given it credit for being, containing endless hints of things to come—if not for the filmmakers (who would never achieve the status that De Palma, Scorsese, and Coppola did), then at least for the actor/star.

DE NIRO'S JEWISH MOTHER:

A family portrait: Ma Barker (Shelley Winters) flanked by her killer brood (Clint Kimbrough, Robert Walden, Don Stroud, and Robert De Niro).

Bloody Mama

(1970)

American International Pictures

CAST:

Shelley Winters (*Kate "Ma" Barker*); Pat Hingle (*Sam Pendlebury*); Don Stroud (*Herman Barker*); Diane Varsi (*Mona Gibson*); Bruce Dern (*Kevin Dirkman*); Clint Kimbrough (*Arthur Barker*); Robert Walden (*Fred Barker*); Robert De Niro (*Lloyd Barker*); Alex Nicol (*George "Pa" Barker*); Pamela Dunlap (*Rembrandt*); Scatman Crothers (*Moses*); Lisa Jill (*Young Kate*).

CREDITS:

Producer and director, Roger Corman; coproducers, Samuel Z. Arkoff and James H. Nicholson; screenplay, Robert Thom, from a story by Thom and Don Peters; photography, John Alonzo; editor, Eve Newman; musical supervision, Al Simms; composer and conductor, Don Randi; running time, 92 minutes; rating: R.

After 1967's *Bonnie and Clyde* surprised everyone by becoming both a financial and artistic success, Holly-wood's "fringe" filmmakers rushed into production with exploitation-flick imitations, movies featuring *Bonnie and Clyde*'s rural Depression-era setting, romanticized rube outlaws, and graphic violence—lacking only the original's admirable artistry and thematic weight. *Bloody Mama* was such a film, hurriedly written only to be shelved for two years after the spring 1968 assassinations of Sen. Robert Kennedy and Dr. Martin Luther King caused even such schlockmeisters to pause and reconsider the effect cinematic gore could have on the country.

Former A-movie actress and two-time Oscar winner Shelley Winters had been approached by quickie-flick producer Corman as his first choice for the title character. Winters often states that she loves giving young talented people (especially males) their first big break, particularly someone as brilliant as she knew De Niro to be. She had cast him in her New York stage show after

39

In the film's most disconcerting scene, Rembrandt (Pamela Dunlap) seduces Lloyd (De Niro), only to realize too late that the man on top of her is a dangerous killer.

Bonnie and Clyde meet Oedipus: Lloyd and Ma enjoy a tender moment.

seeing Bobby perform some forgettable play in a small Greenwich Village loft theater where, she recalls, "when he moved across the stage, it gave me tingles. It was like lightning [striking], and I hadn't [experienced] anything like it since the first time I saw Brando in the forties." Winters then convinced Corman to let De Niro play Lloyd, one of her sons in this fictionalized account of the real-life Barker gang. When Corman agreed, the film—shot in less than six weeks—gave De Niro his first experience working outside of the New York academic/avant-garde style of De Palma.

Bobby's natural tendency to live his roles to the fullest was clear even in this modest gangster mini-epic. The script had his character gradually falling apart, until Lloyd physically all but wastes away. De Niro took that notion quite seriously. He became so frail (losing weight with the same artistic intensity with which he would later gain weight for a far more formidable project, *Raging Bull*) that Winters recoiled in horror at what she still recalls as Bobby's "horribly chalky look," as ugly sores began breaking out all over his body. By the time his character reached his nadir, De Niro had lost a full thirty pounds. Then, Lloyd was killed off, and the crew—Winters included—breathed a sigh of relief, assuming De Niro would now do what an actor on a B picture usually does under such circumstances—go home. Winters proceeded, performing her role in Lloyd's burial

Mona (Diane Varsi) gives Lloyd and Herman something to think about besides robbing banks; a decade earlier, Varsi had been introduced to audiences as the ingenue in the big budget *Peyton Place*, but her career had long since faded, so while on the way down, she met De Niro on the way up.

Lloyd and Herman (Don Stroud) hold up a store.

Mom insists that the boys clean up in the tub, even before they go out to kill.

sequence. As she walked up to the gravesite, her conscious performance of sadness suddenly transformed into real horror as she peered in, expecting an empty hole, instead finding her young protégé lying there, quite still.

"Bobby!" she recalls screaming. "You get out of that grave this very minute!"

But De Niro, insisting on a total integrity that Corman films have never been known for, felt it necessary to see his character through to the bitter end, so Winters and the other performers could react honestly to his presence, rather than merely pretend they grieved for the dead Lloyd. Winters, who takes great delight in remaining coy on the question of whether she was ever romantically linked with De Niro, insists he was a little boy in need of protection: "I'm his Jewish mama. Bobby needs somebody to watch over him. He doesn't even wear an overcoat in the winter." She was stunned to realize while filming *Bloody Mama* that De Niro had been so thrilled

to win the role, he didn't bother to check on how much he would receive. "When I found out how little money they were paying him," she recalls, "I demanded they gave him [something more] for his expenses, at least."

What we see on-screen is sleazy, if never boring. In the opening sequence, an unknown young actress (Lisa Jill) playing Kate, who will eventually become the notorious Ma Barker, is raped by her brothers, egged on by her father. The man (Alex Nicol) she eventually marries and has children with (assuming none are the byproduct of her siblings) is an emasculated and sad excuse for the head of a redneck clan. No wonder, then, that her twisted "killer brood" will include a wide variety of out-of-the-mainstream types, including drug addicts, violent homosexuals, and an outright sadist.

Ma and her boys bid farewell to their shack in Joplin and head through the Ozarks. Petty larceny leads to a ferry-raft incident in which casual killer Herman stomps the neck of another passenger, strangling him to death as the other brothers gather around to watch. Reasoning that you can only be hanged once, the entire family then steals some petty cash from a fireman's picnic. Fred and Herman are captured and incarcerated in a local jail, though Ma, Arthur, and Lloyd plot to rob the Yellville bank and use the cash to buy the jailed boys out, attesting to the corruption of the Establishment: a late-1960s attitude imposed on the period-piece material.

Indeed, the film insults traditional sensibilities whenever it can. During the getaway, Ma takes four little old white-haired ladies as hostages, forcing them to stand on the running board, hanging on for dear life, as the police give chase. When Mama casually begins knocking the old ladies off the moving car, those rare older people who had entered the theater gasped in horror, while many youthful moviegoers loudly shouted their glee at this offhand dismissal of even such harmless Establishment types. With her entire family intact once again, the Barker brood then zips around the Southern back roads in period cars, rob banks, and kidnap various characters. These include a beautiful society girl, and a millionaire played by Pat Hingle, blindfolded and forced to engage in sex with Ma, nonetheless impressing the boys as being the kind of father figure they always wanted but never had. When Sam Pendlebury's $300,000 ransom is paid, the boys disobey their mother for the first and only time, ignoring her instructions that there are to be no witnesses left alive, refusing to touch Sam owing to his strength of character.

Lloyd, Fred, and Herman pause over the body of a victim.

The Barkers engage in some laughably simplistic and overstated pop psychology about the dishonesty of the social system and their outlaw lifestyle as a form of protest. "You had everything and we had nothing and it ain't fair," Ma shouts at policemen—who were probably underpaid themselves—before she blows them away. Herman's jailhouse lover (Bruce Dern) joins the gang only to be seduced by Mama. Later, the sexual revolution of the late sixties is anachronistically imposed on the Depression-era setting when Mona the whore (Diane Varsi, former 1950s A-movie starlet who proved unable to follow up her lead in 1957's *Peyton Place,* drifting into junk movies) would like to marry Herman but practices free love, age-of-Aquarius fashion, with any and all of the brothers who constitute the "outlaw commune."

Ultimately, there's the obligatory slow-motion massacre sequence in which those characters who have not yet been killed are finally finished off in graphically violent fashion. In *Life,* Richard Schickel claimed that *Bloody Mama* "has a certain feverish energy, though it is . . . lacking in moral or esthetic imperatives, badly directed by Roger Corman, whose reputation among cultists continues to mystify me." Charles Champlin of the *Los Angeles Times* referred to it as "Mommie and Clyde" and "a sleek, vile exercise. . . . It is all totally cynical (in attitude) and totally professional (in execution), a piece of pop art from which you emerge feeling depressed, degraded, and diminished." In addition, Champlin's review contained an astute perception: Hollywood movies, which had previously brought all Americans together into a single vast community, had in the late sixties begun to "target" audiences, be they young or old, further dividing an already divided nation: "The audience for which Corman is aiming will love *Bloody Mama* for its cynical sending-up of cinematic pretentions and for its anti-Establishment snarlings. . . . Other audiences will look at the sleazy concoction of sex and sadism which Corman has decided is what [the kids of the early seventies] want and will feel a considerable distaste."

Though he's the first of the brothers to be killed off, De Niro did create a strong enough impression to be singled out by several critics. John Mahoney of the *Hollywood Reporter* disliked the film intensely, but paused in his criticism to note that "Robert De Niro, currently working with Miss Winters on Broadway, is rather good, given the limited dimensions of his junkie role," while the *Motion Picture Herald* cited his acting as "excellent." Indeed, De Niro's sequence with the society girl is the best thing in the movie. Rembrandt (Pamela Dunlap) is a rich beauty who uses her femininity to conquer the insecure redneck Lloyd on a raft at a public beach. When she gradually realizes he is quietly dangerous rather than the sweet and shy boy she believed,

Rembrandt only wants to get away as quickly as possible, but her fear and panic are by then useless. The clan has angrily gathered around her, resenting the condescending quality of her flirtatious seduction of Lloyd. The emotional torture she visited upon Lloyd is then returned to her as outright physical torture. Rembrandt—who had previously entrapped Lloyd, black-widow-spider style, with her body—is bound and gagged, going from all-powerful to totally powerless in a frightfully quick transition. When she is drowned in the bathtub (after being repeatedly raped), we actually share her horrible death, presented through one of the film's few point-of-view shots.

This subplot serves as a fascinating precursor to the De Niro–Cybill Shepherd relationship in *Taxi Driver*, as the powerless rube—seemingly someone who can be manipulated by a self-assured, sexually dominating woman hailing from a higher-class background—rebels against the controlling female. The results here, though, are very different from those in the later film, for her death is what causes Lloyd to descend into hard drugs and eventually die himself. Still, as forgettable and slipshod as the *Bloody Mama* production may have been, it did allow De Niro to create the prototype of Travis Bickle and so many other violence-prone characters he would later incarnate. As Keith McKay put it, De Niro "perfectly portrayed a fractured, disconnected, drug-crazed person. . . . His scenes were imbued with his character's spiritual bankruptcy, with a schizoid, paranoid intensity . . . a stunningly disturbing portrayal." Moreover, it's important to note that as Lloyd, De Niro played the most contemporary of all the sons. While the others are more clearly incarnations of Depression-era outlaws, De Niro's is the drug addict. Lloyd begins by overindulging on Baby Ruth candy bars, moves up to airplane glue, and eventually dies of an overdose of hard drugs. However accidental the casting may be, it's still fascinating that the actor who, more than any other, would effectively portray modern problems on-screen was the one who, in this early nonambitious movie, dramatized a situation that proved frightfully close to what many of the young people in the audience were just then going through. Understandably, then, in a "think piece" for the Sunday *New York Times* theater section, Peter Schjeldahl wrote in the spring of 1970: "Academy Awards have been given away for far lesser efforts than those of . . . De Niro in *Bloody Mama*."

Jon and Judy (Jennifer Salt) attempt a civil date, though the awkward social atmosphere makes that difficult.

Hi, Mom!

(1970)

A Sigma III Release

CAST:

Robert De Niro (*Jon Rubin*); Charles Durnham (*Superintendent*); Allen Garfield (*Joe Banner*); Peter Maloney (*Drugstore Manager*); Abraham Goren (*Pervert in Movie*); Lara Parker (*Jeannie Mitchell*); Jennifer Salt (*Judy Bishop*); Gerritt Graham (*Gerrit Wood*); Nelson Peltz (*Playboy*); Ruth Alda, Carol Vogel, and Beth Bowden (*"Be Black, Baby!" Audience*); Buddy Butler (*"Be Black, Baby!" Actor*); Floyd L. Peterson (*John Winnicove*).

CREDITS:

Writer and director, Brian De Palma, from a story by De Palma and Charles Hirsch; producer, Charles Hirsch; photography, Robert Elfstrom; art director, Peter Bocour; editor, Paul Hirsch; music, Eric Kaz; running time, 87 minutes; rating: R.

Though hardly a blockbuster, *Greetings* had shown enough of a profit that a sequel was in order. Originally to have been called *Son of Greetings*, that title gave way to *Hi, Mom!* Of the three characters from the first

picture, only De Niro's Jon Rubin was featured in the return bout (Gerritt Graham of *Greetings* here plays a new, minor character), suggesting the strong impression Bobby made on filmmaker De Palma and also the public. Jon had been a supporting role in *Greetings*, but it was he—and the actor who played him—that youthful viewers wanted to see more of. So the approach of *Hi, Mom!* is actually a return to the initial concept for *Greetings* in which De Palma hoped to find a Leaud-type actor to express himself, an American Truffaut, through a single evolving character.

A shame, then, that this wasn't continued through a succession of movies during the following decades, for such an autobiographical series might have provided a fascinating portrait of the American scene in transition. Shortly, though, De Palma would instead shift gears and begin his series of technically proficient if intellectually empty Hitchcock homages, while De Niro would discover, in Martin Scorsese, a substance-oriented filmmaker more akin to his own vision. In the meantime,

45

Robert De Niro again as Jon Rubin.

though, Hollywood had begun co-opting the counterculture. Martin Ransohoff of Filmways struck a two-picture deal with youthful producer Hirsch, who remembers being handed "ninety-five thousand dollars under the table to go out and make a nonunion movie in New York," double the budget for *Greetings.* The final shooting budget would top $100,000.

Hirsch and De Palma sketched in a story that begins as Jon, now a veteran of Vietnam, returns home, having metamorphosed into an ultraconservative while under fire. He moves into the only apartment he can afford, in an ugly, crumbling building on New York's Lower East Side. But if he is now a far cry from the lovable leftist we saw in *Greetings,* there is one part of Jon that has not changed: he remains a closet voyeur and potential pornographer. Noticing a sleek new high rise has been erected directly across from his hovel, Jon sets his 8mm camera and records the proclivities, most of them sexual, of his classier neighbors: three attractive girls who continuously slip in and out of their myriad clothes; an aspiring white revolutionary who paints himself black out of guilt; a weird playboy who changes the decor of his room to better fit the personality of each latest girlfriend; and most significantly, a middle-class father who can't enjoy any of the activities of his children firsthand because he's too busy filming them with his home movie

Judy Bishop (center) and her roomates lounge about their apartment, never guessing that Jon Rubin is photographing their every move from across the way.

46

Judy and Jon in a moment of passion.

camera, only relishing those experiences when he eventually watches them on-screen.

Shortly, Jon meets Joe Banner (Allen Garfield), an upscale professional pornographer who explains the techniques of their sleazy trade, ironically doing so with a tone of high seriousness—as if he were the mature Truffaut telling young De Palma how to make an art (in the old-fashioned sense of the term) film. Joe's desire to create the first children's sexploitation flick seemed a far funnier notion in 1970 than it does today, when molestation has become a major issue. At any rate, sensing that he has at last found his calling in life, Jon decides to go pro himself. He becomes fascinated by Judy Bishop (Jennifer Salt, who was featured in De Niro's first picture, *The Wedding Party*), an attractive woman he also lusts after. A bizarre scheme forms in Jon's mind: he will set the timer on his camera, go next door, and seduce Judy while recording their sex act, making him the star as well as director of this improvisational, spontaneous film. In our age, every person with the money to buy a home movie camera becomes an instant voyeur, his favorite subject being himself. Indeed, the recent tendency toward home video porn is something De Palma predicted two decades earlier.

Their encounter remains one of the two most remark-

able and rewarding bits in *Hi, Mom!* as the two engage in much soap-opera-ish, self-indulgent chatter about their missed chances in life, while gorging on everything from sauerkraut to pizza before, during, and after sex—the satisfying of sexual hunger and their parallel hunger for food becoming fascinatingly interrelated. But to his horror, the overenthusiastic girl responds far too quickly, and Jon, knowing the camera is not yet timed to film, makes a desperate excuse, running off to a nearby drugstore where he engages in a bizarre conversation with the druggist (Peter Maloney) about the efficiency of various contraceptives.

Then, Jon rushes back to bed, afterward returning to his own apartment—discovering his camera tilted, yielding up only a Warholian minimalist record of a brick wall. The attitude of the writer/director, as well as an entire generation of film nuts, is perfectly conveyed by the look of horrified disappointment on De Niro's face. Little matter that his seduction succeeded if he doesn't have a permanent record of it to watch and relive over and over as a filmed experience. The seduction (or anything else in his life) does not really count until he also gets to watch it a second time on instant replay; we have become a nation of voyeurs, enjoying the vicarious experience more than the real thing.

Whenever possible, filmmaker Brian De Palma makes the television set a central part of his scene; the movie is essentially about the first generation of Americans to come of age in front of a TV.

47

The cast of the play-within-the-film, "Be Black Baby."

Much of what follows is social satire—some of it splendid, some sophomoric—on everyone from white liberals to black militants. In our age, when *Saturday Night Live* has become a long-established fixture of TV and David Letterman serves up such comedy on a nightly basis, it may be difficult for younger readers to grasp what a jolt such humor provided in 1970. This was a film made by young people who had been weened on *Mad* magazine, then radicalized by the country's dark experiences between the assassinations of JFK in 1963 and RFK in 1968. Shortly, they would become the New Hollywood; in 1970, they were a band of outsiders, railing not only at the Establishment but also at absolutely everything, including themselves. What followed was the film's second brilliant bit, and like the first, it concerned not only society but also the media in the age of McLuhan—the way in which the cinematic capturing of an event takes on more significance than the event itself.

A revolutionary black-theater group, performing off-off-off-Broadway, needs a relatively straight-looking military type to play the villainous policeman ("Pig") in their new production, *Be Black, Baby!* This show, staged by a small clique of radicals, will play to an audience of self-loathing middle-class liberals, who will be insulted throughout the performance and, since this is a "total-organic theater experience," have their faces blackened

by the black actors (wearing whiteface), then actually dragged onto the stage to be force-fed soul food, fondle the actors' Afros ("It feels like angels' hair!"), and be verbally abused. Then, the men are beaten and a woman (Ruth Alda) is stripped and virtually raped, as simulation transforms into actuality. The cop (played by Jon, who is played by Bobby) arrives on the scene and automatically takes the side of those whose faces are white. The sufficiently bloodied theatergoers then exit, thrilled that the play was everything the Clive Barnes review promised, while spouting reactions at once naive and clichéd ("Really makes you think!").

They make such admissions to a documentary film-maker from a TV show called *N.I.T. Journal*—a marvelous takeoff on the actual NET (pre-PBS) programs. NET actually did present just such intellectualized studies of radical street theater. The sequence—a grainy black-and-white TV show within the movie, and a perfectly modulated satire that only slightly exaggerates the actual video vérité approach—remains a dazzling, if now dated, example of media satire.

The black militants invade Jon's apartment house and are mowed down by middle-class residents who have taken up guns. Jon (now married to a respectable, pregnant, whiney Judy), observing as firemen sift through the rubble of his trashed apartment building (a good bourgeoise, he went downstairs to do the wash,

Jon Rubin and his radical friends.

then instinctually blew up the place instead), is asked by a TV reporter if he has something—anything—to say to America. He stares into the camera, flashes what would become De Niro's signature grin, and mutters an enigmatic, unrevealing "Hi, Mom!"

Critic Richard Cuskelly of the (*Los Angeles Herald-Examiner*) argued that "it is an effective, shocking ending, but an incomplete one." Perhaps; then again, Cuskelly may have been hoping for something more in line with the ingenious and ingenuous *Greetings*. This was a different film, about and for a different era. Society was changing so fast that *Son of Greetings/Hi Mom!* could not merely offer more of the same, as the youth audience of 1970 was different from that of only a year and a half earlier. Fortunately, filmmakers De Palma and Hirsch noted this. In the first film, New York is divided up into two sides—the lovably scruffy young and their natural enemies, the older Establishment types—precisely how most people perceived things in 1968. In the sequel, however, there's no sense whatsoever of a community among the young. It's extremely significant that Jon Rubin now stands entirely alone, without his companions from the first picture.

Understandably, then, Richard Schickel of *Life* noted that De Palma had "moved from the relatively cheerful anarchy of last year's draft-dodger comedy to a much more intense, difficult, and daring manner of filmmak-

ing." This is a New York in which drugs have become a bad trip rather than a groovy experience, where violence is enacted randomly instead of being perpetrated on flower-power kids by urban rednecks. Nihilistic graffiti and nonstop crime have replaced the gaily positive psychedelic colorings and love-in-the-streets attitude of the previous year. Nineteen sixty-nine had been the last year of a we-vs.-them mentality for the country's youth; in 1970, that notion had given way to a me-vs.-everybody attitude.

When De Niro's Jon Rubin joins in the theatrical experience, he plays the role of a vicious urban-redneck cop, swinging his billy club at innocent people in the audience. Critic Michael Bliss noted, in De Niro's ferocity, "a terrifying capacity for the depiction of violence-prone individuals," something that would be repeated many times over the years. But it would be the Scorsese films that would milk this potential and make the strongest impression, so it's noteworthy Bliss also picked up on a precursor to that famous *Taxi Driver* scene in which Travis Bickle, always on the edge, tips over a TV set to see how far it can lean without actually falling over, all the while "fondling one of [his] deadly weapons." In *Hi, Mom!* Jon similarly tips over a TV, then puts a bullet through it, as if he can't discern between animate and inanimate objects—causing us to wonder if the remarkable *Taxi Driver* moment really did come

49

from the mind of cowriter/director Scorsese, or whether De Niro was a far more active collaborator than anyone has yet given him credit for being.

Since he was the centerpiece of the picture, De Niro was finally singled out by critics, who mostly had only positive things to say—even if they still sometimes managed to mangle his name. John Mahoney of the *Hollywood Reporter* noted that "Nero [*sic*], who is very much like Alan Alda [?!], performs well in his many character shifts," while "Rick" of *Variety* similarly commented that "De Niro's character is really a series of separate acts, and he is very capable of each one of them." In the *Motion Picture Herald,* Lewis Archibald wrote: "Robert De Niro does a fine job as the hero in what amounts to a series of improvisations on different themes. Whether an aw-shucks kid, a pursed-lip uptight, or a spare-time cop, De Niro always extends the comedy with his own fine sense of timing." How fascinating that De Niro, who would impress audiences and critics alike with his ability to become a totally, convincingly different person for each film, would in his initial lead play a person who, like himself as an actor, cannot be pigeonholed as any single personality, but shifts, chameleon-like, throughout.

It's worth noting, though, that De Niro also had his first major experience with negative reviews, when Stanley Kauffmann of *The New Republic* claimed that "the weakest element is that the weight of the picture rests on De Niro, who was very good as part of a troika in the first picture but lacks the range and appeal to sustain a film more or less by himself." At least Bobby could take pleasure in knowing that Kauffman would eventually have to eat those words!

A HEROINE ON HEROIN:

The original Taxi Driver: Robert De Niro in his initial incarnation of the gypsy cabbie who drives Marcus Rottner (Michael Brandon) around the city.

Jennifer on My Mind

(1971)

A United Artists Release

CAST:

Tippy Walker (*Jennifer Da Silva*); Michael Brandon (*Marcus Rottner*); Lou Gilbert (*Max Rottner*); Steve Vinovich (*Sigmund Ornstein*); Peter Bonerz (*Sergei*); Renee Taylor (*Selma*); Chuck McCann (*Sam*); Bruce Kornbluth (*Larry Dolci*); Barry Bostwick (*Nanki*); Jeff Conaway (*Hanki*); Robert De Niro (*Mardigian*); Erich Segal (*Gondolier*).

CREDITS:

Director, Noel Black; producer, Bernard Schwartz; screenplay, Erich Segal from the novel *Heir* by Roger L. Simon; photography, Andy Laszlo; art director, Ben Edwards; editor, Jack Wheeler; music, Stephen J. Lawrence; running time, 90 minutess; rating: R.

In the late sixties, drugs briefly seemed an acceptable part of the flower-power mentality that suffused the peace/love counterculture; films including *Easy Rider* and *Alice's Restaurant* portrayed drug use matter-of-factly. By the early seventies, however, bell-bottom jeans, psychedelic shirts, and antiwar pendants—the charming, idealistic aspects of the youth revolution—slipped out of sight. But drugs remained, no longer seeming innocuous. Movies necessarily commented on the growing problem of a down-and-out druggie subculture, including the still-powerful *Panic in Needle Park*. Robert De Niro had already offered a harrowing performance of a drug-addicted youth in *Bloody Mama*, though that film placed the problem in a period-piece context.

So the announcement that producer Bernard Schwartz, president of Joseph M. Schenck Enterprises, had purchased the screen rights to Roger Simon's first published novel, *Heir*, for $50,000 boded well. Roger O. Hirson was originally signed to write the screenplay, which United Artists put on their slate as a $2-million-

La Dolce Vita by way of Erich Segal: Tippy Walker (as Jennifer Da Silva) and Michael Brandon.

plus film. "I want to make *Heir* the way it is," Schwartz stated, "the real thing about two youngsters, where money is no problem but who grow up without family affection and go on drugs. It's the kind of picture I've always wanted to do."

Jennifer on My Mind certainly sounded like a potentially powerful film. The director, Noel Black, had created a cult sensation several years earlier with the black comedy *Pretty Poison.* The final writer was Erich Segal, whose *Love Story* had recently broken box-office records by effectively updating the old *Dark Victory* weeper for contemporary audiences. The top-billed star was Tippy Walker, delightful ingenue from *The World of Henry Orient,* and Robert De Niro received nineteenth billing! If any movie seemed likely to impress critics and overpower audiences, it was *Jennifer.*

Instead, the film barely received release. A total failure, the movie simplified the issues, presenting them through contrived drama, offering characters who were both uninteresting and unsympathetic. As Kevin Thomas wrote in the *Los Angeles Times, Jennifer* "could just as easily have been called *Drug Story* and been hyped, you should pardon the expression, with the slogan 'Love means never having to ask for a fix.'" *Cue* nodded to Segal's previous hit by tagging this "a love story without love and without a story." Segal once again wrote about the privileged upper class, focusing on a leading lady named Jenny who dies, as well as the young man who

52

So young, so beautiful, so rich, so unhappy; a desperate Jennifer flirts with death.

The age of addiction: Marcus realizes that Jennifer has been shooting up again, in one of the numerous early-seventies films to provide a cautionary fable about drugs.

afterward recalls her; this time, however, it is not cancer but hard drugs that do her in. *Jennifer* features a heroine on heroin. "You would think," Thomas continued, "that filmmakers would have learned by now you can't sentimentalize drug-taking (and that it is irresponsible to try). But *Jennifer* [preaches against drugs] to the point of threatening us with an overdose—of saccharin."

In Segal's earlier and more commercially successful film, he had featured a preppyish boy and a blue-collar girl. This time, he reversed that, making Jenny Da Silva a descendant of people who were on the *Mayflower,* and Marcus Rottner (Michael Brandon) the grandson of a Jewish racketeer. Both are wealthy, though she radiates Waspish class while he has the street-tough blood of his parents, creating the necessary contrast. They have something else in common: each is neglected, lost, and lonely. "Every month I get this big check from my trust fund," he complains, "so big I couldn't possibly spend it all." Jenny, suffering from ennui, sighs, "I was on one of

my tours of Southern Europe, moving aimlessly from Spain to Italy to Greece and back to Italy again."

Their story is told in annoying flashback fashion. We first see Marcus driving around in his sports car and can't grasp why he looks so unhappy. We soon realize why: Jenny's corpse is in the trunk. Flashbacks then reveal how they met, fell in love, swam in a Venice canal, then shared marijuana, only to lose their chance for happiness owing to Jenny's growing addiction to hard drugs. Segal set the story in Venice (and made a cameo appearance as a gondolier), perhaps hoping the gorgeous settings would make up for the lack of substance.

The film attempts to make the audience weep for the main characters—difficult, seeing as they come off not as the victims of an unfair adult society but as self-indulgent brats we can't care about. "All others [in the story] are reduced to caricatures in order to bolster sympathy for [the leads], always a sign of a bad movie," Thomas wrote. That included De Niro, all but wasted in a bit role. Whatever limitations there may have been to *Bloody Mama,* it depicted the horrors of drug addiction far more effectively than this supposed A movie did.

Having already played several leads or key supporting parts in left-of-center films, young De Niro considered himself lucky to be cast in an A feature, at the very least getting the experience of working in a large-scale production, however awful the results. He was not alone— the supporting cast (see listing above) featured numerous other young actors who would also shortly make their mark on the entertainment business, if none so notably as Bobby. Yet even his most devoted fans will be hard-pressed to sit through *Jennifer* waiting for a brief glimpse of him as, intriguingly enough, a semicrazed gypsy-cab driver—a cameo portrait of Travis Bickle in embryo. At one point, Mardigian's wildly painted taxi lurches up to a New York streetcorner when hailed by the hero, who enters. The cabbie then grins strangely and announces, "Hey, man, I think I should warn you—I'm very high!" To which Marcus replies, "So am I."

Brief as his part is, De Niro was singled out by Craig Fisher of the *Hollywood Reporter,* who wrote: "There is one memorable, original character in *Jennifer on My Mind,* the gypsy-cab driver/speed freak played by Robert Deniro [*sic*]. . . . Apart from Deniro, there's not much that's memorable—such a fey, weird concoction that it almost defies description. Watching it is like mainlining taffy." If the film were available on home video, the recommendation for De Niro fans might be to fast-forward to his single scene.

A WILD MAN IN EMBRYO:

George Segal as the junkie antihero, Jay Jay; Though the film was not successful, Segal did deliver one of his better performances.

Born to Win

(1971)

A United Artists Release

CAST:

George Segal (*Jay Jay*); Karen Black (*Parm*); Jay Fletcher (*Billy Dynamite*); Hector Elizondo (*The Greek*); Marcia Jean Kurtz (*Marlene*); Irving Selbst (*Stanley*); Robert De Niro (*Danny*); Paula Prentiss (*Veronica*); Sylvia Sims (*Cashier*).

CREDITS:

Director, Ivan Passer; producer, Philip Langner; coproducers, George Segal and Jerry Tokofsky; screenplay, David Scott Milton; photography, Jack Priestly and Richard Kratina; art director, Murray Stern; editor, Ralph Rosenbaum; music, William S. Fisher; running time, 90 minutes; rating: R.

Bobby's leading roles in such little youth movies as *Greetings* had not catapulted him into the fame that Dustin Hoffman enjoyed after *The Graduate*, so he took what roles he could get, including some that were little more than bit parts. His policeman in this early 1970s antidrug treatise is an example of De Niro working in a film with meritorious ambitions but minor impact, at least allowing him to play the kind of tough, insistent, threatening character he would develop in such little movies as *Taxi Driver*—though most often, he would be cast as a loner who runs afoul of the law rather than as a plainclothes cop.

As compared to De Niro's previous antidrug film, *Jennifer on My Mind,* this one certainly seemed to be shaping up as something special. Author David Scott Milton clearly knew what he was talking about here, basing his characters on drug addicts who had frequented the New York restaurant he owned. His film, based on his off-off-off-Broadway stage play, was at one point to have been called *Scraping Bottom*, eventually changed to *Born to Lose*—and then, when that, too, seemed too pessimistic, to its final title. Well, not quite final—recently, the movie has been released on home

research for the film; they'll work with professional actors." Together, Passer and Milton (whose play *Duet for Solo Voice* was just then opening at the American Place Theatre) interviewed ex-addicts at Phoenix House and, as Milton put it, "learned how these people exist, including the way they're pushed into crises and how they survive."

In the film, Jay Jay (George Segal) and Billy Dynamite (Jay Fletcher) are New York junkies who became hooked in the late sixties, when drugs seemed trendy, even political. Now, lost in a life of crime, they will do absolutely anything to procure the next fix. In the film's opening sequence, they are robbing a Broadway diner; no sooner have they grabbed all the money and rushed out the door than they slam into the police. The film was

Robert De Niro at about the time when *Born to Win* was filmed; the actor who had played several leads was, at the moment, glad to be working even in minor roles.

video under the title *Addict*, with De Niro's name listed above the title, as if he played the leading character!

Then there was the director, highly acclaimed thirty-six-year-old Czech filmmaker Ivan Passer, whose 1965 movie, *Intimate Lighting*, had received ecstatic reviews. Passer hailed his first American project as a touching blend of drama and comedy: "I guess you could call it a drama about drug rehabilitation—on the surface, but it's more about junkies I've been meeting, whose values are more real and stable than those of many other people. I plan to use actual [druggies] I've run into while doing shot as a downbeat antidrug movie, but certain parties at United Artists got cold feet and decided no one would ever pay to see such a depressing picture. So the movie was recut, its comedic elements played up. In fact, nobody came to see the film, as it arrived after one too many other antidrug films had already surfeited the market. Instead of a movie with integrity that no one wanted to see, the result of postproduction monkeying was a compromised movie nobody wanted to see. Too bad for Segal, who delivered what was perhaps his finest performance; also for two interesting actresses, Paula Prentiss (who, as Segal's ex-wife, received star billing but was virtually cut from the film) and Karen Black (she plays his kooky, accommodating new girlfriend).

Charles Champlin of the *Los Angeles Times* wrote that

Director Ivan Passer coaches George Segal on the playing of a particularly gruesome shoot-up sequence.

Jay Jay collapses in the arms of Parm (Karen Black) and Billy Dynamite (Jay Fletcher).

"*Born to Win* leaves no doubt that Ivan Passer is a topflight director with a special capacity for handling close relationships and intense private moments. But here . . . his observant eye seems to have watched not American life but movies and TV purporting to be about American life." Nick Yanni of the *Hollywood Reporter* complained that "Passer's direction seems strangely unfocused [so] much of the picture comes off as phony and ill-conceived. . . . It's unfortunate that a sensibility as fine as Passer's has gotten bogged down in a film that is so cliché-ridden." If handled properly, this might have been a black comedy, but that is not the result. At times, the movie turns into a vivid, harrowing case study of an addict and his craving on the order of *The Man With the Golden Arm*. At other moments, it transforms into a Feifferesque example of edgy humor about a lovable Jewish schnook trying to survive in the ever-more-threatening Manhattan, like *Little Murders*. Occasionally, it's supposed to be a romantic comedy about a Neil Simonish guy and his girls. We're left with the impression that the filmmakers set out to make one sort of movie, were persuaded to do something else entirely after they had started shooting, then changed their minds a third time when things were clearly not working out and everybody became desperate. When the scenes were finally edited together, the result was a mishmash, a total mess—but not without flashes revealing the talents of all involved.

Perhaps the best comic moment occurs when a detective catches Jay Jay, who is hiding from him in a washing machine until it is suddenly activated. Likewise, the best dramatic scene was Billy's death—the elevator doors endlessly opening and closing on his body—providing actor Jay Fletcher with his best moment ever on-screen.

Of marginal interest to De Niro fans is his hard-edged policeman, who—with a partner—continually closes in on Jay Jay. Whereas the partner is relatively quiet, Bobby's cop flashes a cruel smile; he bullies and cajoles, continually threatening to break into wild violence that even his partner would not be able to restrain. Though Bobby is always in the background and has only a few minutes of screen time, he does present an embryonic portrait of the wild men he's always been most associated with—despite the long line of quiet characters he's also played.

Jay Jay is assaulted by the hoodlums and dealers.

A posed publicity shot, in which Kid Sally (Jerry Orbach) and Baccala (Lionel Stander) argue, while other assorted Runyonesque characters mill about. That's De Niro, second-from-left, romancing Leigh Taylor-Young.

The Gang That Couldn't Shoot Straight

(1971)

A Metro-Goldwyn-Mayer Release

CAST:

Jerry Orbach (*Kid Sally*); Leigh Taylor-Young (*Angela*); Jo Van Fleet (*Big Momma*); Lionel Stander (*Baccala*); Robert De Niro (*Mario*); Irving Selbst (*Big Jelly*); Herve Villechaize (*Beppo*); Joe Santos (*Ezmo*); Carmine Caridi (*Tony the Indian*); Frank Campanella (*Water Buffalo*); Harry Basch (*DeLauria*); Sander Vanocur (*TV Reporter*); Phil Bruns (*Gallagher*); Jack Kehoe (*Scuderi*); James Sloyan (*Joey*); Burt Young (*Willie Quarequio*); Jackie Vernon (*Herman*); Michael Gazzo (*Black Suit*); Elsa Raven (*Water Buffalo's Wife*).

CREDITS:

Director, James Goldstone; producers, Robert Chartoff and Irwin Winkler; screenplay, Waldo Salt, from the novel by Jimmy Breslin; photography, Owen Roizman; art director, Robert Gundlach; editor, Edward A. Biery; music, Dave Grusin; running time, 96 minutes; rating: GP.

The first *Godfather* film had been nervously greeted by Italian Americans, ready to accuse it of being offensive to their sensibilities. But upon watching Francis Ford Coppola's movie, such self-appointed watchdogs quickly concluded it was a great cinematic work of art, in no way worthy of admonition. Shortly before, though, loud and angry indignation was taken toward *The Gang That Couldn't Shoot Straight,* an unrelentingly stupid portrait of Italians as mobsters, based on Jimmy Breslin's well-regarded book of the same name but turning his clever ethnic comedy into broad, vulgar burlesque of the lowest order. "You don't have to be Italian to hate *The Gang That Couldn't Shoot Straight,"* Jay Cocks wrote in *Time,* "although that gives you a distinct edge. The movie's febrile witlessness easily transcends all ethnic boundaries and comes guaranteed to outrage virtually everybody. . . . [Waldo] Salt's chaotic script turns Bres-

Robert De Niro, hitting the big time at last when Al Pacino dropped out of this film to do a bigger one: *The Godfather*.

lin's characters, which were already caricatures, into vicious racial stereotypes."

Most other critics felt pretty much the same way. Though the movie is an utter embarrassment for all involved, it's worth noting that the initial ambitions were grand. Salt had recently won an Oscar for adapting another novel, *Midnight Cowboy,* to the screen, while director James Goldstone had been praised for his gentle coming-of-age film, *Red Sky at Morning.* A sufficient budget was raised by independent producers Chartoff and Winkler so that the film could, for authenticity's sake, be shot entirely in New York, with most of the location work done in the Red Hook section of South Brooklyn. That did not prove to be an easy task, for Goldstone immediately found himself at odds with Manhattan's unions in general, and the International Alliance of Theatrical Motion Picture Machine Operators, Local 52, in particular. He loudly complained that "we had a Cinemobile with a phenomenal driver provided by Cinemobile Systems, but we were required to have three standby drivers—and none of them drove." *Gang* deserves a footnote in film history as the straw that

Mario, the first of De Niro's phony priests, listens intently as Baccala explains the game plan; Kid Sally (standing) listens in.

Most critics reserved their faint praise for the young lovers; surprisingly, pretty and talented Leigh Taylor-Young would soon disappear from movie screens.

broke the cinematic camel's back; during the next decade, numerous other New York films would be shot in Baltimore, Toronto, and other cities to avoid the hassle and expense encountered on this project.

Gang was clearly a New York fable. A pathetic gang of maverick gangsters, led by the hapless Kid Sally (Broadway's Jerry Orbach, in a role originally slated for Marcello Mastroianni), find themselves at odds with Baccala (Lionel Stander), the local big boy and a religious fanatic to boot: he has a neon-lit, life-size statue of St. Anthony in his office. It's less that Kid Sally is ambitious, more that his mother, Big Momma (Jo Van Fleet), into lasagna and larceny, prods him to take over local criminal operations from his sometimes boss. But Baccala is not an easy guy to get; fearful of being bombed, he sends his wife out each morning to start the car while he hides under the dining room table. As part of an elaborate (and impossible to follow) scheme, Mario (De Niro), a young six-day bike racer, is brought over to America to race, creating a bridge between the two gangs. When he's not busy stealing everything in his hotel suite, Mario romances Kid Sally's kid sister.

Though, among other things, the actors' accents were widely attacked as being stereotyped, it's worth noting that De Niro, upon learning he'd been cast in the film, immediately reached into his own meager savings and paid for a trip to Sicily, to master the speech patterns so his work would be authentic. This was yet another early example of his total dedication to a role and the film containing it, giving his all even for a project that many others would have thought of as nothing more than a source of a paycheck. *Playboy* acknowledged that a star equal to Hoffman and Pacino was in the making, as Bruce Williamson reported that "attention is sure to settle on Robert De Niro, an amiably handsome recruit from the New York movie scene, who contributes a socko performance as Mario—an Italian bicycle rider with a penchant for petty theft and a yen for Kid Sally's sister. In this kind of movie, romance usually poses a problem, but De Niro and Leigh Taylor-Young are so attractive a couple that they almost walk off with the picture." Williamson was not alone in citing the young couple as the high point. Cocks noted in *Time:* "Robert De Niro, as a kleptomaniacal bicycle rider, and Leigh Taylor-Young as his perennially startled paramour, somehow manage to bring a small degree of charm and reality to the lamentable goings-on."

Taylor-Young drifted out of the limelight, even as De Niro emerged as the equal of Hoffman and Pacino. So it's intriguing to note that the role of Mario had been slated for Pacino, who achieved full-fledged stardom a few years before Bobby thanks to the first *Godfather* film. Lawyers for Pacino and MGM engaged in nasty bouts over his refusal to appear in several of the company's films, beginning with *Gang*—which he presumably felt would be a stigma on his career, and rightly so. Fascinating, though, that the actor who, in flashbacks, would shortly play Pacino's father in the second *Godfather* installment was brought in to replace him. Indeed, De Niro made such an impression in this otherwise muddled, minor gangster film that it helped him win the coveted role of Don Corleone.

In many respects, this serves as a dry run for that part, since Mario is charming and sinister, able to sweetly court a pretty young woman (and strike us as absolutely sincere when doing so) only to, a moment later, engage in some nefarious, even deadly, criminal activity. Mario is a convincing contradiction in terms rather than the inconsistent character he might have been. Certainly, we expect a good actor to do good work in a good movie; but turning in a fine performance in a dreadful film allows us to see a performer going above and beyond the call of duty. De Niro was singled out for praise even by those critics who rightly trashed the film. Richard Cuskelly of *Los Angeles Herald-Examiner* hailed "Robert DeNiro [*sic*], the handsome young Italian whose antics and sense of comic timing nearly steal the picture." Likewise, *Variety* briefly halted their panning of the picture to note: "Particularly good is Robert De Niro, the irreverent, thieving immigrant who's quick to learn the ropes." Charles Champlin of the *Los Angeles Times* mentioned that "De Niro, stealing everything in sight, has a raffish charm." Ann Guarino of the New York *Daily News* pointed out that Orbach, whose bid for movie stardom this was, "goes too far" in making his character a bungler and "gives the film away to Robert De Niro." In *Films and Filming,* Peter Buckley noted that the acting "ranges from the charmless broad to the blatantly bad," but hastened to add that "only Robert De Niro manages to give any sort of dimension to his cardboard character, and his Italian accent is quite perfect."

At the very least, most of the critics spelled his name right this time around. Shortly, they would even begin to leave the proper space between the De and the Niro. What better proof could Bobby have asked for that he'd finally arrived?

DUSTIN HOFFMAN, MOVE OVER:

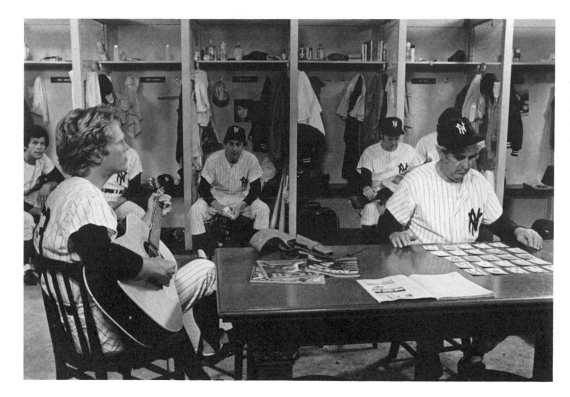

The title sequence: a cowboyish ballplayer, unaware of Pearson's terrible predicament, sings a ballad about dying young.

Bang the Drum Slowly

(1973)

A Paramount Pictures Release

CAST:

Robert De Niro (*Bruce Pearson*); Michael Moriarty (*Henry Wiggen*); Vincent Gardenia (*Manager, Dutch Schnell*); Phil Foster (*Coach Joe Jaros*); Ann Wedgeworth (*Katie, Bruce's Hooker Girlfriend*); Patrick McVey (*Pearson's Father*); Heather MacRae (*Holly, Henry's Wife*); Selma Diamond (*Tootsie, Switchboard Lady*); Barbara Babcock, Maurice Rosenfield (*Team Owners*); Tom Ligon (*Piney*).

CREDITS:

Director, John Hancock; producers, Maurice and Lois Rosenfield; screenplay, Mark Harris, adapted from his novel; photography, Richard Shore; production design, Robert Gundlach; editor, Richard Marks; music, Stephen Lawrence; running time, 96 minutes; rating: PG.

If there has been a limitation to De Niro's career, it's the rarity with which he's played sympathetic characters.

Perhaps his utter lack of sentimentality as an actor draws him to more complex, ambiguous, even dark types. But on those rare occasions when his character has been mostly likable and easily accessible—*Falling in Love, Awakenings*—De Niro has effectively approached what could easily have become soap-opera-ish roles in such a circumspect and original manner that he's prevented the parts from lapsing into the maudlin. His first major effort in this direction was in *Bang the Drum Slowly*, his initial mainstream movie lead as well as his premiere performance as a nonthreatening character.

Though the title suggests a western (deriving, as it does, from the old ballad, commonly called "The Streets of Laredo," about a young cowboy who dies young), this was in fact a baseball movie. The film dealt with the unexpected friendship that develops between two members of the fictional New York "Mammoths," the uneducated Bruce Pearson (De Niro) and his roommate, a

Robert De Niro as Bruce Pearson.

Joe Jaross (Phil Foster, right) is amazed to realize that classy Henry Wiggen (Michael Moriarty) has become best friends with Bruce, the team outcast.

Bruce attempts an awkward romance with Katie (Ann Wedgeworth).

more sophisticated young man, Henry Wiggen (Michael Moriarty). *Drum* was supposed to have been made much sooner; Mark Harris's novel had been published in 1956. Shortly thereafter, the story had been dramatized on television's *Playhouse 90* (with then-youthful Paul Newman and Albert Salmi playing the roles that would later go to Moriarty and De Niro). Owing to strong ratings and fine notices, the movie rights were swiftly optioned. But, due to various circumstances, the picture was not immediately shot, with the script then passing through the hands of numerous companies.

The timing could not have been better for De Niro, whose strong work in *Greetings* and *Hi, Mom!* had earned him enough critical and industry attention that he was being hyped as a young "comer," allowing for precisely the sort of star-on-the-rise casting that the producers—the wife-and-husband team of Lois and Maurice Rosenfield (he the controversial lawyer who once successfully defended Lenny Bruce on an obscenity charge)—wanted. Big names would have been beyond their budget, while total unknowns would have had no marquee value.

Michael Moriarty was, in the early seventies, then being hyped—much like Bobby—as one of the potentially great actor/stars for the new decade; his excellent work here should seemingly have solidified that reputa-

tion. Watching De Niro and Moriarty together at this time was, in the minds of many serious moviegoers, akin to what it would have been like to see Marlon Brando and Montgomery Clift on-screen together in the early fifties. Surprisingly, though, Moriarty's film career never did take off in a big way.

De Niro's Bruce Pearson is a catcher on a bush-league baseball team. Uneducated, with no taste in clothing and wearing his hair in an out-of-date greasy pompadour, with a thick Georgia accent to boot, Pearson is a bungler and a rube, so unsophisticated that his teammates want little to do with him. The person who would seem least likely to befriend Pearson is pitcher Henry Wiggen (Moriarty), the most glib, worldly team member, and the one who certainly seems to have bigger things in store. Initially, Wiggen does actively resent Pearson, whereas the other team members merely ignore him. But a believable if unlikely relationship forms, as Wiggen not only learns to tolerate Pearson but also deeply like, then love, the man. Wiggen becomes so totally attached to the

Realizing he is doomed, the inarticulate Bruce burns his most prized possessions.

Dutch Schnell (Vincent Gardenia, right) realizes that the odd couple will not allow themselves to be split up, under any circumstances.

pathetic Pearson that he is willing to turn down considerable money under a transfer deal if Pearson cannot go, too.

Then, Pearson develops Hodgkin's disease. Though it would be easy to win over the sympathy of the other team members now by simply telling them of the terrible situation, Pearson might very well be dropped from the team if the owners ever suspected how sick he is. Instead, Wiggen helps Pearson to both maintain his position and see his fate through with his dignity intact as they keep the sickness secret. This allows Pearson to win respect without resorting to the sentimental emotions that always—and easily—pour out for anyone who is known to be dying, while continuing to play ball for as long as possible.

Also basic to the drama is the fact that Pearson is simply too unintelligent to fully grasp the implications of his disease, though he does understand enough to feel a general resentment toward his predicament, referring to himself as "doomeded." It is Wiggen who goes through the greater anguish, constantly wrestling with the oncoming death that is about to strike down his best friend.

Drum resembled the disease-of-the-week films just then becoming popular as TV fare, and though there were virtually no negative reviews, the few critics who tempered their positive reactions cited this as the reason. Tagging *Drum* "as perfect a piece of mindless entertainment as one could wish for," Peter Schjeldahl

of the *New York Times* complained that the TV influence was far too obvious: "directed by John Hancock with the kind of pacing that makes you anticipate commercial breaks." However, not everyone agreed, *The New Yorker* insisting "this film is no tearjerker about a doomed athlete" but rather is "about friendship." That, of course, tied *Drum* in to a theme explored in previous De Niro vehicles (*Greetings, The Wedding Party*) and later ones (*Mean Streets, The Deer Hunter, GoodFellas*): male bonding.

One strong example of how a film that might have turned maudlin managed to avoid that through the emotional complexity of the scenes, and De Niro's playing of them in particular, occurred in the title sequence. A rookie player, who does not know of Pearson's situation, picks up his guitar and begins to sing "The Cowboy's Lament." Pearson is aware that he's dying, but does not know that, one by one, his teammates have learned of his fate, though out of respect for the way he has chosen to see this thing through, none have given him any inkling. The words of the song of course touch the doomed Pearson, who—though hardly bright—understands how this coincidentally sung ballad brushes up against his sad fate. Pearson cannot completely hold all his emotions in, though he tries, and the others, likewise touched by the beautiful, bittersweet ballad, feel guilty about their previous cruel treatment of Pearson as well as remorse for his fate and struggle—

each in his own way—to keep from revealing their emotions.

In retrospect, *Drum* might seem to be a throwback to the older Hollywood sports movies about baseball players with physical or mental problems—*Pride of the Yankees, Fear Strikes Out.* But it was not merely a redo of them. *Drum* retained the young, dying athlete theme while featuring a sense of honesty that was quite remarkable—and groundbreaking. The team owners, for instance, were neither the loving, supporting types nor the exploitive villains they would simplistically have been played as in earlier pictures, but rather complex characters: out for the money, but not caricatured and certainly not entirely unsympathetic. Likewise, the players themselves used rough language, quite impossible before the Production Code died in 1967. Perhaps the single scene that best represents the integrity of the film is the one in which the national anthem is played before a big game. In previous Hollywood baseball pictures, the team members would have been seen standing at proper patriotic attention, though here some are busily scratching their crotches and thinking of a variety of other things while halfheartedly attempting to appear in a serious mood for the spectators in the stands. The ideals of the old Hollywood had been replaced by a desire to show life as it actually is—even in formula films and tearjerkers.

If there is a single notable flaw to the film, it's that the novel *Drum* was set in the 1950s but was filmed in the 1970s. How much better this might have been if the budget had allowed for a period-piece approach. Then, the emotions and ideas expressed—so right for the fifties, so false for the seventies—would have felt true in context. Instead, these are Eisenhower-era people who walk around in a 1970s world, as if oblivious to all the changes that tore through society during the intervening decades. Throwing in a few four-letter words and a couple of quick references to recent things, as well as using modern cars and clothing, does not effectively update a story about not only a particular place, but also a singular time.

As for Bobby, he appreciated from the first that Moriarty would play the more "normal" character—one upscale audiences could easily associate with—while he would (as he would later again in *Awakenings*) take on a role that could be called "the other"—a lovable mutant, someone who is clearly different from most of us. Early on, Bobby made a decision that causes the film, even when viewed some twenty years later, to ring true. "I didn't play dumb," he claims, understanding that for an intelligent person to try to portray his notion of a dumb person would result in a patronizing performance. Instead, Bobby played a man who is, in his own mind, perfectly normal, though not in tune with the intelligence level of everyone else around him. It is the context, the situations that Bruce Pearson finds himself in, that cause him to appear dumb.

Though he was playing a minor league athlete, De

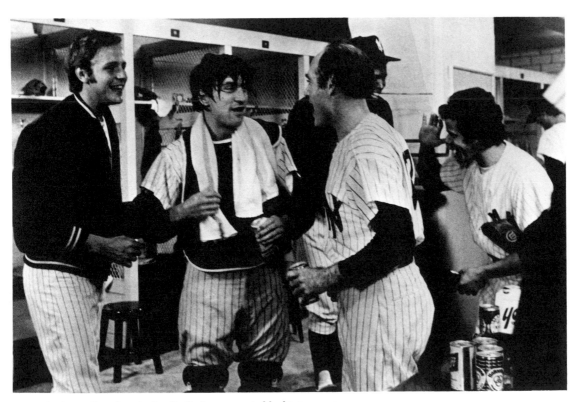

Bruce (with towel) realizes he has finally been accepted by his teammates.

67

Niro was now in the big leagues so far as movies were concerned, allowing him to take his dedicated approach to creating a total character further than he had been able in his earlier low-budget work. De Niro traveled, with director John Hancock and other cast members, to Clearwater, Florida, weeks before shooting was to commence, to inundate themselves in baseball and provide as authentic performances as possible. The actual shooting was done later at Shea and Yankee stadiums in New York, with members of the Yankees, Mets, and other teams constantly giving the actors pointers on how to make it look real. During the rehearsal period, the performers all played baseball for two hours a day before director Hancock allowed them to go over their lines, so that they might get into the proper spirit.

For the other actors, this sufficed. But not for De Niro. Since his character hailed from a small town in Georgia, Bobby—upon learning he had the role—immediately departed for the South, where he took up residence in a rural community not far from Atlanta,

Bruce (De Niro) and Henry (Michael Moriarty).

pretty much like the one his character would have come from. There, De Niro rented an apartment, purchased clothes of the type worn by the locals, and spent all his time chatting with the cracker-barrel crowd at the country store. The people there, understanding what he was up to and accepting him, were happy to help him master the local speech patterns. "Most everyone was remarkably friendly," Bobby would later recall. "I wanted to listen to the way Georgians really talk, [so] I carried a tape recorder around with me into bars, gas stations, and hotels. I told them I was an actor preparing for a role and even went so far as to ask a couple of guys if they'd mind reading lines from the script into my recorder."

The only problem came when De Niro realized during this period that his character would chew tobacco and decided he had to take up the habit, too. Unfortunately, it made him sick. Yet, as ill as he became, he would not stop, so dedicated was he to the performance. At one point, he even tried to mix tobacco with more tolerable substances: first licorice, then tea leaves, finally bubble gum. Bobby later recalled, "Then I got sticky and sick, too. Besides, nothing works like the real thing." Only when a local doctor assured him that chewing the tobacco would make his teeth a bright white did he find the nerve to continue.

Later, when in front of the cameras, De Niro's dedication to actually becoming the character rather than merely playacting became a significant concern. To portray Bruce's illness, he spun around again and again until he was nauseated, so that what was captured on camera was actual illness rather than pretend, allowing De Niro to feel it rather than fake it. Meanwhile, he remained totally submerged in his character, rarely if ever taking off his baseball uniform, practically living in it the entire time he was on the film.

Not all the reviews were raves. *Variety*, for instance, reported that "De Niro is very good, his character unfortunately being too gauchely defined (we could do without some of his social and personality weaknesses, and still get the point)." But Kevin Thomas of the *Los Angeles Times* found Bobby's performance "ingratiating," while Joy Gould Boyum noticed the "nicely understated [performance] by Robert De Niro." In his begrudgingly positive *New York Times* piece, Peter Schjeldahl wrote: "What elevates [the film] is mainly a deeply humorous performance by Robert de [sic] Niro . . . who bears a striking resemblance to Jughead [and] may be destined to replace Dustin Hoffman as our foremost portrayer of wacky, guileless dolts." More correctly, De Niro would—like Hoffman—prove to be a "character lead" who could convincingly play absolutely anything at all.

Lonely, alienated, individualistic: the first true De Niro hero.

Johnny Boy frightens his friends with an unexpected burst of violence.

Mean Streets

(1973)

A Warner Brothers Release

CAST:

Harvey Keitel (*Charlie*); Robert De Niro (*Johnny Boy*); David Proval (*Tony*); Amy Robinson (*Teresa*); Richard Romanus (*Michael*); Cesare Danova (*Giovanni*); George Memmoli (*Joey Catucci*); Vic Argo (*Mario*); Robert Carradine (*Assassin*); Jeannie Bell (*Diane*); D'Mitch Davis (*Cop*); David Carradine (*Drunk*).

CREDITS:

Director, Martin Scorsese; producer, Jonathan T. Taplin; executive producer, E. Lee Perry; screenplay, Scorsese and Mardik Martin; photography, Kent Wakeford; editor, Sidney Levin; running time, 110 minutes; rating: R.

Mean Streets deserves a sizable footnote in film history as the movie that began the De Niro–Scorsese collaborations; more significant, this little movie stands as a major milestone of contemporary cinema. Lest we forget, the studio system had been in gradual decline throughout the fifties, then collapsed in the late 1960s when such innovative, unconventional films as *The Graduate* and *Bonnie and Clyde* shook the industry. When, in 1969, the radical-druggie-biker flick *Easy Rider* proved an immense box-office success even as the latest Julie Andrews musical—*Star!*—floundered, a whole new era had seemingly begun. *Time* rushed to judgment, tagging *Easy Rider* "the little film that killed the big films."

Not quite. Only one year later, a glossy commercial item, *Airport*, was the hit box-office attraction, while the rash of post–*Easy Rider* youth films—*The Strawberry Statement, Getting Straight*—fizzled. By 1972–73, after three awkward years for the American movie industry, critics and audiences hungered for breakthrough films. They came in a pair of movies—one big, one small—that remain legendary: Coppola's *The Godfather* and Scor-

A posed publicity shot of the youthful cast: De Niro, in his hat, takes the center spot, even though
Harvey Keitel (to his right) had the ostensible lead.

sese's *Mean Streets*. Whereas Coppola combined the best of the old gangster epics with a more honest approach to such stories, likewise mixing old stars such as Marlon Brando, Sterling Hayden, and Richard Conte with fresh faces (Pacino, Keaton, Duvall, Caan), Scor- sese—with his tighter budget—opted for a different approach. Like France's Truffaut, he created a script based on his own life experiences; like Truffaut, he made the very business of watching a movie the ultimate subject of his movie.

Charlie (Harvey Keitel) realizes his best friend is mentally unbalanced.

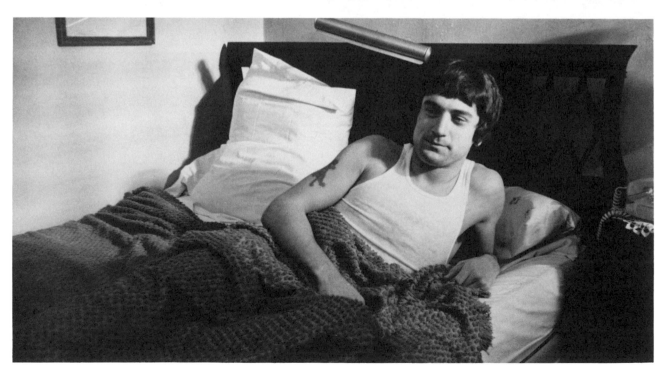

Sullen even when sleepy, Johnny Boy wakes to face another crazy day in the streets of Little Italy.

Mean Streets begins with a motion picture projector pouring light, color, and imagery onto a screen—Scorsese's loving acknowledgment of the medium he's working in. But are those images from home movies or a theatrical film? It's difficult to tell, precisely the point of the sequence; the movie being projected—like the one we are watching—immediately makes such past distinctions obsolete. Scorsese stood at the forefront of the new breed of filmmakers, redefining our ideas of cinema even as we watch his movies; such directors created not only a new form of film, but a new audience as well. No wonder, then, that opinion-shaper Pauline Kael in *The New Yorker* hailed the film as "a true original of our period, a triumph of personal filmmaking. It has its own hallucinatory look; the characters live in the darkness of bars with lighting and color just this side of lurid. It has its own unsettling, episodic rhythm and a high-charged emotional range that is dizzyingly sensual . . . by the end, you're likely to be openmouthed, trying to rethink what you've seen."

The arrogantly youthful and upwardly mobile Charlie (Harvey Keitel) marches into one of the Little Italy bars he likes to frequent, clowning with friends and flirting with the topless dancers. What immediately marked Scorsese as an artist of the first order—and what would be basic to the appeal of his most successful work—was the sensation of his thrusting us directly into a world he obviously knows fully, rather than slowly, conventionally introducing us to that world, step by step, so that we can gradually adjust to it. Previous movies had been set in Little Italy, but they had always treated the film's viewer as an outsider, allowed to gaze in on a fascinating lifestyle, as if through a window. Here, the camera forces us to live the lifestyle—experience rather than observe the textures of sight and sound, which include garish colors and nonstop rock 'n' roll music. Like several other films of the same period—George Lucas's *American Graffiti*, Stephen F. Verona's *The Lords of Flatbush*—*Mean Streets* would focus on the bonding of four very different male heroes, their offbeat friendships and difficult dealings with women. None of the other "pack" pictures, however, conveyed the same sense of raw intensity and personal integrity as *Mean Streets*. If *Graffiti* was the more easily accessible and commercially successful, this was the more aesthetically satisfying.

Here, the foursome consists of the ambitious, arrogant Mafia turk Charlie—who looks like a sly, starving shark in his slick suit—his somewhat more serious but usually jocular barkeeper friend Tony (David Proval), the petty, pompous, self-important number-running hustler Michael (Richard Romanus), and the crazy, out-of-control compulsive gambler Johnny Boy (De Niro). Though Johnny Boy is named after Charlie's uncle Giovanni (Cesare Danova), the local godfather to all, as well as Johnny Boy's own actual godfather, Johnny Boy is on the outs with this soft-spoken but deadly man owing to Johnny Boy's outrageous and intolerable behavior. Uncle Giovanni wants Charlie to sever his relationship with Johnny Boy and also break off a romantic relationship with Johnny Boy's cousin Teresa (Amy Robinson), a nice Italian Catholic girl, rejected as a possible wife for Charlie only because she happens to be epileptic. Charlie is torn between sincere feelings for the two and his petty ambitions to own a restaurant his uncle has promised him—if he will first prove that he's willing to take Giovanni's orders on every issue, including his personal life.

Johnny Boy—maniacal enough to drop bombs in mailboxes and run away, gleefully laughing at the destruction—at first seems the least gratifying of the film's roles, and perhaps a letdown for De Niro. Bobby did indeed express enthusiastic interest in playing Charlie, but learning that Scorsese had already cast Keitel in the pivotal role, agreed instead to take on this zany part—a kind of cruel, meanspirited Marx Brother. In fact, though, the role proved so remarkable—and De Niro so mesmerizingly energetic—that Johnny Boy, who all but explodes on-screen, like a stick of dynamite, ended up as the most memorable part in the picture, despite the overall sense of high-quality acting. As Kael put it: "When you're growing up, if you know someone crazy-daring and half-admirable (and maybe most of us do), you don't wonder how the beautiful nut got that way; he seems to spring up full-blown and whirling, and you watch the fireworks and feel crummily cautious in your sanity. That's how it is here. Charlie digs Johnny Boy's recklessness. De Niro's Johnny Boy is the only one of the group of grifters and scummy racketeers who is his own man; he is the true hero. . . . De Niro here hits the far-out, flamboyant [note] and makes his own truth. He's a bravura actor, and those who have registered him only as the grinning, tobacco-chewing dolt of that hunk of inept whimsy *Bang the Drum Slowly* will be unprepared for his volatile performance. De Niro does something like what Dustin Hoffman was doing in *Midnight Cowboy*, but wilder; the kid doesn't just act—he takes off into the vapors. De Niro is so intensely appealing . . . " In *Newsweek*, Paul D. Zimmerman likewise praised the character as written and performed: "Johnny Boy—an erratic, foolish, endearing, debt-ridden loser, [with Charlie] trying to straighten him out every time Johnny Boy steps out of line, which is all the time. Beautifully realized in all his self-destructive flamboyance by Robert De Niro, Johnny Boy is a parody of the cool mafioso—checking his pants instead of his coat at the door, pushing a poolroom negotiation over an unpaid debt into

Johnny Boy (De Niro, far left) studies the pool table while his pals argue.

a brawl, finally goading and belittling Michael into a violent climax." In the *Hollywood Reporter,* Vincent Canby noted that "De Niro has an exceedingly flashy role and makes the most of it."

Even the rare critic who panned the film praised Bobby. Though Stanley Kauffmann, in *The New Republic,* dismissed the work as "theatrical in the wrong way, both lumpy and discursive," he added that "*Mean Streets* has some ragged, intermittent flashes of fire, particularly in a poolroom brawl triggered by De Niro in his angry explosion at a usurer. In *Drum,* De Niro understood what he wanted to do as the dumb, doomed Southern catcher; he simply couldn't summon up enough of the juices and flavors. Here he is wild and strong. It's a flash part, and every actor who sees it will gnash his teeth because he'll know that anyone with any talent at all could score in it. The part is a success; De Niro happens to have it. He uses it very well, but, without putting him down, I note that he's had some good luck in casting lately; a sweet guy doomed to die and a loose, pathetic, obscene quasi-maniac. What actor could ask for more?"

One thing he could ask for is a more sensitive critic. Kauffmann seems naive in ascribing the quality of the Johnny Boy we see to the writing alone. Though the Scorsese–Mardik Martin script suggests a fascinatingly flamboyant character, it's difficult to imagine anyone else—even Hoffman or Pacino—coming close to Bobby's gleeful demon in terms of force and impact. A critic ought to grasp that the ultimate test of a great actor is his ability to make a difficult role look easy and effortless, as if any boob could have hopped up and done it as well.

Frank Rich (writing in *New Times*), another of the film's rare detractors (acknowledging it as a film of "decent intentions and real integrity," but lambasting Scorsese's "scattershot" technique), at least admitted that "the best of these vignettes invariably involve Johnny Boy, the gang's depressed loser, who has trouble walking down any block without encountering a creditor. The role is played by Robert De Niro . . . rapidly becoming the movies' foremost embodiment of sublingual schleppyness. Pasty-faced and greasy, De Niro walks and talks with a good-natured slovenliness not unreminiscent of Art Carney's sewerman on the old Jackie Gleason *Honeymooners.* At one point in *Mean Streets,* he haltingly approaches Diane (Jeannie Bell), the black go-go girl at the neighborhood joint, to tell her she's 'a terrific performer.' Her response is not overwhelming, but Johnny Boy mumbles on, expanding his spiel to include an offer of a gig as a hostess of the big nightclub he says he'll open uptown someday . . . Still, on he goes, even to the humiliating point of promising that the club will serve the Chinese food Diane says she likes."

In fact, Rich errs here: It is Charlie, not Johnny Boy, who approaches Diane. Still, if we keep in mind the fact that De Niro desperately wanted to play the Charlie role, then it's fascinating to relate this scene to De Niro's later life: He would meet and wed an equally statuesque black woman with the same name as the character here. Diahnne Abbott even looks enough like onetime Playmate of the Month Jeannie Bell to be her sister. In retrospect, one can't help but wonder whether the initial conversation between De Niro and Abbott took similar turns, or whether Chinese food was ever mentioned.

This was also one of the first times that critics felt compelled to compare De Niro with Brando—notably, before he played the Brando role in *Godfather II*. In a Sunday *New York Times* think piece, Foster Hirsch noted: "De Niro is a virtuoso actor, but as Johnny Boy, he's not an original; the territory has already been staked out, classically, by Marlon Brando in *On the Waterfront*. De Niro uses the same slum-drenched diction, the same restless, shifting movements, the same distracted sidelong glances. He's unquestionably found a rhythm for his character, he's obviously explored motivation, but his work, for all its terrific pace and energy, for all its bravura

histrionics, is marked indelibly as Brando-imitative. Like the movie in which it's the glittering centerpiece, the performance is too studied, too influenced by too many movies."

In fact, though, it may be more true to say that any aura of Brando in De Niro's work is quite in keeping with the director's overall vision, which is a commentary on the way movies impact on our lives. The male characters continually go off to see movies together (*Point Blank, Husbands*); their attitudes are derived from their favorite films. Both Scorsese and De Niro, as collaborators, are on the same track, then, when they contain homages to past pictures; doing so is basic to what their work is all about. Hirsch is wrong about something else, too: Johnny Boy is less the center of the film's dramatic action than the catalyst. When his compulsive gambling leaves him deeply indebted to Michael (who feels such a situation causes him to lose respect), Johnny Boy desperately turns to pal Charlie. The obvious way to help would be by borrowing money from his wealthy uncle Gio-

Teresa (Amy Robinson, center) cringes in fear as Johnny Boy and Charlie fight; Robinson would give up acting to become a successful producer of films.

vanni. But he can't do that, for Giovanni would feel he hadn't been shown the proper respect within the Family's code. Charlie's desperate indecision causes the final burst of irrational violence with which the picture ends, as the three attempt to escape over the Brooklyn Bridge but are shot down by Michael and his henchman—seemingly, not so much because of the gambling debts as because they would actually consider leaving their tightly ordered, self-contained world. Then, Scorsese returns us to an image of the movie projector, reminding us that in the evolving American cinema of the seventies, it is the medium itself that, as McLuhan would have put it, is central to the message.

There are other themes here as well. Like *The Godfather, Mean Streets* is essentially a movie about Italian males, and the ability of some such individuals to exist in a Jekyll/Hyde duality—devout Catholics and career criminals—without, seemingly, sensing any irony or incongruity at all. But the filmmakers certainly were aware of it and made that paradox the basis of their films' moral sensibility. Also, though the exteriors were mostly shot on actual locations, Scorsese nonetheless makes abundantly clear that we are not looking at this demimonde objectively, but through his eyes. This is not an unbiased portrait of Little Italy, but his personal vision—nostalgia critically undercut by moral consideration—of it. Purposefully garish lighting and lurid colors—even more extreme than would exist in a real-life mafioso bar—are used throughout. While the camera angles are never so offbeat as to call obvious attention to themselves, they also contribute to an ever so slightly stylized quality. In particular, the red light always on in the topless bar suggests this is truly hell on earth—the very place that the priest in church warns the boys against.

Scorsese's use of rock 'n' roll standards as his sound track (an innovation at the time, simultaneously employed in Lucas's *Graffiti*) led to Scorsese's ongoing employment of popular music in his movies, a natural accompaniment to the now-accepted hand-held-camera techniques that had been found only in European art-house films a few years earlier. If the contemporary cinema was to be about the older movies that shaped our sensibility, it is also about the rock 'n' roll music that began in 1955. What we hear at any point is not necessarily meant to be the music playing on the radio at that moment, but the music going on in the characters' heads—the music they heard on the radio earlier that day. It's the same music that the relatively young audience for *Mean Streets* had stuck in its head, which is the way Scorsese allowed people from all over the country, whose backgrounds have nothing to do with the unique codes and value systems of Little Italy, to warily enter this world.

Ultimately, this oftentimes grim movie is a fascinating blend of street realism and heightened expressionism; it is the daily life of a young mafioso as reimagined in his later nightmares. Scorsese scrupulously avoids anything hokey, never projecting a sense that gangsters are glamorous, as Coppola did (however unintentionally) in *The Godfather. Mean Streets* is honest and unsparing in a way no other gangster movie had ever dared to be.

Scorsese, who was thirty at the time of filming, had graduated from New York University, then returned to teach there, between gigs as a film editor (*Woodstock*) and a director of Cormanesque B movies (*Boxcar Bertha*). He had managed to make one offbeat art film—*Who's That Knocking at My Door?*—which had also

The final confrontation: While trying to spirit Johnny Boy away, Charlie and Teresa find themselves ambushed.

Robert De Niro as Johnny Boy.

starred Keitel, but though he and Mardik Martin had completed the script for *Mean Streets* in 1966, they were not to find funding for another six years. Scorsese had to shoot the film on a small budget (for somewhere between $350,000 and $480,000, depending on whom you are talking to) and tight schedule (twenty-seven days). In fact, only six days of shooting were actually done in Little Italy, the larger portion of the time being given over to a Hollywood studio shoot—including all those scenes inside Tony's bar. Scorsese himself plays the vicious triggerman who fires the shot that kills De Niro's Johnny Boy—though whether this was merely a money-saving fact of life or a statement about the relationship of director and actor is difficult to say.

Young Clemenza (Bruno Kirby) approaches Vito on the crowded streets of New York.

The Godfather, Part II

(1974)

A Paramount Picture

CAST:

Al Pacino (*Michael Corleone*); Robert De Niro (*Vito*); Diane Keaton (*Kay*); Robert Duvall (*Tom Hagen*); John Cazale (*Fredo*); Talia Shire (*Connie*); Lee Strasberg (*Hyman Roth*); Michael V. Gazzo (*Frankie Pentangeli*); G. D. Spradlin (*Sen. Pat Geary*); Richard Bright (*Al Neri*); Gaston Moschin (*Fanucci*); Bruno Kirby (*Young Clemenza*); Morgana King (*Mama*); Francesca deSapio (*Young Mama*); Troy Donahue (*Merle Johnson, Jr.*); Mariana Hill (*Deanna*); Fay Spain (*Mrs. Roth*); Harry Dean Stanton (*FBI Agent*); Roger Corman, Phil Feldman (*U.S. Senators*); Danny Aiello (*Tony Rosato*); James Caan, unbilled (*Sonny*).

CREDITS:

Producer and director, Francis Ford Coppola; coproducers, Gray Frederickson and Fred Roos; screenplay, Coppola and Mario Puzo; based on the novel *The Godfather* by Puzo; photography, Gordon Willis; production designer, Dean Tavoularis; edited by Peter Zinner, Barry Malkin, and Richard

Marks; costume design, Theadora Van Runkle; music, Nino Rota; additional music, Carmine Coppola; running time, 200 minutes; rating: R.

From the moment thirty-three-year-old director Francis Ford Coppola agreed to do a *Godfather* sequel for Paramount production chief Robert Evans, the intense, intelligent filmmaker loudly announced that his decision to sign on was "not commercialism at all," a claim that proved true. While the studio might have been happy with any film which allowed them to capitalize on the vast success of the first *Godfather*, Coppola was far less interested in the financial rewards of a sequel (though they were certainly considerable) than in the opportunity to protect the integrity of his much-respected film while improving on its various shortcomings. However inadvertently, *The Godfather* had romanticized Mafia life; audiences viewed the Corleones as

Robert De Niro as Vito Corleone.

The Kiss of Death.

A sedate Vito.

unlikely heroes, more than one critic referring to the film as "the *Gone With the Wind* of gangster films."

So in addition to telling earlier and later stories about the same characters—tales every bit as compelling as those in the first picture—Coppola wanted to correct his earlier miscalculation, making us aware, through a far darker and unsparing work, that what these people did was evil, and that they had corrupted themselves beyond redemption. Understandably, then, the *Hollywood Reporter* would eventually note, with some surprise, that the sequel was "a more personal film. This movie's huge world audience may see it less as entertainment than as condemnation of the American corporate power structure." Here Michael Corleone (Al Pacino) projects none of his boyish charm or eventual elegant sophistication from the first film, rather impressing us as an icy, black-hearted character, aloof from everyone who might love him. He seals off his wife, Kay (Diane Keaton), and eventually orders the execution of his own brother Fredo (John Cazale), the final shot depicting him as an absolute nihilist—an island unto himself, physically and symbolically.

Likewise, Coppola's more mature understanding of his material dictated the director's approach with the young Don Corleone in the scenes depicting Vito's initial journey to America and his lifelong quest for vengeance on those who executed his family in Sicily. The director intended that this tale of Vito's gradual rise to power in early twentieth-century America parallel the story of Michael's decline in post–World War II America, through his involvements with such key historical happenings as the Kefauver crime hearings, the overthrow of the Batista regime and subsequent emergence of communist Cuba, and the virtual creation of the city of Las Vegas. In perfect symmetry, Vito's story here is that of the early immigrant experience gone sour, the American dream in its initial stage of corruption. We see wonderfully vivid and richly textured sequences depicting the new arrivals, from various nations, pouring through Ellis Island and into New York City, their diverse cultures enriching and expanding the American character. Then, there is a remarkable shot of young Vito (Oreste Baldini), all alone on the boat with the Statue of Liberty framed behind him, awaiting possible deportation back to Sicily. The little boy looks so vulnerable that we can't help but be moved by his plight, hoping customs officials will overlook his sickliness and allow him in.

Then we recall whom he will grow up to be: Vito is the rotten apple who will spoil the barrel of America's melting pot; he will bring corruption to these shores in the form of the Black Hand. The sequences in which Bobby's Vito wanders through Little Italy, planning his ascent to power, are indicative of the remarkable density

An energetic Vito.

81

A pensive Vito.

A pensive Vito.

of this film, combining a Brueghelian sense of richly textured place with a Dickensian feel for diverse characters, drawn quickly, sharply, broadly, without ever degenerating into caricature. De Niro's scenes are striking; one, in which he slithers along the rooftops to calculatedly kill a loan shark (Gaston Moschin) who has been bleeding his neighborhood, is unforgettable. We see the sequence through a striking double vision that Coppola clearly intended: Vito establishes himself as an urban Robin Hood to the common men and women down below, a folk hero ridding them of an evil oppressor; we see it, too, through our memory of what Vito—as cold-bloodedly out to achieve power for himself as he is to help the downtrodden—will become in his later years.

If the first film had been an epic of sorts, this new one aimed for full-blown tragedy. The fascinating approach was to feature a dual hero; instead of the rise and fall of a great man, we witness the fall of Michael as set against the rise of Vito, with constant dissolves from one man's face to the other's. That was the end result in 1974. But in '72, Coppola's first chore came in reassembling his original cast and crew, or at least rounding up as much of the old gang as possible. The first notable loss was Al

A dangerous Vito.

Ruddy, who had produced *The Godfather*; this time around, Coppola would assume production chores as well as direct. The success of the first film had transformed him from a young Hollywood hopeful, almost fired during production, to one of the key power brokers in the new, emerging Hollywood of the early seventies.

The shooting schedule for *Godfather II* was an unheard of eight months, during which time cast and crew journeyed all over the globe: Lake Tahoe, Las Vegas, Los Angeles, Miami, Santo Domingo, New York's Little Italy, Trieste, and at last Sicily. In Santo Domingo, Pacino became ill, further slowing down the proceedings, while New York's unpredictable weather did not cooperate either. The cost of the film, budgeted at a then lofty $6 million, soon skyrocketed, ultimately totaling more than $11 million. Adding to the headaches was the writers' strike, which made it all but impossible for Coppola to discuss his project in public at the very time when he ought to be in preproduction.

Marlon Brando seemed the most insurmountable

A wary Vito.

problem. Coppola's original concept was to have Brando, so brilliant as the elderly don, return as Vito in his thirties, again proving his remarkable abilities by playing a man younger than himself, just as in *Godfather* he had played someone older. Coppola openly admitted that "it will hurt me personally if Marlon doesn't repeat the title role," though signing Brando was "not my end of it"—that remained the job of the Paramount power brokers. However, Brando—whose faded career had been revived by *The Godfather*—displayed little loyalty to the project or to Coppola. He approached this strictly as a business deal, demanding $500,000 plus 10 percent of the gross for a sequel. Today, when flash-in-the-pan actors receive multimillion-dollar deals for films, that seems less than exorbitant. At the time, it was inconceivable that any studio would pay the price, even for Brando. For a moment, the immense project seemed stymied by one person: after all, how could you do *The Godfather* without "The Godfather"?

Where there's a will, there's a way; if Coppola provided the will, De Niro offered him the way. Coppola's statements of the time suggest that, however hurt he may have been by Brando's attitude, he was able to accept that unpredictable, iconoclastic actor's final decision: "He just doesn't want to work. I know, because this happened to be a project that really excited him. Early on, we met a couple of times about the sequel and he came up with some terrific ideas. Many of them have been incorporated into the screenplay [they were, reportedly, the dialogue suggesting that Mafia life is not alien to normal American business and political procedures, but emblematic of it.] Then he and Paramount had a big falling-out—over money, probably—and he was no longer available to us." That's when Coppola recalled the brilliant young actor who had appeared in the powerful little film *Mean Streets* by his friend Martin Scorsese, reminding Coppola—like most of the film's viewers—of the young Brando.

"When that [Brando's walkout] happened," Coppola continued, "we decided to make Vito as young as he was in the early section of the book and go with De Niro. I'd been familiar with his work before *Mean Streets* and *Bang the Drum Slowly* brought him to the fore. In fact, I signed him to do a small part in the first *Godfather*—he was to play Carlo Rizzi, the brother-in-law who set Sonny up for the kill." In other interviews, Coppola has indicated that it was the role of Paulie Gato, the chauffeur and bodyguard, that he was considering De Niro for; De Niro wanted to play Sonny, but Coppola wasn't sure he was right for the part. Meanwhile, Coppola was insisting to the Paramount brass that he wanted Pacino for Michael, though some studio powers were lobbying for Dustin Hoffman—a bigger name, and a similar actor, though not an Italian American.

At this time, Pacino—offered the young lead in *The Gang That Couldn't Shoot Straight*—was all set to take it when Coppola was given permission to sign him for Michael. The casting now seemed complete, until De Niro asked to be released. A leading role had just been offered him in a film called *The Gang That Couldn't Shoot Straight,* since the actor who had been set for that part had, for some reason, just dropped out. Coppola, appreciating the irony and lunacy of all this, recalled, "He wanted to do that instead, so I released him. He got the part, but I got something, too. I got Bobby in *Godfather II,* which I couldn't have done if I'd held him to his commitment in *Part I.*"

Coppola cast De Niro after a single screening of *Mean Streets*—without so much as a screen test. While on location, Sicilian consultant Romano Pianti glanced at De Niro—sporting a cigarillo slim mustache and wearing a white cardboard shirt collar—listened to the young actor's fluent Sicilian, then confided to Coppola, "If you'd asked me if it was possible that an actor master a language like Sicilian in such a short time, I would have said, 'Never, impossible.' But this De Niro has done it." Bobby spent eighteen months in preparation for the part. Most of Vito's scenes are set in the Italian American New York ghetto, in the years 1918–23, where Vito struggles to support his wife and three small sons, Santino, Fredo, and Michael. Vito masters the English language only after his experiences take him out of this all but hermetically sealed world. To perfect his Sicilian, De Niro took some preliminary instruction at Berlitz, then studied intensely with Pianti, who helped Bobby understand that Sicilian "is not just another Italian dialect, like a Southern accent in America—Sicilian is another language." The people have been somewhat separated from the Italian mainland and subject to numerous invasions over the centuries. As a result, the vocabulary is rich in words from the Greek, Arabic, Phoenician. The word *mafia,* for example, is Arabic for protection.

While Coppola, Pacino, and company headed for Lake Tahoe to shoot the contemporary scenes, De Niro grabbed a tape recorder and headed for Sicily, beginning his quest for authenticity in the capital city of Palermo. In time, he would visit Romano's relatives in Trapani, then briefly settle into the coastal towns of Scopello and Castellammare del Golfo. Finally, he visited the village of Corleone—listening carefully to the way in which the populace pronounced their words, requesting that they read his lines from the script so that he could record and later study their inflections. He did not pretend to be anything other than what he was, in keeping with his approach while researching in Georgia for *Bang the Drum Slowly.* "I was always up-front about what I was doing," he later explained. "I felt it would be under-

Vito, the doting father.

handed not to say anything. I'm just an actor doing my work. I've found people enjoy helping you, if they understand what you're looking for, you save a lot of time and unnecessary suspicion." The honesty paid off; the people invited him into their homes, though he noticed that the ancient Sicilian fear of foreigners could also be observed, however subtly: "Although they are very cordial to you as a tourist, Sicilians have a way of watching without [appearing to be] watching. They'll scrutinize you thoroughly and you won't even know it." That "you," however, did not apply to Bobby, who watched them watching him—and made that a key factor in his interpretation of Vito. In Vito's eyes, we always see a "peasant shrewdness," the basis for his ruthless drive to first survive, then prevail.

De Niro had already been compared to Marlon Brando by several critics before *Godfather II*. After he accepted the role, then went on to win a Best Supporting Actor Oscar—the first time in the history of the Academy Awards that two performers won Oscars for playing the same part in different pictures—the comparison would be not only obvious and unavoidable but also mandatory. And—perhaps surprisingly—positive; for if Coppola fashioned a sequel that creatively expanded on and improved upon the original, so did De Niro come up with a performance that in no way mimicked Brando's legendary part, but likewise expanded on it in satisfying ways.

"Brando's creation of Don Vito Corleone exists and that is my guideline," De Niro said at the time. "Brando played Vito as a man in his late fifties. For me, Vito is twenty-four years old, a Sicilian emigrant getting established in America. Going backwards in time, I must find the threads of that man in his early life that created the older Godfather." Director Coppola spoke, before principal shooting commenced, about the need for De Niro to "evoke that character without doing an imitation of him." Coppola said something else of great significance: "De Niro's features reminded me of Vito Corleone, not Brando. The accented jaw, the kind of funny smile, the strong cheekbones and jowls." Which helps explain why actor and director decided that any elaborate makeup, to create a closer resemblance to Brando, was not only unnecessary but also wrongheaded.

Just as wrongheaded would be the extremes of either avoiding or emulating Brando. Some actors would have resisted the temptation to go back and look at Marlon's performance for fear of being overwhelmed and enslaved by it. De Niro studied a *Godfather* videotape, knowing he would never repeat the mannerisms, though it would be absolutely necessary to suggest them. Which explains why, when the two films were reedited into *The Godfather Saga* for television, with the previously jumbled story line turned into a straight, conventional narrative, the effect was as seamless as everyone had hoped it would be—and initially feared it could not be. De Niro's approach resembled "being a scientist or a technician," in the actor's own words. "Audiences already know Vito Corleone. I watch him [on videotape] and I say, 'That's an interesting gesture. Now, when could he have started to do that? And why?' It's my job as an actor to find things I can make connections with. I must find [such] things and figure out how I can use them, in what scenes, to suggest what the older man will be like."

Writing about Vito in contrast to Michael—the ostensible romantic hero of *The Godfather*—the *Hollywood Reporter*'s John H. Dorr noted that in the first film, it was Don Vito who appeared corrupt, while Michael—at least in his early scenes—was innocent. That situation was neatly reversed here: "Ironically, the romantic figure is De Niro, with whom the audience can sympathize as the oppressed immigrant learning how to deal with a threatening culture on its own hard terms. De Niro carefully prefigures mannerisms that will age into Brando and acts out the original of 'I'll make him an offer he can't refuse.'" In *The New Yorker*, Pauline Kael took that concept further: "As Vito, Robert De Niro amply convinces one that he had it in him to become the old man that Brando was. It's not that he looks exactly like Brando but that he has Brando's wary soul, and so we can easily imagine the body changing with the years. . . . [He] has the added wonder of suggesting Brando, not from the outside but from the inside. De Niro's performance is so subtle that when he speaks in the Sicilian dialect he learned for the role, he speaks easily, but he is cautious in English and speaks very clearly and precisely. For a man of Vito's character who doesn't know the language well, precision is important. . . . Like Brando's Vito, De Niro's has a reserve that can never be breached. Vito is so secure in the knowledge of how dangerous he is that his courtliness is no more or less than noblesse oblige." Charles Champlin of the *Los Angeles Times* wrote: "It is a sensational performance, advancing Corleone (the character receives that name from an Ellis Island clerk, who identifies Vito by the nine-year-old boy's hometown) from the thin, pale youth working for pennies in a grocery store to the solid leader of his family, returning in triumph to settle the old score in Sicily, parlaying thievery and murder into power and respect. DeNiro [*sic*], hoarse-voiced and imperiously handsome as he grows in assurance, does an amazing job of preparing us for the Brando we remember."

Alone among A-list critics, Vincent Canby of the *New York Times* trashed not only the film (referring to it as "a mess") but also De Niro's performance. According to Canby, Bobby played young Vito "with a fascinating, reserved passion . . . until the shadow of Brando's earlier performance falls over it and turns it into what amounts to an impersonation." It is doubtful anyone else who ever watched the film—critic or casual viewer—could arrive at such a preposterous conclusion.

The two films, merged together, form a work that is not only epic and tragic but, also, beyond that, mythic and operatic—with the eventual third installment, arriving on theater screens in 1990, adding to that larger-than-life effect. Interestingly enough, De Niro did, at one time, express interest to Coppola in returning for the third film in the role that eventually went to Andy Garcia; as Vincent, he would have played the grandson of his character from *Godfather II*. That's the kind of acting challenge Bobby would have relished: making us believe that Vincent had enough in common with Vito to truly be his grandson, but being most careful to create an entirely new character. Had *Godfather III* been shot a few years after the original films—with the same two-year period that had elapsed between I and II—that concept might have worked. But during the sixteen-year gap, De Niro had aged enough that the youthful role of Vincent was, simply, not right for him. Ironically, Coppola had to turn down the finest of his previous *Godfather* actors, whereas in the past, it had always been the actors—including lesser talents—who had passed on the opportunity to do the successive *Godfather* films.

Vito, man of the streets.

Alfredo and Olmo Dalco (Gerard Depardieu), in Bertolucci's overly-schematized study of the aristocracy on the decline, socialism on the rise, in the Twentieth Century.

1900/Novecento

(1976)

PEA (Rome); Artistes Associés (Paris); Artemis (West Berlin)

A Paramount Release

CAST:

Robert De Niro (*Alfredo Berlinghieri*); Gerard Depardieu (*Olmo Dalco*); Dominique Sanda (*Ada*); Burt Lancaster (*Alfredo Berlinghieri I*); Donald Sutherland (*Attila*); Sterling Hayden (*Leo Dalco*); Stefania Sandrelli (*Anita*); Alida Valli (*Signora Pioppi*); Laura Betti (*Regina*); Werner Bruhns (*Octavio*); Ellen Schwiers (*Amelia*); Anna Henkel (*Anita*).

CREDITS:

Director, Bernardo Bertolucci; producer, Alberto Grimaldi; screenplay, Bernardo Bertolucci, Franco Arcalli, and Giuseppe Bertolucci; photography, Vittorio Storaro; production designer, Ezio Frigerio; editor, Franco Arcali; costume designer, Gitt Magrini; music, Ennio Morricone; various running times, 320 minutes, 278 minutes, 245 minutes; ratings: R (1977), NC-17 (1991).

In some ways a masterpiece and in others an absolute mess, *1900* stands as one of the cinema's remarkable failures. Like other projects ranging from D. W. Griffith's *Intolerance* (the screen's first glorious disaster) to, more recently, Francis Ford Coppola's *One From the Heart* and Michael Cimino's *Heaven's Gate, 1900* is a film of major ambition and minor achievement, a huge undertaking ultimately seen by a relatively small audience. This was an attempt, from day one, to make one of the great films. Part of the reason it falls so flat and fails so dizzyingly is that the movie can't come even close to realizing the lofty intentions of director/cowriter Bernardo Bertolucci, who clearly hoped to top his then-recent critical and commercial success *Last Tango in Paris*, just as it had outdistanced his earlier cult/critical

De Niro as Alfredo: The Last Aristocrat of Italy was Bobby's first screen character with class.

Alfredo and his beautiful bride, Ada (Dominique Sanda).

Alfredo under the gun.

hits, *Spider's Stratagem* and *The Conformist*. The idea was to make a movie that would live forever in the hearts and minds of people who appreciate serious cinema. But this is hubris, pure and simple; the results, then, were understandably tragic.

Incredibly enough, this doomed project began with happy feelings as well as high hopes. Producer Alberto Grimaldi and Bertolucci announced, following the screening of their joint venture *Last Tango* at the 1972 New York Film Festival, that they would shortly set to work on an $8-million epic. Originally conceived as a six-part Italian-TV miniseries, *1900* would instead be transformed into a feature film, thanks to Bertolucci's sudden post-*Tango* marketability. So Paramount put up a substantial amount of the necessary money (Grimaldi was to raise the rest in Europe), agreeing to release a normal-length film in the United States. The movie was to have starred Jack Nicholson and "some Russian actor" (in order to contemporize the theme of capitalism vs. socialism through the casting) in the roles eventually played by De Niro and France's Gerard Depardieu, but preproduction dragged on so long that the announced stars necessarily moved on to other work. Those were not the only cast changes: Burt Lancaster appeared in a role originally intended for Orson Welles, while Stefania

Sandrelli stepped into the part written specifically for Bertolucci's *Tango* protégée, Maria Schneider—who stormed off the set in a tantrum and, apparently, out of the movie business altogether.

But the sparks really began to fly after the film was finally in the can. Paramount executives decided in the fall of 1976 that they would not honor their original intention to release *1900* owing to a length that violated their contract. Twentieth Century-Fox announced plans to pick it up (United Artists already had European distribution rights), though that never happened. By March 1977, even movie business insiders were confused as to how long the movie was. By this time, Bertolucci's five-hour-eleven-minute cut was playing in Italy, France, Germany, and Switzerland, shown in two separate parts on successive nights. A three-hour-fifteen-minute version existed, which Grimaldi had created (without Bertolucci's cooperation and against the director's wishes) at the request of Paramount; and a four-hour-thirty-minute print representing a begrudging compromise between the Bertolucci and Grimaldi cuts had also been prepared.

Bertolucci had shot the film in the gorgeous green-and-russet-tinged regions of North Italy, a rural area of

Alfredo confronts evil incarnate, in the presence of the Nazi leader Attila (Donald Sutherland).

It's almost impossible to tell the nearly-lifeless owner Alfredo from all the statues in his collection; the comparison is intended—even insisted on—by Bertolucci.

the Po Valley known as Emilia-Romagna—the very place where the director, himself highborn, had grown up. This helps explain why the sense of place is, in all three versions, one of the strong points. The story chronicles nearly fifty years of history, as seen through the eyes of two families: the local landowners, the Berlinghieris, symbols of the ruling class, and the Dalcos, who work for them. Old Alfredo (Lancaster), last of the nineteenth-century padrones, commits suicide following the turn of the century, sensing that his way of life is inexorably coming to an end. His friendly adversary, the working-class Leo (Sterling Hayden), represents in his grumbling rebelliousness an embryo of the socialist wave that will, a generation later, sweep the land. Their respective grandsons—born on the same day in 1900, this "coincidence" being one of the film's many overobvious symbols—are Alfredo (De Niro) and Olmo (Depardieu), who as children play together. Their lives take separate courses as they grow up and face both inherent class responsibilities and unexpected social changes, from Mussolini to Marxism.

Even their respective wives are more effectively seen as symbols than as flesh-and-blood people. Alfredo marries Ada (Dominique Sanda), the superficially liberated young woman of the 1920s, who embraces hedonism and decadence (cocaine, kinky and nonreproductive sex) before she ultimately walks out on her wishy-washy husband, a bourgeois liberal. Olmo marries Anita (Sandrelli), an intellectual schoolteacher who turns the somewhat inarticulate man on to the joys of socialism between bouts of healthy, productive working-class sex. Then fascism rears its ugly head, represented by the monstrous foreman-turned-brownshirt Attila (Donald Sutherland), who all but drools at the thought of sodomizing an innocent young boy before bashing his brains in. The fundamentally decent but weak-kneed Alfredo does nothing to stop the horrors, so it is up to the courageous Olmo to organize his comrades and fight back. On liberation day, 1945, Attila is finally killed, spineless Alfredo removed from his position of power, and the country turns to communism—with a hint that utopia is just around the corner. Years later, Alfredo and Olmo—now old men—sit in the sun and endlessly argue, much as their grandfathers once did—the dialectic between capitalist and laborer taking on a cyclical quality.

But this doctrinaire approach caused the drama to suffer. Bertolucci so busied himself with tightening the strings of his big political statement that he allowed the narrative to unwind. What could and should have been the film's most memorable scenes (such as the death of Olmo's wife) take place offscreen, the time and space they ought to have occupied instead given over to naive speeches in which textbook socialism is spouted. Even on the less-than-lofty level of hackwork historical drama, the film fails, since the embarrassingly named villain Attila (so caricatured that he practically curls the ends of his mustache) never represents any kind of a threat to either of the two heroes, only to the general populace. Way back in silent movie days, Griffith and DeMille always threw their central characters into direct conflict with the villain.

On the positive side, 1900 is a film of brilliantly complex visual panoramas (thanks to the exquisite camera eye of cinematographer Vittorio Storaro). The end result is part peasant pageant, part grand opera, part polemic, and part cheap melodrama peopled with cardboard characters. Tagging it "a fabulous wreck" and an "extravagant failure," *Time*'s Frank Rich praised the film's "brute poetic force" but complained that "by the time 1900 reaches its flag-waving climax, the [political] sloganeering and [narrative] confusion are almost unbearable."

Adding to this irony is the fact that 1900, largely funded with American cash, was headlined by America's bright young actor/star—De Niro—in part owing to his formidable talent, in part because of his box-office allure. This compromised the project from its very conception: 1900 was the first international work of communist propaganda ever to be financed by a Hollywood studio. A pre-*Time* Richard Corliss tagged it "an alfresco operatic version of *Das Kapital*" in *New Times* magazine, while Pauline Kael of *The New Yorker* added: a "gigantic class-struggle puppet show." As Bertolucci would later reflect in 1991, on the eve of the uncut film's long-delayed release: "I wanted to do a movie with a political meaning and [dramatic] energy that could be seen by a large audience. Maybe I became a little [idealistic] about it. In 1900, I wanted to conjugate a very strong political message with Hollywood storytelling. In other words, I wanted to marry socialist realism to *Gone With the Wind*. I think of it as my impossible film." Impossible to make, at least successfully, for Bertolucci, and impossible to sit through for most viewers.

Owing in part to the investment strategies planned by producer Grimaldi and in part to the director's vision—this was meant to be a mind-expanding, consciousness-raising viewing experience—1900 was always conceived as an international coproduction, which helps explain why the two Italian leads were played by a Frenchman and an American. The result was a problematic style of shooting, in which the various actors (American, Canadian, French, Italian, and German) each spoke his native tongue, with the understanding that they would then redub their voices—again, each in his native language—for the print to be shown in their homelands. In the

Olmo on the far right, Alfredo on the far left, with much symbolic space (along with two women) between them; throughout the film, Bertolucci placed the characters in positions that represented their political positions.

American version, then, we hear De Niro's own voice (as well as those of Lancaster and Hayden), though the "English" voice coming out of Depardieu's mouth is clearly another actor's. The strangest aspect to such a scene is that De Niro's voice almost—but never quite—fits his lip movements. Bobby dubbed in his final voice track nearly a year after shooting the scenes, and the synchronization is, at best, imperfect. As Kael wrote, this makes us "aware of the actors as actors, and of their different cultures. They're not all sure what they're meant to be conveying. And we're not, either."

No wonder, then, that Stanley Kauffmann of *The New Republic* felt compelled to complain that "that fine actor Robert De Niro has been inadequately directed. That's the only explanation I can find for the fact that, in addition to his feeble grip physically on the role of the rich youth/man, he has no distinction in speech. 'Lea' me alone,' for instance. No one who knows Europe can doubt that, though both boys might have shared a local dialect, the rich and educated boy would speak the general language with distinction." This assessment is on target, indicating a sad state of affairs, since the "stretch" here for De Niro—who had already played a poor native-born Italian in *The Godfather II*—was to show he could perform as a highborn aristocrat. De Niro arrived several weeks before shooting (at his own expense) to painstakingly prepare. But whatever he said on the set has been lost; when he redubbed one year later, he slipped into what critic Arthur Knight criticized in *Saturday Review* as "his own Lower East Side variant of Italo-American." Bobby appears to have been thwarted in his actor's ambition less by any limitations in his abilities than by Bertolucci's postdubbing, the norm in Italy.

In fact, the performance was doomed long before that. De Niro has always been at his best with what he considers "collaborative" directors, those who work closely with him, as equals, to "find" the character. On the other hand, Bertolucci—despite his supposed communist viewpoint—proved virtually dictatorial in his approach, Bobby later recalling that Bertolucci would "instruct" the actor how to say a line, practically giving him a "line reading" as to what he wanted for a scene, allowing Bobby little freedom much less any sense of creative collaboration.

Why did De Niro want to do this role? As always, in large part for "the stretch": Alfredo is not merely soft-spoken, but soft—this was De Niro's first (and inciden-

Alfredo the aristocrat.

"bought" the movie would also appreciate De Niro's work. In the *Hollywood Reporter,* Ron Pennington called *1900* "magnificent" and "a masterpiece," suggesting that there was indeed an arc—if a subtle one—to Alfredo: "Robert De Niro gives subtle expression and remarkable development in his characterization of Alfredo, whose early sympathies for the farmers eventually give way to the ineffectualness of his ancestors." Likewise, critics who detested the film overall tended to be harshest on Bobby. Stephen Farber, tagging *1900* "not just a disappointment—it's a disaster," concluded that "Robert De Niro's performance is an embarrassment."

Pauline Kael took Bertolucci to task for having employed De Niro, then refusing to allow him to do what he does best: "He has cast De Niro, an actor whose responsiveness to the camera derives from his reserves of passion, and, having cast this man, has not allowed him any passion. Bertolucci, locking himself away, locked out De Niro as an actor—gutted him. His Alfredo is an unfinished man: a man who hasn't tested himself. He's too emasculated even to suffer. Alfredo is the pampered, bourgeois liberal that Bertolucci guiltily fears himself to be." However, Caryn James, reviewing the

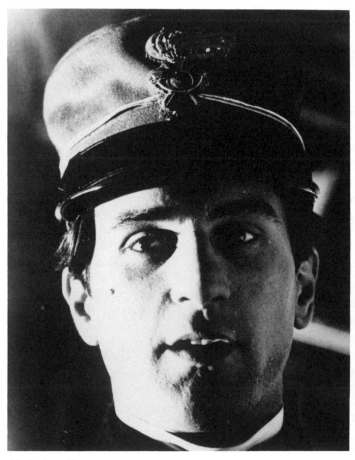

Alfredo the soldier.

tally, only, to date) absolute weakling. That caused problems for *Variety,* which noted: "A sober De Niro is somewhat overshadowed by a role condemning him to passivity." Taking a more involved, complex view of that very problem, Richard Corliss criticized the characterization of Alfredo thusly: "Alfredo is a curiously passive character to build a film around. From childhood to middle age, he does nothing, thinks little, feels hardly at all. As the padrone of a huge estate, he is given things (by his family), loses things (his wife), is finally stripped of things (by his peasants)—but to what effect? It is Bertolucci's point . . . that this representative of the ruling class is too weak to fight either the proletariat (Olmo) or the fascists (Attila), and that Alfredo learns nothing from his own and his country's tumultuous history. But must he be so boring? De Niro has played quiet characters before . . . [but] there was always a residue of strength, a hint of obsessiveness, a sense of personal pride. Alfredo has none of these qualities, and De Niro has no hook to hang his own outsized but narrow-ranged talent on. His performance is as boring as his character."

It made sense, though, that the rare critic who

film for the *New York Times* when it was rereleased in 1991 in a five-hour-eleven-minute version, saw it quite differently, in retrospect: "Alfredo is Robert De Niro, whose American accent adds an unsettling whiff of modernism to his role as the last padrone. . . . Mr. De Niro's portrayal is the strongest because his ultramodern presence works against all expectations. Alfredo may be the watered-down last generation of feudalism, but the actor's vibrant presence suggests the tenacity of his class."

That longer version contains a great many more didactic political speeches and near-pornographic scenes than the 1977 American release print, causing the rating to be changed from R to NC-17. The sex and socialism are awkwardly at odds with one another throughout—suggesting that the filmmaker may have been at odds with himself in ways he failed to realize, especially since his sequences depicting the hedonism of Ada are the most memorable, while the political correct-

ness of Olmo comes off as downright dull. There's something out of whack with a work of communist propaganda that leaves us liking the decadent capitalists far more than we do the common-man hero. In 1977, critic Farber took that aspect a step further, writing: "There's something deeper than politics behind Bertolucci's confusions. His movies are full of homoerotic moments: In *1900,* when Olmo returns from World War I, he wrestles with Alfredo in the hay, and Alfredo cries, 'Kiss me, my hero.' Yet Bertolucci struggles to repudiate his own sexual ambivalences. Focusing on robust, rutting peasants, *1900* is his unconvincing celebration of healthy heterosexuality. Bertolucci wants to champion the normal even while he's secretly fascinated by the abnormal, the atypical. He's an artist in desperate conflict with himself." That conflict impacted not only on the film, but also on De Niro's work; though he has been in other failed films, this is one of the few times when his performance must also be deemed a failure.

Olmo rises to power, even as Alfredo falls from grace.

A FACE IN THE CROWD:

Travis eyes a particularly strange client, played by director Martin Scorsese.

Taxi Driver

(1976)

A Columbia Pictures Release

CAST:

Robert De Niro (*Travis Bickle*); Cybill Shepherd (*Betsy*); Jodie Foster (*Iris*); Peter Boyle (*Wizard*); Albert Brooks (*Tom*); Leonard Harris (*Senator Palantine*); Harvey Keitel (*Sport*); Murray Moston (*Timekeeper*); Richard Higgs (*Secret Service Agent*); Martin Scorsese (*Weird Passenger*); Joe Spinell (*Personnel Officer*).

CREDITS:

Director, Martin Scorsese; producers, Michael and Julia Phillips; screenplay, Paul Schrader; photography, Michael Chapman; visual consultant, David Nichols; art direction, Charles Rosen; editors, Marcia Lucas, Tom Rolf, and Melvin Shapiro; music, Bernard Herrmann; running time, 114 minutes; rating: R.

In the opening scene of *Taxi Driver*—the most praised and damned movie of the 1970s—a cab winds its way down one of New York's mean streets, past steam billowing out of a manhole. The image—powerful or pretentious, depending on your point of view—is undeniably a vision of the contemporary city as hell on earth. Roaming this world like a wolf about to display the first signs of rabies is Travis Bickle (De Niro), an introverted Vietnam vet who hails from the Midwest but has settled in this squalid stinkhole, which he detests—especially for its easy availability of sleazy sex, something he watches being sold on streetcorners from the relative safety of his cab. Travis has taken the job as night rider because of insomnia. Since he can't sleep, he might as well do the work no one else wants, which at least allows him to wander into the sordid, grungy neon demimonde of the flesh that simultaneously fascinates and repels him.

Travis jots down his thoughts in a journal, where his tone of voice borders on the mock-poetic; however, he's

Robert De Niro as Travis Bickle.

Travis maintains simultaneous relationships with society-girl Betsy (Cybill Shepherd) . . .

. . . and underage street-prostitute Iris (Jodie Foster).

Travis remains distant even from his fellow taxi drivers, including Wizard (Peter Boyle); director Scorsese establishes Travis's alienation by visualizing the fact that this character remains physically apart from his peer group.

practically inarticulate when dealing with others, even fellow cabbies such as the self-proclaimed philosopher Wizard (Peter Boyle). Despite his low social status, Travis manages to charm a bored socialite and sometime political activist, Betsy (Cybill Shepherd) into a date, overcoming the protestations of her friend and fellow office worker Tom (Albert Brooks). But Travis makes the mistake of taking the goddesslike Betsy, always dressed in immaculate white, to one of the porno palaces he frequents when not railing against overly permissive sex. Her amusement at the offbeat date quickly turns to repulsion. She leaves, refusing to see him again.

Intriguingly, Travis has been leading a double dating life. While trying to move up the social circle with Betsy, self-defeatingly bringing the high-society girl to a low-life movie and dashing his chances, he has also been seeing a twelve-and-a-half-year-old street prostitute, Iris (Jodie Foster). Perhaps Travis has heard the old adage about succeeding with women by always treating a lady like a whore and a whore like a lady. When with the sleazy Iris, he's a perfect gentleman, attempting to persuade the child to return to her family, much to the chagrin of her pimp, Sport (Harvey Keitel). Sport threatens Travis, but Iris has already made clear she likes doing what she's doing and does not want or intend to be "saved."

Most critics agreed that this portion of the film—an insightful, unforgettable portrait of one of those anonymous, vaguely threatening characters we brush up against on the big-city streets every day, coupled with simultaneous cross-cultural "romantic" relationships on both ends of the social spectrum—was extraordinarily well written by Paul Schrader and vividly brought to life on-screen by director Martin Scorsese. What transpired next is what divided critics and audiences. Rejected by both Madonna and Whore, Travis becomes manic. He shaves his head to a radical Mohawk cut, dons paramilitary clothing, outfits himself with an arsenal of pistols and knives, then begins stalking the political candidate (Leonard Harris) Betsy works for, with plans of assassinating the man to prove and announce his own existence—making people at last take note of Travis Bickle. That never happens, as a Secret Service agent (Richard Higgs) notices Travis as a particularly menacing face in the crowd and scares him away.

Thwarted in his twisted ambition, Travis then turns his fury on the lowlifes who have no protection, invading Sport's little world and killing four people in a wave of violence. Some critics found the violence mindless not only on the part of Bickle, but also the filmmakers. Richard Schickel of *Time* argued that "Travis's failure [with Betsy] as presented is more farcical than tragic, and it never adequately explains his becoming a killer. . . . [*Taxi Driver*] is all too heavy with easy sociologizing to be truly moving. . . . It is a conflict [Scorsese] can resolve only in a violence that seems forced and— coming after so much dreariness—ridiculously pyrotechnical." Most critics, typified by Judith Crist in *Sat-

urday Review, rejected the violence toward the end ("one of the most revolting outbursts of blood ever to splatter a non–'martial arts' movie") as excessive, overdone, even angering. Crist ultimately tagged *Taxi Driver* "a completely fascinating and ultimately unsatisfying film"—which, in retrospect, seems a fair, balanced, right-on assessment.

In the film's epilogue—which proved even more controversial than the post-Peckinpah bloodletting— Travis is not prosecuted but rather rewarded for his actions, lauded as a popular hero and media celebrity for ridding the world of some scum. He's seen driving his cab, as if nothing happened; by accident, Betsy steps in, now treating him as someone special, though he rejects her and drives away. Whether he's been "cured" through his cathartic killing or is just waiting to erupt again is impossible to tell. And that's the most problematic part of *Taxi Driver:* in addition to an irony that doesn't come off as intended, Scorsese and Schrader apparently do not fully understand their own striking, even significant, creation.

Perhaps that's because they were the oddest collaborators ever to join forces for a contemporary film, considering Scorsese's rich Catholic upbringing and the violence he witnessed daily in Little Italy, often while on the way to his favorite pastime, the magical world of the movies. His experience was directly opposed to that of Schrader, who knew only a Calvinist Midwestern background of sexual repression. In sharp contrast to Scorsese, Schrader never even saw a film until he was over twenty-one, then not for simple entertainment but as a conscious act of rebellion toward his parents and upbringing.

Once he saw his first film, though, Schrader was addicted. By the early seventies, critic (*Transcendental Style in Film: Ozu, Bresson, Dreyer*) turned screenwriter Paul Schrader had already sold several scripts to the major studios (*The Yakuza, Obsession*). Still, he fell into a deep despair that led to obsessive behavior, including regular visits to porno theaters, with recurrent fantasies of violence and suicide. Schrader turned his unhappy experiences as an isolated loner into a script about an ignored malcontent who actually lives out the author's darkest fantasies. Though Schrader had never actually driven a taxi, he did seize on the notion of a taxi driver as the perfect contemporary equivalent of Dostoyevski's underground man, the anonymous person who drifts through the modern city without ever making viable contact with his surroundings, first imploding, then exploding when the alienation becomes too much. The finished script was handed over to his *Obsession* director, Brian De Palma, who chose not to make the movie but was intrigued enough to share the work with the producing team of Tony Bill and Julia and Michael

Phillips, who read it and were likewise impressed.

But in the summer of 1972, they were hard at work on two projects (*The Sting,* a hit, and *Steelyard Blues,* a flop). *Taxi Driver* was put on the back burner, with such questions as star and director left in the vague-discussion stage. One studio offered them a deal if *Taxi Driver* could be packaged as a vehicle for director Robert Mulligan (*Summer of '42*) and actor Jeff Bridges; but the producers had given Schrader veto power, and he recoiled at the very thought of that combination. Then, as *Sting* and *Steelyard* neared completion, the trio happened to catch a much-heralded little art-house item called *Mean Streets.* There was no question among the producers that *Taxi Driver* should be directed by this bold new talent Scorsese, or that his scene-stealing actor Robert De Niro was perfect to incarnate Travis Bickle, the desperate loner. Schrader, who also saw *Mean Streets,* agreed, making the decision unanimous.

The independent team swiftly received an offer from Warner Brothers that would have extended $500,000 for the film's budget, the WB brass also having seen *Mean Streets* and presuming that *Taxi Driver* would likewise be an artistically ambitious film shot on a minuscule budget. But Bill and the Phillipses decided to pass, believing *Taxi Driver* should and could be something more than just another gritty, realistic melodrama. If things worked out right, this could be an icon-making film, a key motion picture of the decade—an era in which the peace-and-love hopes and hypes of the late sixties had been swallowed up by the harsh realities of street crime and widespread drug addiction.

Eventually, executives at Columbia Pictures were convinced of the movie's major potential, agreeing that *Taxi Driver* should have a budget in excess of a million dollars, then still considered a hefty sum. But all was not easy yet, for De Niro—riding high on the success of *Godfather II*—had departed for Italy to headline Bertolucci's *1900,* while Scorsese had used his post–*Mean Streets* clout to land a more mainstream studio feature, *Alice Doesn't Live Here Anymore,* an uncharacteristically gentle feminist-era fantasy of a woman's rediscovering herself, which won Ellen Burstyn a Best Actress Oscar. It also won Scorsese a reputation as a cop-out among some die-hard fans, who disdained his move toward overtly commercial fare. De Niro, meanwhile, had not been as pleased as he'd hoped when working with Bertolucci. Eager to salvage their reputations—and to recapture the joys of collaborating—Scorsese and De Niro saw *Taxi Driver* as a means of redeeming themselves, an interesting irony as the movie itself is about the strange redemption of Travis Bickle. Columbia, meanwhile, raised the budget somewhat, considering the suddenly elevated status of star, director, and producers since the project's inception. Still, they all worked far

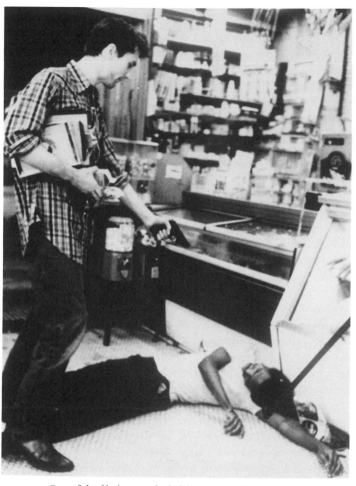

One of the film's more frightful moments: Travis executes a would-be mugger.

more cheaply on *Taxi Driver* than they might ordinarily have agreed to, owing to their collective deep-seated belief that this might turn out to be a movie on the order of *The Wild One* and *Rebel Without a Cause* from the fifties, or *The Graduate* and *Easy Rider* from the sixties—cinematic anthems that, through one particular story, say much and imply even more about our society at a key moment in time.

The possibility that they had succeeded became clear when, in May of 1976, *Taxi Driver* took the top prize, the Palme d'Or, at the Cannes Film Festival. Yet the controversy that would always surround this movie also erupted at Cannes, when the president of the festival's jury, playwright Tennessee Williams, broke the customary vows of silence to articulate his concern over the direction in which our most serious filmmakers were moving. Though *Taxi Driver* was not singled out by name (in fact, the diatribe that followed could also have described various other movies from diverse countries), there seemed little doubt it was the key film to make Williams admonish the then-emerging collective attitude of young filmmakers even while admiring their technical and aesthetic abilities. Williams and the Ecumenical Jury bemoaned the fact that the midseventies "has been marked by serious films without hope, some of which reflected a violence seldom seen before. We are well aware that this violence and hopelessness reflect the image of our society. However, we fear that violence breeds violence and that, instead of being a denunciation, it leads our society to an escalation of violence. The jury . . . expresses its wish that the cinema not become a source of hatred." Those words would prove prophetic

Wizard (Peter Boyle) attempts to reason with Travis, to no avail.

Travis in his cab.

some five years later, when it was announced in the press that John Hinckley, who attempted to assassinate President Reagan to impress actress Jodie Foster, was clearly inspired by *Taxi Driver,* a film in which she had co-starred and which offered him the blueprint for his actions.

It was impossible for the filmmakers ever to answer completely the charge that they were in some way responsible for Hinckley's actions. Untold millions of people can watch a film like *Taxi Driver* and take it as art and/or entertainment, though one deranged soul can always accept it as a catalyst for a descent into insanity. Importantly, though, the filmmakers all agreed that the movie was essentially religious in tone. "The problems that the character has stem from religious ones—religion taken to the extreme," Schrader said. For Schrader, this has to do with his Calvinist urge to repress sexuality, until the decent Christian intention threatens to destroy him, as it did televangelist Jimmy Swaggart, who turned from preaching to prostitutes. Scorsese had a more Catholic approach. "The whole idea," the director has said, "was to make a story of a modern saint—a saint in his own society, [which] happens to be [filled with] gangsters." In other words, Travis is a saint because he wants to save the girl, the problem being that she doesn't

De Niro as Travis, brooding.

101

When he is rejected by Betsy . . .

. . . Travis vents his repressed sexual rage through his gun .

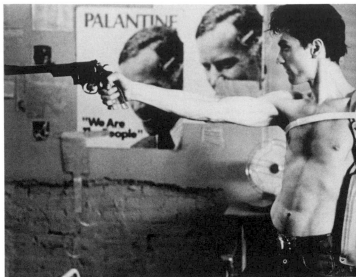

. . . then becomes a dangerous face in the crowd . . .

102

. . . and finally loses all control.

want to be saved. Vincent Canby, in the *New York Times,* also noted this religious angle, arguing that it was a film about "a Manhattan cabbie who finds salvation through slaughter."

De Niro, sensing he had to respond to both collaborators—their agreement that this was a religious allegory, but also their different, even opposing, concepts of religion—worked both ends of the allegorical street. The key to Travis is that nobody listens to him; De Niro's interpretation of the script was that Travis used his gun the way Schrader had used his talent—to get someone to listen. Bobby knew that Scorsese believed making the film was, for him, an "exorcism" from the more commercial ventures he had been tempted by, helping us understand why De Niro's character must exorcise himself through brutal violence. Scorsese opted for a combination of the gritty street realism he'd perfected in *Mean Streets* and the more fluid camerawork of a studio film such as *Alice.* He chose not to use a single hand-held-camera shot in the entire film, dollying even when necessary. He is a good and growing actor, as *Godfather II* showed, but there is nothing here that Robert Blake or Jeff Bridges (who are much less) couldn't have handled." No matter how much one agrees with Kauffmann about

the movie's limitations and disappointments, his comments on De Niro seem out of line. It is inconceivable that either of those other actors could have incarnated Travis Bickle with the precision, texture, depth, and edginess De Niro brought to the role.

Other critics—both those who were kind and unkind to the film itself—had only superlatives for De Niro's performance. *Variety* insisted that "De Niro gives the role the precise blend of awkwardness, naïveté, and latent violence which makes Travis a character who is compelling even when he is at his most revolting." Arthur Knight echoed those words in the *Hollywood Reporter,* writing that as this self-appointed "avenging angel," the star "manages to make a repulsive character constantly credible and sometimes even sympathetic," noting that otherwise it would have been impossible for an audience to stomach the burst of violence with which the film ends.

In *Newsweek,* Jack Kroll wrote that "first and last, *Taxi Driver* belongs to Robert De Niro, the most remarkable young actor of the American screen. What the film comes down to is a grotesque pas de deux between Travis and the City, and De Niro has the dance quality that most great film actors have had, whether it's allegro like Cagney or largo like Brando. De Niro controls his body like a moving sculpture. Once, seething with frustration, he takes a swig from a beer can and his head snaps into a quick, complex spasm of thwarted rage. Trying to ingratiate himself with a Secret Service man, his entire conversation comes out of a tilted-up, twisty-smiling face that's a diagram of social unease. By the time he's through, De Niro has created a total behavioral system for [Travis], which has a macabre comedy."

Pauline Kael of *The New Yorker,* in her last days as a De Niro defender, wrote: "Robert De Niro is in almost every frame; thin-faced, as handsome as Robert Taylor one moment and cagey, ferrety, like Cagney, the next. . . . As Travis, De Niro has none of the peasant courtliness of his Vito Corleone in *The Godfather, Part II.* Vito held himself in proudly, in control of his violence; he was a leader. Travis is dangerous in a different, cumulative way. His tense face folds in a yokel's grin and he looks almost an idiot. . . . Some actors are said to be empty his camera was inside the cab, while somehow retaining the documentary flavor of his earlier work. But while responding to this, Bobby also adopted Schrader's clothing from his depressed period, as well as his manner and attitude. De Niro's Travis Bickle is a psychological combination of Bobby's two very different collaborators, a Jekyll and Hyde character.

Stanley Kauffmann, who panned the film in *The New Republic,* did not so much disparage De Niro as he claimed the actor was above such fare: "De Niro was not vessels who are filled by the roles they play, but that's not what appears to be happening here with De Niro. He's gone the other way. He's used his emptiness—he's reached down into his own anomie. Only Brando has done this kind of plunging. . . . By drawing us into his vortex it makes us understand the psychic discharge of the quiet boys who go berserk."

This was the first film for Diahnne Abbott, De Niro's wife, who played the small role of the porno theater cashier; it was the last for famed composer Bernard Herrmann, who died on December 24, 1975, only hours after completing the sound track. De Niro had, of course, taken the route of careful preparation from the moment he'd signed on, actually driving a cab around Manhattan at night so he'd be able to make his role totally real. One of Bobby's real-life fares was an obscure (but employed) actor who immediately recognized the star of *Godfather II,* asking if this was indeed Robert De Niro in the front seat. Bobby admitted that yes, it was; the actor nodded understandingly, sighed, and muttered, "Well, that's acting. One year, the Oscar—the next, you're driving a cab!"

De Niro was nominated for Best Actor, his first in that category; the award that year went posthumously to Peter Finch for *Network. Taxi Driver*—though nominated for Best Picture—lost out to the contemporary fairy tale *Rocky.* That year, De Niro was picked as Best Actor by the New York Film Critics Circle. The most memorable moments of the movie were improvised, and today, Scorsese and De Niro both admit it's impossible to determine who came up with which bit. The more practical course is to assume it was their unique collaboration that led to the classic takes: De Niro, experimenting to see how far he can tilt a TV set before it crashes down, recalling Henry Fonda's Wyatt Earp in John Ford's *My Darling Clementine,* leaning back on a chair to see how far he can go without falling; De Niro, staring into his reflection and repeating, again and again, the line: "You talkin' to me?" Whether the line actually comes from Schrader, Scorsese, or De Niro finally matters less than that it sums up what the film is all about: communication, or the lack of it, and what the encroaching silence means to those alienated, nearly invisible characters in our society—so lost and lonely that they cannot conceive of even being addressed by the "normals." Occasionally—as in the case of Travis Bickle—they do break out in grotesque violent reaction in order to be noticed, heard, counted.

De Niro as Travis, pensive.

THE MAN IN THE SUIT:

The Last Romantic: Monroe sees Kathleen Moore (Ingrid Boulting) as the love of his live, his first wife reborn.

The Last Tycoon

(1976)

A Paramount Pictures Release

CAST:

Robert De Niro (*Monroe Stahr*); Tony Curtis (*Rodriguez*); Robert Mitchum (*Pat Brady*); Jeanne Moreau (*Didi*); Jack Nicholson (*Brimmer*); Donald Pleasence (*Boxley*); Ingrid Boulting (*Kathleen*); Ray Milland (*Fleishacker*); Dana Andrews (*Ridingwood*); Theresa Russell (*Cecilia*); Peter Strauss (*Wylie*); John Carradine (*Guide*); Jeff Corey (*Doctor*); Anjelica Huston (*Edna*).

CREDITS:

Director, Elia Kazan; producer, Sam Spiegel; screenplay, Harold Pinter, based on the unfinished novel by F. Scott Fitzgerald; photography, Victor Kemper; production design, Gene Callahan; art direction, Jack Collis; costumes/wardrobe, Anna Hill Johnstone, Anthea Sylbert, Thalia Phillips, and Richard Bruno; editor, Richard Marks; music, Maurice Jarre; running time, 122 minutes; rating: PG.

De Niro had long since proven his ability to play characters living on the edge; indeed, he literally had the market cornered following *Taxi Driver*. But as the latter-day Brando, he felt as constrained by this dubious status as Marlon had after *The Wild One, Waterfront,* and *Streetcar* all cast him as an inarticulate man in a T-shirt.

The Last Tycoon was not a box-office success, or a critical one for that matter, but it served De Niro's purpose perfectly. He needed to prove he could convincingly play a soft-spoken, even sentimental man, one who wore a suit well. If he didn't make clear that he could comfortably do such a part at this key juncture in his career, he might never get another chance. And while the reviews of the film were mostly negative, nearly every critic paused to point out how effective Bobby was as Monroe Stahr, a thinly disguised version of that much-revered Hollywood producer of the 1930s,

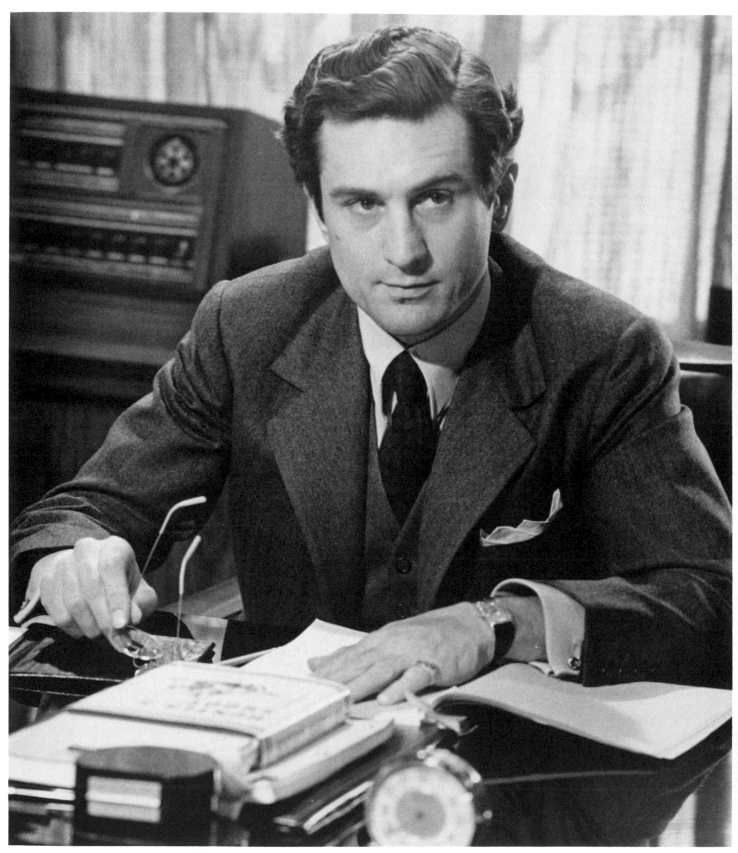

Robert De Niro as Monroe Stahr.

A star is born: De Niro, front and center, is flanked by such Hollywood luminaries (now reduced to supporting roles) as Tony Curtis and wife Leslie, Ray Milland, Jeanne Moreau, and Robert Mitchum, plus newcomer Theresa Russell.

Irving G. Thalberg, who as head of production at MGM fought for quality—even literary—projects, oftentimes against the wishes of studio boss and moneyman Louis B. Mayer, with whom he often found himself in conflict.

F. Scott Fitzgerald fictionalized that conflict, making it the subject of his final (and unfinished at the time of his death) novel, *The Last Tycoon*. The book was an accurate portrayal of Tinseltown, owing to the fact that Fitzgerald spent several unhappy years working there, though his delicate prose never quite fit in with the tough-guy slang styles of the day. Perhaps *Last Tycoon* had never been filmed before because in its heyday, the old Hollywood could not deal with a book so critical of its money mentality. But as the studio system came crashing down during the sixties, it suddenly seemed a fit subject for the New Hollywood, so *The Last Tycoon* became a hot property. What would once have been compromised if it were filmed at all could now be brought to the screen in an age of new freedom. *The Last*

Tycoon might have emerged as a movie that, like the best of the new films, was at once honestly critical of the way things had been, yet at the same time nostalgic for the more glamorous past. What the film all but screamed out for was a youthful director, one who caught the spirit of the 1970s in terms of temperament and technique, but who also appreciated the epic scope and classical style of the best of the old films. One look at *The Purple Rose of Cairo, New York, New York*, or *The Godfather, Part II* makes clear that Woody Allen, Martin Scorsese, and Francis Ford Coppola were just such directors.

However, *The Last Tycoon* was made not by talented members of the New Hollywood, but by holdovers from the past, who attempted to transfer the techniques of high-quality 1950s moviemaking to the present, with results that can only be considered bland and mediocre. Everything on view oozes quality: from the stellar cast to the production values and costume design, each element is meticulous. Yet the overall effect is of a misconceived

107

Cecilia Brady (Theresa Russell) attempts to seduce Monroe . . .

. . . but he is drawn to the ethereal, mysterious Kathleen.

movie. One mistake was the choice of screenwriter: Harold Pinter, best known for his minimalist approach in *The Birthday Party* and *Accident,* in which what is left unsaid by the characters always seems far more important than what is spoken. Pinter was hardly an appropriate writer to bring Fitzgerald's upscale purplish prose to the screen. Equally unlikely was the director, Elia Kazan, who had guided Brando through two of his best early performances in *Streetcar* and *Waterfront.* But following his disastrous 1969 screen version of his own novel, *The Arrangement*—a dreadful mishmash of 1950s kitchen-sink melodrama styles and late-sixties psychedelia—Kazan appeared a once-important artist who had lost touch with the state of the art of the medium he had, two decades earlier, helped redefine.

Variety tagged this "a handsome and lethargic film," Kazan's direction "unfocused though craftsmanlike," noting that "nothing lifts the Paramount release above a level of polite indifference"—which is the way most audiences treated the project upon its release. On-screen, De Niro did have the opportunity to play more intense romantic scenes than ever before—though not with Theresa Russell (playing Cecilia), who, as the daughter of the Goldwynish studio boss Brady just arrived from Bennington, harbors a schoolgirlish crush on Stahr and pursues him incessantly, turning the quietly appealing producer off completely. Rather, De Niro coupled with Ingrid Boulting, British fashion model and daughter of the esteemed English film producer Roy Boulting. As Kathleen, she portrayed the elusive mys-

tery woman whom the romantically inclined Stahr conceives of as his dream girl. And with good reason: the first time he sees her is on the eve of a California earthquake, less a natural occurrence here than a metaphysical act of the gods. When Stahr goes out to inspect his movie set, she—an extra—literally rides toward him down an artificial river atop the head of a goddess left over from some epic picture. She not only appears ethereal, but also reminds Stahr of his deceased wife— the woman he loved, lost, and secretly hopes to somehow magically recover. Stahr invests Kathleen with all sorts of magical qualities that exist only in his romantic imagination; he falls in love not so much with her as with an idealized image of her.

It is her character, more than any other, that throws

the project off-kilter, even suggesting Fitzgerald's work is unfilmable—since the very same problem existed in the production of *The Great Gatsby* shot two years earlier. Whether it is pretty, pouty, but untalented Boulting here or the far more accomplished Mia Farrow there, the problem is that the filmmakers find themselves unable to show on-screen the dual vision of the woman as created by Fitzgerald in words. In both movies, the female lead is presented to us as the hero sees her—an image of perfection—whereas in the books, we simultaneously see his subjective obsession with her surface attractiveness and the less flattering objective truth about her. In the novel, that was achieved by having Cecilia serve as the narrator; her unfulfilled romantic obsession for Stahr makes her a particularly intriguing person to comment on Stahr's romantic obsession with Kathleen. In the film, Cecilia does not narrate—and only seems an unrealized, unnecessary,

irritating minor character. So there's nothing of that complexity of vision here; when De Niro and Ingrid Boulting make love in a beach house, the sequence is played as a romantic cliché, bordering on upscale soft-core porn: a sweet, sexy, superficial image of lovemaking.

If there was any value to the film, it was in getting to see De Niro hold his own against various heavyweights, including Robert Mitchum as the Mayerish character, Jeanne Moreau as a Garbo-esque fading star, Tony Curtis as a Latin lover who fears he's going bald on-screen and impotent offscreen, Dana Andrews as an alcoholic director, Ray Milland as an arrogant studio lawyer, and John Carradine as an actor turned tour guide. Though these cameo roles by onetime major movie stars made clear that De Niro—all but unknown only a few years before, when they were still on top—was now one of the big boys, they play less as revealing

Monroe meets and greets the elite of 1930s Hollywood.

109

Monroe experiences his ultimate romantic dream come true.

character cameos than as roman-à-clef walk-ons, allowing knowledgeable moviegoers to guess which celebrities from the past the fading celebrities of today are impersonating. Far more intriguing was the brief on-screen coupling of De Niro with Jack Nicholson, as a socially oriented and politically idealistic labor union activist. Their scenes together provide the sparks missing in so much of this elaborately empty, handsomely hollow film—and make us wonder about how exciting the results might be if the two were ever to costar in a film that provides each with a suitable character.

Still, De Niro's performance here is the centerpiece. It's worth noting that he was signed for the role only after Dustin Hoffman declined owing to other projects and Al Pacino failed to respond to Spiegel's inquiries. As the third edge of the superstar pyramid of the seventies, De Niro was the last great hope. He proved enthusiastic, understandable since the other two actors were constantly being offered such "suit" roles, while he still had to prove himself here. His reviews ran from mildly

Monroe cannot understand why everything seems to be going wrong.

positive to ecstatic. *Variety* considered "De Niro's performance as the inscrutable boy-wonder of films" only "mildly intriguing," adding, "De Niro's characterization does project, through a kind of constipated visual expression, a combination of quiet ruthlessness, nervous interpersonal relationships, extreme arrogance, and brilliant knowledge of the film medium. . . . De Niro cannot fairly be belled with the failure here." Judith Crist of *Saturday Review*, furious that the "faithful" but "bloodless" film "reduced what has endured as an insightful study of a man and an industry into an insipid little love story," found De Niro to be "at best adequate as the slight, brooding producer and moonstruck lover, never quite encompassing the inner fire and outer strength that gave Stahr such a literary distinction." Charles Champlin of the *Los Angeles Times* claimed that "De-Niro [sic] as Monroe Stahr [is] tough and introspective, sensitive and headstrong, romantic and ruthless . . . the movie's most successful element. He looks the part and delivers the man. . . . *Tycoon* is a major and wasteful disappointment, stranding a fine central performance in contrived, tone-dead, and totally uninvolving situations, missing both the romance and reportage of Fitzgerald's work."

Though Stanley Kauffmann of *The New Republic* found the film "weak" and "flawed," he nonetheless insisted that "De Niro does excellently as Stahr but cannot give a really excellent performance. This pat contradiction simply means that, as the part is written (by Pinter, not Fitzgerald), De Niro cannot realize it . . . either as a character in depth or as a dynamic in a web of actions. But he accomplishes two things beautifully. He is completely convincing in his enchantment by Kathleen; he almost seems to have moved into a fine mist. And if you remember him in *Mean Streets* and *Godfather II*, you will see how he has altered the use of his body. In those pictures his body was the source of everything; his physicality was his power. Here his body is merely some necessary equipment for a man whose mind and concerns are elsewhere. De Niro's performance is the chief reason for seeing this film." Indeed, the only reason!

Monroe fleetingly believes he will be able to recapture the gone glory of his lost love.

In their happy, early days, Jimmy and his love Francine Evans (Liza Minnelli) make beautiful music together.

New York, New York

(1977)

A United Artists Release

CAST:

Liza Minnelli (*Francine Evans*); Robert De Niro (*Jimmy Doyle*); Lionel Stander (*Tony Harwell*); Barry Primus (*Paul Wilson*); Mary Kay Place (*Bernice*); Georgie Auld (*Frankie Harte*); George Memmoli (*Nicky*); Dick Miller (*Palm Club Owner*); Murray Moston (*Horace*); Lenny Gaines (*Artie*); Clarence Clemons (*Cecil*); Diahnne Abbott (*Singer*); Larry Kert (*Dancer in 1981 home video release version*).

CREDITS:

Director, Martin Scorsese; producers, Irwin Winkler and Robert Chartoff; screenplay, Earl MacRauch and Mardik Martin; story, Earl MacRauch; photography, Laszlo Kovacs; production designer, Boris Leven; costume designer, Theadora Van Runkle; editors, Irving Lerner, Marcia Lucas, Tom Rolf, B. Lovitt, and David Ramirez; musical director, Ralph Burns; new songs, John Kander and Fred Ebb; choreography, Ron Field; various running times, 153 minutes (1977), 137 minutes (1978), 164 minutes (1981); rating: PG.

After playing the well-meaning weakling in *1900* and the sensitive soul of *The Last Tycoon*, De Niro tackled a considerably less sympathetic character in *New York, New York*, which also marked his return to the fold of filmmaker Martin Scorsese. His role as tenor saxophonist Jimmy Doyle is an uncompromising yet off-putting portrait of a self-absorbed talent—a man of immense surface charm that masks internal anger, self-pity, and a short-fuse temper that at times leads to brutal behavior, most of it directed at his wife, Francine Evans (Liza Minnelli), also a jazz artist. The fact that Francine's style of pop singing is more mainstream than Jimmy's esoteric jazz, logically leading to superstardom for her even as Jimmy receives only cult attention, hardly works in favor of their relationship. Nor does the fact that when they first meet (at an exuberant VJ-day celebration), he seems on his way up the ladder to remarkable success, she

Robert De Niro as Jimmy Doyle.

Director Martin Scorsese films the golden days of radio with a haze that captures his sense of nostalgia . . .

. . . and overly-stylizes many of the scenes, including this meeting of Jimmy and Francine in the woods, which looks like something out of an old Hollywood musical.

appearing only a minor artist, lucky just to ride along on his coattails.

The pivotal moment in the film comes when Francine, pregnant, willingly retires as a singer with Jimmy's band (at least temporarily) to stay home and raise their child. The moment she's gone, the band slips in popularity, making abundantly clear that Francine was not a sidelight, but in fact the basis of their appeal. Unable to admit this to himself, much less willing to articulate it to Francine, Jimmy expresses his frustration the only way he can, by verbally abusing their child and physically abusing her: a pre–*Raging Bull* portrait of the type of character De Niro and Scorsese would closely study in their upcoming La Motta movie.

Many critics complained that the very integrity with which the dislikable character of Jimmy was portrayed (he's a composite of various real-life jazz artists) ultimately hurt *New York, New York*'s chances for box-office success. Stanley Kauffmann spoke not only for himself but also the vast majority of reviewers—and casual viewers—when he wrote: "They tried to make it a tough-sentimental showbiz story . . . moving in and out of the texture of a musical. . . . But the sentiment doesn't take, and what's left isn't tough—it's occasionally repellent but mostly tedious and trite. . . . De Niro is not a personality actor (in terms of charmingly conventional movie-star charisma), he's a [serious] actor. . . . De Niro just becomes a nuisance." De Niro himself attempted a justification of the performance by claiming, "If you saw enough of this guy's life, maybe in a twenty-four-hour film, you'd see his better side."

That defense, however, does not suffice. It was the job of De Niro and Scorsese to show enough of Jimmy's good side so the audience considered Jimmy if not entirely sympathetic, then at least a worthwhile human being, with some sort of balance between the good and the bad. As is, there's so little to admire about Jimmy the person (as opposed to Jimmy the artist) that the critics' complaints seem justified. He's simply an unregenerate jerk, however fine his music may be. It's true that the later Jake La Motta characterization likewise gives us little to like, other than his abilities as a fighter. Still, there, the grim black-and-white world of that film—as well as the boxing milieu itself—sets us up for such a situation. Also, De Niro and Scorsese there managed to endow the character with a tragic stature and primal empathy missing here. *New York, New York*'s show business setting—and the assumption of audiences, especially older audiences, that any $8-million film (then still considered a huge budget) featuring Liza Minnelli and the Big Band sound of the 1940s (twenty-four oldies, plus four originals) should ultimately be a "nice" experience—left viewers feeling violated by the results, however powerful and/or honest.

When, toward the end, Liza dazzlingly performs the title number (which really did sound of a piece with the period music), the film briefly promised to pay off with a reconciliation that might have made up for much of the shrill melodramatics and numbing domestic violence along the way. But the filmmakers, hoping to maintain integrity, flatly refused to do that. Though Francine and Jimmy plan a meeting for after her performance to try to patch things up, each independently decides to take a powder.

The difficulty of maintaining a personal relationship (much less a marriage and home life) under stressful show-biz circumstances is basic to this musical drama, set against the changing times (1945–1960) and concurrent transformations in popular musical styles. No director of our time is more attune to this music than Scorsese. In *New York, New York*, the music moves beyond simple nostalgia, effectively serving as a metaphor for the movies. Jimmy Doyle says at one point, "You know, all my life it was the big bands. Then, just when I was ready, the war comes along. And now that the war's over and I'm ready, the bands are over. . . . It's funny. The bands were always my dream, and now they're finished." Merely change *music* to *movies*, and this can be taken as the lament of Scorsese, who grew up loving the glossy Hollywood films, craving to someday make them himself. Then, just as he reached a stature in the film business where he could actually direct, the studio-

style was gone, replaced by a new realism he helped initiate.

If De Niro's music-oriented character is a thinly disguised spokesman for moviemaker Scorsese, then the schizophrenic style Scorsese employed for *New York, New York* expresses his own ambiguous attitude: simultaneously wanting to make a gritty, naturalistic drama and a Tinseltown fairy tale for adults. No wonder, then, that the film features nearly incomprehensible scenes in which the characters speak overlapping dialogue (the actors improvising as they tentatively interrupt one another, the most realistic way in which screen people can talk) while standing on self-consciously phony papier-mâché sets, with overobvious back-projection behind them.

Little doubt also that De Niro, Scorsese, and writer Mardik Martin were—despite the fictional characters and the period-piece setting—making a work about their own problems in maintaining normal home lives while also surviving the wild roller-coaster ups and downs of show business success and failure. Scorsese's reflections on the film make clear that, in rendering this story about a couple of equally ambitious jazz artists, he was in fact telling his own earlier story, as well as that of collaborator De Niro: "It's about the period in your life when you're just [on the edge of] making it [big]." More generally, *New York, New York* tells the story of all artists ("It's really about everything everybody goes through—directors, musicians, writers, everyone"). The wives of both Scorsese and De Niro became pregnant during filming, so the reaction of the two men to such a situation informed the film they were making, which is about men emotionally torn apart by the seemingly mutually exclusive (but equally appealing) demands of domesticity as opposed to the freedom necessary for artistic integrity.

The film also featured a sense of social comment, suggesting what the public's taste in seemingly escapist entertainment tells us about the nation at the time. When the story begins, in the mid-forties, the trend is still toward big bands; when it ends more than a decade later, there's an emphasis on solo performers. Likewise, the national mood went from an emphasis on communal behavior (so necessary to win the war) to one of rugged individualism (the "lonely crowd" mentality of the 1950s Cold War era). As Colin L. Westerbeck, Jr., wrote in *Commonweal:* "The incompatibility of Jimmy and Francine is prefigured in the film as a whole by the incompatibility of swing and bebop."

Moments of brilliance appear throughout *New York, New York*, attesting to Scorsese's artistry and ambitions, yet there is a pervasive inconsistency in tone, perspective, and purpose, suggesting the film was not well thought out in advance. Liza Minnelli recalls that, deep

Violence erupts when Jimmy and Paul Wilson (Barry Primus) argue over Francine.

into the actual filmmaking, "the changes came constantly, from everyone's imagination and enthusiasm. After a while we were all running around with tape recorders so we wouldn't lose ideas." Liza's contributions, certainly, derived from the tradition of Hollywood musicals she grew up with, having been on the set with actress/singer mother Judy Garland and world-class director father Vincente Minnelli.

Despite its title, *New York, New York* was shot in Hollywood, on old film sets that had been used in 1940s and 1950s studio pictures about Manhattan. Scorsese has admitted to having been highly influenced by the Hollywood studio films he saw about New York as a child: "New York on-screen was more real to me than New York itself, even though I lived there." At times, the New York in Scorsese's film is the New York of his boyhood, essentially realistic if somewhat nostalgically portrayed. At other moments, it is the New York of movie mythology—*On the Town, It's Always Fair Weather*—glorious studio facsimiles that idealized the city. This concept of two distinct New Yorks might have made for a profound film indeed; the title—*New York, New York*—could have rung with brittle irony, as the film explored the distinction between the real New York and the Hollywood dream-factory version. But even the most devoted Scorsese–De Niro fan would be hard-pressed to find any rhyme or reason to the erratic bouncing back and forth between realism and fantasy

here. One moment, the characters are performing in a kitchen-sink drama set on real streets; the next, they walk through a fantasy world, composed of cardboard cutouts and painted backdrops, incongruously still speaking street-wise dialogue.

Throughout the filmmaking, Scorsese appears to have waffled between wanting to re-create the romantic attitudes of the 1940s and to reject those very attitudes as unrealistic. It must have hurt him deeply when the lavish "Happy Endings" production number was hacked away by United Artists on the eve of the film's theatrical release, even though it had been the film's raison d'être. Indeed, the film's "real" unhappy ending only makes sense when seen in contrast to the appealing phony myth—enshrined here, with just a tinge of satire—that a happy ending is indeed always possible. At the time, Scorsese absolutely defended UA's decision to cut: "Though this was the first sequence we planned, the movie which had in time evolved was something quite different, and it no longer fit in." He did an about-face when an extended version of the film was released on home video, with that sequence reinserted: "At last, people can see the film as I wanted them to see it."

Theatrical viewers in 1977—particularly mature viewers—were hooked while watching the animated opening, in which the cartoonish letters in the title "New York, New York" swayed to the Kander/Ebb tune that would quickly become a pop standard; they loved the

116

re-creation of such musical hot spots as the Rainbow Room and Harlem jazz cellars. De Niro's wife of that time, Diahnne Abbott, is perfectly cast as the beautiful Lena Horne look-alike who performs "Honeysuckle Rose." Audiences loudly applauded at such moments. But the Liza Minnelli character, badly beaten by her husband, ended up serving as a symbol for the audience itself. Viewers who, early on, rejoiced, eventually crawled out of the theater feeling brutalized by the shrill, unsparing, nasty, downbeat work they were stunned to experience.

However, an indication of the film's ability to elicit strong reactions to this day is that Leonard Maltin, in his widely used encyclopedia of minireviews, was forced by a landslide of indignant letters to change his rating on *New York, New York.* The 1981–82 edition of *TV Movies* tags the film as a BOMB, the lowest possible rating, stating, "Scorsese creates a milestone: the first sick Hollywood musical. . . . Overlong [and] meandering." However, in the 1987 edition (now called *TV Movies and Video Guide*), the film is begrudgingly upgraded to a °½ rating (out of a possible four), the capsule commentary revised to: "Elaborate but off-putting musical drama. . . . Some people consider this film extraordinary, but we're not among them; kudos, though, to production designer Boris Leven, music arranger Ralph Burns, and the Kander-Ebb title song."

Pauline Kael, who had not yet turned on De Niro, was a staunch defender of his performance here, if not the movie itself, which in *The New Yorker* she abruptly dismissed as an ill-conceived pastiche: "The best thing about [*New York, New York*] is De Niro's firm, rapid performance. He is a wonderful actor . . . he convinces the movie audience of a sort of desperation underpinning his talent." In addition to the opportunity to work again with Scorsese, De Niro agreed to play Jimmy in anticipation of the painstaking preparation this role required, including playing a musical instrument on a professional level. Though many actors might have simply faked it, De Niro took a more meticulous approach, hanging out in various jazz clubs to soak up the unique ambience, practicing up to six hours a day on the sax, learning the correct finger control and breathing. He studied for three months with a veteran jazz musician Georgie Auld (who had played with Artie Shaw and Benny Goodman and has a featured role in *New York, New York*) to completely master the instrument. Though it's Auld's sax-playing we hear in the film, De Niro would later insist, "I played the same material and had to synchronize to what Georgie recorded. I can't read music, but Georgie helped me pick out the right kind of sax and taught me to play phonetically. I've learned to do the phrasing and breathing exactly the way Georgie does." Auld reflected that "Bobby had actually done a little music training on the clarinet. Still, it's incredible the way he learned. He'd find himself a little hideaway and practice until midnight. . . . He improved from advanced to amateur to good." In time, though, De Niro's attention to detail and desire for perfection unnerved Auld, who complained, "[He] asked me ten million questions a day. It got to be a pain."

Jimmy and Francine meet the legendary Tommy Dorsey (William Tole).

Vronsky and pals (from left, Christopher Walken, Chuck Aspegren, John Savage, John Cazale) at the mill, before war changes their lives forever.

The Deer Hunter

(1978)

A Universal Film

CAST:

Robert De Niro (*Michael Vronsky*); John Cazale (*Stan/"Stosh"*); John Savage (*Steven*); Meryl Streep (*Linda*); Christopher Walken (*Nick*); George Dzundza (*John*); Chuck Aspegren (*Axel*); Shirley Stoler (*Steven's Mother*); Rutanya Alda (*Angela*); Pierre Segui (*Julien*); Mady Kaplan (*Axel's Girl*); Amy Wright (*Bridesmaid*); Joe Grifasi (*Bandleader*); Ding Santos, Krieng Chaipuk, Ot Palapoo, Chock Chai Mahasoke (*VC Guards*); Hillary Brown (*Hillary Brown*).

CREDITS:

Director, Michael Cimino; producers, Barry Spikings, Michael Deeley, Michael Cimino, and John Peverall; screenplay, Deric Washburn, from a story by Cimino, Washburn, Louis Garfinkle, and Quinn K. Redeker; photography, Vilmos Zsigmond; production designers, Ron Hobbs and Kim Swados; costume design, Eric Seelig; editor, Peter Zinner; music, Stanley Myers; running time, 182 minutes; rating: R.

In the midnineties, it's difficult for many people (especially younger moviegoers) to grasp the impact of *The Deer Hunter* in 1978. Simply, there have been so many movies made about Vietnam (ranging from the realism of Oliver Stone's *Platoon* to the fantasy of Sylvester Stallone's *Rambo*) that the subject has, if anything, been all but worn out. But other than John Wayne's ultrapatriotic *The Green Berets* and several underground antiwar diatribes, few films were done about Vietnam in the midsixties, while the war raged. Even in the midseventies, as America gradually disassociated itself from Vietnam, our involvement remained such a sore spot that filmmakers were not yet willing to squarely face the issue. Finally, *The Deer Hunter* and *Coming Home* appeared in 1978, with Francis Ford Coppola's *Apocalypse Now* following a year later. From

Robert De Niro as Michael Vronsky, deer hunter . . .

. . . turned Vietnam warrior.

that point on, filmmakers felt free to dramatically explore the frightful impact of the war on Americans of all political persuasions. But when *Deer Hunter* appeared, it stirred interest as much for being the first major commercial movie to seriously study Vietnam as for any qualities of filmmaking. Technical and aesthetic issues aside, it rates as a classic movie owing to the issues writer-director-producer Michael Cimino, then thirty-seven, dared to deal with.

De Niro said, "I thought that the war was wrong, but what bothered me [most] was that people who went to war became victims of it; they were used for the whims of others. I don't think that the policymakers had the [necessary] smarts. I didn't respect their decisions, or what they were doing. And it was a right of many people to feel, 'Why should I go and get involved with something that's unclear—and pay for it with my life?' It takes people like that to make changes." So his involvement with *The Deer Hunter* came as no surprise. Though this

119

is not a knee-jerk antiwar didactic piece in the way *Coming Home* was, *The Deer Hunter* does portray the negative impact of the Vietnam experience on working-class Americans who allow themselves to become involved, without ever quite grasping what's happening.

The plot of the movie can be described succinctly, as it's the texture and detail with which the characters and situations are fleshed out that gives *The Deer Hunter* its complexity—and created the controversy. The story begins in 1968. The protagonists are all descendants of Slavic immigrants, blue-collar residents of Clairton, Pennsylvania, the men working in the steel mills, the women marrying young and having babies who will grow up to repeat the life cycle of their parents and their parents' parents. In the opening, these various blue-collar types prepare for the Russian Orthodox wedding of Steven and Angela, a key family-oriented ritual in their ultratraditional lives. The long, involved wedding sequence introduces us to all the key characters and their relationships. When the wedding is over, Steven's longtime buddies—Michael, Nick, Stan, John, and Axel—slip off into the nearby mountains where they have always been happiest, hunting deer. The brutal, basic masculine bonding/blood ritual—performed in the innocence of nature, far from the grim city that consumes their daily lives—is what sustains them. While deer hunting, Michael is the perfect killer, totally disciplined and in control; he prides himself on always bringing down a buck with a single, clean shot.

Shortly, though, they will encounter something far more bloody—and considerably less happy. Steven and their ever-so-slightly-feminine, soul-of-a-poet friend

Nick (Christopher Walken) are drafted and sent to Vietnam as airborne infantrymen, while Michael joins the Green Berets. All three are eventually captured and tortured by the monstrous Vietcong, who keep the boys in pens where they are nibbled by rats and in danger of drowning, then forced, along with other prisoners, to endlessly play Russian roulette while the captors bet on who will live and who will die. Through the heroic Michael's efforts, the three eventually escape, Michael even managing to return home where he receives a hero's welcome. There, Michael senses that something essential, if intangible, has been lost during the Vietnam experience.

In 1975, on the eve of the fall of Saigon, he returns to Nam to try to bring Nick back with him, in part motivated by the fact that he has always coveted Nick's fiancée (Meryl Streep). But now, the once jovial Nick is cynical and drug-addicted, working in a Saigon gambling club as a "performer" who endlessly restages his Russian roulette experiences. Michael attempts to disengage Nick from the nihilistic lifestyle, even playing the game with him. But, as always, Michael survives, while Nick perishes of a self-inflicted wound, dying in the arms of this friend who loves him like a brother—the ultimate act of male bonding. In time, Michael does return to his old job, old friends, even his old hobby of deer hunting. But it is not the same anymore; though he goes through the motions, he is, like so many of the walking wounded who blithely went off to the Nam and returned home with some aspect of himself still missing in action, never again able to enjoy his simple life in the same old way. It's even impossible for him to take pleasure in shooting a deer, since he himself has been one of the hunted; now, he fires over a deer's head.

But being simple Americans, he and his friends cannot resist performing the old rituals, however hollow they may now be. *The Deer Hunter* ends with the survivors singing, in all seriousness, "God Bless America," though the innocence with which they—and all people like them—once sang this song has been forever dashed.

Initial reaction to the dazzlingly edited, powerfully photographed film was mostly positive. Critic Arthur Lubow hailed *The Deer Hunter* as "the first postwar Vietnam epic, a film that tries to say it all." In *Time*,

Vronksy in action.

Vronsky finds himself caught up in the tide of history.

Frank Rich called it "the first movie about Vietnam to free itself from all political cant. . . . [*The Deer Hunter*] demolishes the moral and ideological clichés of an era: it shoves the audience into hell and leaves it stranded without a map." The movie went on to win the New York Critics' award for Best Motion Picture of the Year, Cimino—who had directed only one previous feature, *Thunderbolt and Lightfoot* with Clint Eastwood—being hailed as a great new American director, along with Coppola and Scorsese.

Shortly, though, a reaction against the film set in, especially in the liberal monthlies and quarterlies, where the movie was perceived (in comparison to *Coming Home* with Jane Fonda, about middle Americans radicalized by the war and loudly repudiating it) as tacitly supporting American involvement while portraying the Vietcong in a simplistic racist fashion. In *Harper's,* Tom Buckley—who covered the war for the *New York Times*—complained that "by implication, the truth is turned inside out. The North Vietnamese and the Vietcong become the murderers and torturers and the Americans their gallant victims." Frances Fitzgerald, Pulitzer Prize winner for the Vietnam study *Fire in the Lake,* dismissed *Deer Hunter* as "a grade-B western . . . wholly implausible." Similarly, Colin L. Westerbeck, Jr., of *Commonweal* attacked the movie as being "ready to indulge in every kind of self-delusion to ease the pain [of Nam]. . . . What *The Deer Hunter* quickly turns into is a western in which the Vietnamese communists are the Indians, the vicious savages who have to be mowed down."

On the other hand, conservative critics—likewise judging more on the degree to which the film conformed with their politics rather than as to its artistic merits—tended to praise those aspects the liberals attacked. Richard Grenier of *Commentary* happily noted that *The Deer Hunter* was "imbued with a kind of primary patriotism, even a florid patriotism. For Cimino, the root, the home base of this nationalist ardor, is in America's working classes, for whom America is not yet something to be taken for granted. . . . The film is very admiring of what it holds to be working-class strength and vitality." Then, presaging the election of Ronald Reagan a mere two years later, Grenier saw in the film's box-office success a premonition of the neoconservatism that would blossom during the next decade: "To judge by the surprisingly strong positive reaction to *The Deer Hunter,* the ardent patriotism it expresses is not so dead a commodity in today's America as some might have thought."

A few critics, though, took nonpolitical stances, including Peter P. Schillaci of *The Christian Century,* who saw it as "a revival of the genre in an innovative format that does for the war film what *The Godfather* did for the gangster movie" by redeeming, via a contemporary approach, what was best about the genre; "*The Deer Hunter* retains many features of the classic war film—not least its refusal to render an overt moral judgment on the war or its participants." Pauline Kael also approached *The Deer Hunter* in this manner, admiring it as "a romantic adolescent boy's view of friendship, with the Vietnam War perceived in the Victorian terms of movies such as *The Lives of a Bengal Lancer*—as a test of men's courage. . . . [Cimino's] new film is enraging, because, despite its ambitiousness and scale, it has no more moral intelligence than the [Clint] Eastwood action pictures. Yet it's an astonishing piece of work, an uneasy mixture of violent pulp and grandiosity, with an enraptured view of common life—poetry of the commonplace."

Much of the controversy surrounding *The Deer Hunter* derived from the famed Russian roulette sequence. There's no record the Vietcong ever engaged in anything like this, as numerous POWs would dutifully explain to the press. Compounding this is the film's realistic style (if not necessarily substance), which caused moviegoers to believe what they saw. The grim, unrelenting portrait of the steel town, along with the vividly realized and unsparing portraits of the people, immediately set the naturalistic tone. There's a tendency—however dangerous—to trust that a movie which announces such a heightened realism early on will indeed be realistic in all respects throughout.

The writing team concocted the sequence as a symbol, Cimino explaining it as a visual representation of "men blowing their brains out for money while nations commit suicide in war." *Time* interpreted the sequence thusly: "The roulette game becomes a metaphor for a war that blurred the lines between bravery and cruelty, friends and enemies, sanity and madness." That's all well and good, except for the fact that trusting, believing viewers were outraged to discover the sequence they'd strongly reacted to was nothing more than a screenwriter's invention. Such revelations, incidentally, were announced after the voting was completed for the Academy Awards. The film was in tight competition in most categories with *Coming Home.* On Oscar night, a split took place: though Jon Voight and Jane Fonda won Best Actor and Best Actress, *The Deer Hunter* took Best Director (Cimino), Best Supporting Actor (Christopher Walken over *Coming Home*'s Bruce Dern), and Best Picture of the Year, along with two lesser awards. A furious Jane Fonda immediately announced to the media that *The Deer Hunter* was both sexist and racist, eventually admitting that she hadn't actually seen the film, but had heard this from reliable sources. When a nasty anti–*Deer Hunter* attitude set in the day after the

The wedding party (Chuck Aspegren, De Niro, John Savage, Rutanya Alda), one last moment of happiness for the unsuspecting blue-collar young people.

Oscars, many astonished Academy members asked why they had not been told any of this sooner, insisting that the voting would have gone differently.

Ignored in the politicized debate was the performance by De Niro as Michael Vronsky, which earned him a Best Actor nomination. Not to take anything away from Jon Voight's superb Oscar-winning work in *Coming Home,* but Bobby's performance is not only one of his greatest, but also in many respects the finest performance by an American actor during the 1970s. His work as Michael works on two levels, being marvelously specific, a truly unique character study, yet remarkably universal, by implication a portrait of all those blue-collar youths who went off to serve in Nam when their country called and were forever scarred not only by the experience of combat but also by the terrible letdown of their return home. *Film Library Quarterly* caught this universal-within-the-unique aspect of De Niro's performance beautifully, commenting: "When Michael reenters the fire of Vietnam . . . he is playing out a fantasy which flashes in the mind of many Vietnam veterans . . . the survivor guilt fantasy, the desire to go back and bring through combat buddies who didn't make it." How many films have, since *The Deer Hunter,* played out variations of this theme (*Missing in Action, Uncommon Valor,*

Vronsky saves Steven's life.

123

The helicopter sequence, which called for such close shooting that stunt people could not be used.

Rambo: First Blood Part II) without any of the artfulness?

Critics were dazzled by De Niro's work, hailing him as one of those rare performers who delicately treads a tightrope between character actor and leading man—a "character lead" in the best sense of the term. Jack Kroll of *Newsweek* wrote that "De Niro's acting is perhaps his purest yet. What Michael the 'control freak' is controlling is himself—you sense a power in him that he fears could bring disorder and even evil into the lives of himself and his friends. When he allows the power to break loose, raging against the Vietcong torturers . . . he is terrifying; sublimating his love for Linda he is poignant and gentle." The repressed violence that Kroll notes in the character could also, with a few minor changes, effectively describe other De Niro characterizations as diverse as Travis Bickle and Mendoza in *The Mission*. Though the challenge for De Niro the serious actor is in

The epic scope of the film . . .

. . . and the intimacy.

EMI Films present
ROBERT DE NIRO IN THE DEER HUNTER
A MICHAEL CIMINO Film

creating successive characterizations that are, at least on the surface, as varied as could possibly be, a certain artistic integrity is to be found in that a psychological pattern recurs in many roles. He was obviously attracted to Michael and *The Deer Hunter* because it approached such other recurring De Niro themes as Catholic rituals and male bonding.

Schillaci noted the heroic qualities of the characterization: "A riveting performance by De Niro, who invests his charismatic role with nobility and grace. His heroics save his buddies, but there is no victory—and this realization amounts to a conversion for Michael." Westerbeck took the film's title literally and, likewise stressing the larger-than-life aspects of Michael, interpreted Bobby's character as a contemporary Natty Bumppo: "Behind the notion of the deer hunter in this movie is James Fenimore Cooper's deer slayer, who was himself a prototype of the cowboy. Before he ever goes to Vietnam, Michael is already a legendary figure back home because of his skill in stalking a deer. . . . This quality he shows as a hunter is what gets him through Vietnam." Buckley, who did not like the film, carried his negative reaction over to the performance: "De Niro, who for some reason wears a beard and mustache, must be close to forty and looks it—too old to be playing a draftee. Far from seeming Slavic, he remains what he is ineradicably by birth and upbringing. That is, the big-city Italian-American he has played in virtually all his films. De Niro is, nonetheless, a powerful screen actor, and his presence gives *The Deer Hunter* whatever flickering life it possesses."

To prepare, De Niro traveled to Mingo Junction and Steubenville, Ohio, towns not unlike the one that would be the focus of the film. Interestingly enough, though, the Method actor never did get around to working a regular shift at one of the mills, even though that would have seemed likely. Rather, he hung out at the places where the mill workers ate and drank, spoke with them at length, learned their attitudes while observing their manner, and regularly played pool with the young men to get a sense of the way they talked and reacted during off-hours. Certainly, the casual pool-shooting sequence early in the film is one of the most memorable in the entire movie, despite the extreme violence and melodrama of the later scenes. To make his transformation into Michael Vronsky complete, De Niro turned in his New York driving license for a Pennsylvania one, like-wise picking up a Pennsylvania gun license, which he carried during the hunting sequences. "Sometimes, I practice the nature of a person's lifestyle," he explained. "The main thing is to put in the time—even if it's boring. Then you know you've covered every possibility. . . . I've done this in my characterization of Michael."

Cimino likewise worked for a base of authenticity, hiring parishioners of the neighborhood church that they chose for the film as performers in a folk-dancing sequence. The only time that De Niro, Cimino, and the crew "faked it" was when, owing to budget restrictions, they had to film the frigid winter sequences during a particularly hot summer. Bobby and the other actors, bundled up in winter garb, were all but suffocating while getting those shots. Yet despite the impact of what they achieved, Cimino's career would shortly curdle. Two years after *The Deer Hunter*, his minimalist western *Heaven's Gate* would all but bankrupt United Artists. Later films—*Year of the Dragon, The Sicilian*—boasted plenty of flourish but no real sense, substance, or style at all.

The Deer Hunter's vividness was achieved only at great risk to all involved. In one shot where De Niro and costar John Savage leap from a helicopter, the actors came frightfully close to losing their lives in a near-accident that predated the one that would claim actor Vic Morrow and two children on the set of *Twilight Zone—The Movie* some five years later. Bobby would tensely recall, "The helicopter pilot didn't want to go too low because there were rocks on two sides, and a narrow passage where the water rushed through. The runners underneath the helicopter caught under the bridge's cable, and without knowing it, the pilot lifted the whole bridge and twisted it around while John and I were hanging from it. It was dangerous. I looked down and shouted, 'Drop!' and we just dropped. We came up out of the water and . . . I thought the helicopter would drop down on us. That happens in movies; you have to be very, very careful. Nobody plans an accident; and the thing is, sometimes the stunts don't even look like anything [special] on film. Or the shot isn't even used. You could die doing one of those stunts, and when people look at it, they don't even know how dangerous it was."

Of his work in *The Deer Hunter*, De Niro has been uncharacteristically unhumble: "My role in this movie is the best performance I've ever given."

Director Martin Scorsese sets up a
scene with Robert De Niro.

Raging Bull

(1980)

A United Artists Release

CAST:

Robert De Niro (*Jake La Motta*); Cathy Moriarty (*Vicki*); Joe
Pesci (*Joey*); Frank Vincent (*Salvy*); Nicholas Colasanto
(*Tommy Como*); Theresa Saldana (*Lenore*); Frank Adonis
(*Patsy*); Mario Gallo (*Mario*); Johnny Barnes (*Sugar Ray
Robinson*); Martin Scorsese (*Barbizon Stagehand*).

CREDITS:

Director, Martin Scorsese; producers, Irwin Winkler and
Robert Chartoff; screenplay, Paul Schrader and Mardik Martin; based on the book *Raging Bull* by Jake La Motta, Joseph
Carter and Peter Savage; photography, Michael Chapman;
production designer, Gene Rudolf; costume designers,
Richard Bruno and John Boxer; editor, Thelma Schoonmaker;
music, Pietro Mascagni; boxing technical adviser, Al Sil-
vani; consultant, Jake La Motta; running time, 129 minutes;
rating: R.

De Niro's next was yet another collaboration with
Martin Scorsese and, to date, ranks as their greatest:
Raging Bull, the story of Jake La Motta, a Bronx-born
prizefighter who proved even more violent in his home
than in the ring, abusing his wife, Vicki (Cathy Moriarty),
and brother, Joey (Joe Pesci), literally driving away
everyone capable of loving him. The film was framed by
the aging, overweight La Motta recalling the ups and
downs of his life in a nightclub setting, when at New
York's Barbizon Plaza he became a self-styled freak
show, performing a quasi-autobiographical one-man
show, reciting lines from Shakespeare while flashing
back over the years to reveal his early boxing career
culminating in the 1949 middleweight championship
bout, a title he lost a mere seven months later. The
pugilist, who initially believed in the fight game wholeheartedly, once compromised himself by throwing a
bout for the Mafia, leading to his subsequent fall and

decline, personally and professionally. Eventually, he was convicted on charges that he'd allowed a fourteen-year-old girl to work as a prostitute in his Miami Beach bar.

The material hardly seemed promising, yet Scorsese and De Niro wrought from it a remarkable work of art. *Raging Bull* rates as the greatest single American film since *Citizen Kane*, with which it has much in common. The project was initiated by Bobby, who brought a copy of La Motta's "as told to" autobiography (ghosted by Joseph Carter and Peter Savage, the latter a pen name for La Motta's boyhood friend Pete Petrella) to the director while Scorsese was working on a non–De Niro project, *Alice Doesn't Live Here Anymore*. One thing that attracted both De Niro and Scorsese to the material was its episodic nature, the way in which the book perfectly captured and communicated La Motta's vision of his life as a series of vivid fragments, only loosely connected. This was not a book that, in retrospect, imposed an order on La Motta's life; rather, it forced

A closet romantic, Jake pursues his dream girl Vicki (Cathy Moriarty).

Robert De Niro as Jake La Motta.

readers to enter the man's mind and see his past in the punchy, distorted way he saw it. During the following year, Scorsese's old film-school buddy and sometimes collaborator Mardik Martin (*Mean Streets*) worked on a script. Then in 1977, Paul Schrader (*Taxi Driver*) did a second draft, coming up with a story structure that De Niro and Scorsese approved of. Martin and Schrader then retired to the Caribbean together, where they wrote the third draft, maintaining most of Schrader's story structure but reintroducing a stronger sense of

Brother Joey (Joe Pesci) is the only man Jake can trust, until he begins believing that Joey has been flirting with Vicki.

powerful moments, connected only by a purposefully slight narrative line, which had initially so impressed them.

That helps explain why in the finished film, La Motta's first wife seems to disappear virtually without a trace. Though some critics complained her sudden absence wasn't properly explained, they missed the point, for this was how Jake dimly remembered it all in 1964. That is where the film begins, following a title sequence in slow motion revealing De Niro as the young La Motta, doing his boxer's dance in slow motion, transformed into a ballet owing to the playing of the intermezzo from *Cavalleria rusticana* on the sound track. His graceful movements are then strikingly contrasted against those of the older La Motta (Bobby gained over fifty pounds for those sequences) preparing to deliver a monologue in a sleazy nightclub. Originally, Scorsese planned to contrast the young and older Jake throughout, but after shooting the film from fall 1979 through winter 1980, he realized in the editing room the contrast was so strong that the effect proved confusing. The flashback approach was cut out; instead, the 1964 sequences were used only at the beginning and end, as a framing device.

De Niro had seen Joe Pesci on late-night television in a little low-budget movie about the Mafia called *Death*

Kitchen-sink melodrama: Jake snarls at the beratings of his suspicious first wife, Irma (Lori Anne Flax).

128

Jake does a victory dance after knocking down Tony Janiro (Kevin Mahon), even as the referee (Martin Denkin) rushes in to halt the carnage.

Collector, suggesting to Scorsese that this might be the right person to play Joey. Pesci was called in and asked to read, but as he turned out to be several years older than Joey should be (especially in relation to Bobby's age at that time), Scorsese and De Niro were uncertain whether it would work. Putting off a decision, they asked Pesci to come back and read several more times. Numerous other actors were considered, but De Niro and Scorsese finally decided Pesci was the only person to play Joey. Once set for the film, Pesci brought Cathy Moriarty around. Though she had no previous acting

experience and was only sixteen years old (reportedly, Pesci discovered her in a disco), Moriarty conveyed precisely the natural quality De Niro and Scorsese wanted for Vicki. Her thickly accented, nasal Bronx voice—such a gravelly turnoff in comparison to the perfect looks—was precisely right to convey the reality of the girl in contrast to the surface image of a goddess.

Many of the De Niro/Pesci scenes were improvised, and a problem arose in shooting their endless arguments. Because the filming was done in small rooms of actual houses to add to the authenticity, it was often impossible to bring the usual two cameras in; fitting one into a space so small was difficult enough. De Niro would improvise a line while the camera filmed him, and Pesci's spontaneous reaction would be priceless. Unfortunately, it could not be captured. When the entire sequence had been shot with the single camera trained on De Niro, the crew then had to break down the setup, train the camera on Pesci, and have De Niro feed him his lines, with Pesci reacting—trying hard to redo the fabulous reactions, so spontaneous the first time. At a key moment in the film when it was necessary to have Pesci respond strongly to De Niro's accusation that Joey had been sleeping with Jake's wife, Pesci was unable to come up with the necessary sense of shock. On the next take, De Niro changed his line, altering it so that Pesci was questioned about whether he had slept with his own mother, and his stunned expression was real, priceless, and usable.

At one point, though, the improvisation went further than intended. When the two brothers spar, Bobby hit Joe harder than he meant and broke Pesci's rib by accident. The squeal of pain we hear in the film is actual, though not even De Niro and Scorsese, with their desire for realism, wanted things to go quite that far. Ironically, it proved to be the only accident that occurred, despite the fact that most of the ring scenes appear far more brutal than this innocent bit of "friendly" sparring. As for the bouts themselves, Scorsese was inspired by a book of photographs called, simply, *Fighters*. The boxing sequences were all shot in L.A., one in an auditorium, the rest on movie soundstages. Five weeks had been scheduled for these scenes, but they proved such a technical challenge that the shooting took twice that long. For the sake of realism, the fighters were all professionals, the referees all actual refs. Rather than shoot with several cameras, then move into the editing room to see which combinations of shots would work out best, Scorsese, De Niro, and company planned—all but choreographed—the fights in advance, then filmed most of the bouts with a single overhead camera, knowing precisely what they needed and wanted. This amounts to doing the editing before filming.

But as realistic as the ring scenes may at first seem, they are highly stylized—since, like the movie itself, they convey not what really happened but the way it all appeared to La Motta. The camera is kept inside the ring at all times, with none of the longer shots from the crowd that are the hallmark of the *Rocky* films; here, we participate rather than observe. The actual ring is not as realistic as it initially appears; to lend the arena that distorted quality it would offer a punchy pugilist, Scorsese actually cut it into quarters, then added extra space, creating a surreal set rather than filming a real set with a surrealistically inclined fish-eye lens. For the second bout with Sugar Ray, Scorsese filmed De Niro's fighting over a flame, to convey that Jake is burning up inside. The sound track is not realistic in these scenes but highly stylized. Sound editor Frank Warner created a different sound for each punch—slicing a cantaloupe for one, coming up with other slushing sounds so unique that he would not tell anyone how they were achieved—while adding animal screeches to enhance the theme that lends the film its title, then cutting to total silence, communicating the mind of a fighter who has just been smashed in the head. Scorsese augmented all this with operatic music by Pietro Mascagni to convey the grandeur La Motta finds in the ring—if nowhere else in his life.

What could have become a major problem—all fight scenes look pretty much alike to the nonfan—was dazzlingly handled by shooting and editing each in a totally different way. One is a succession of still photographs, another done entirely from an anxious "down" angle. Better still, the form and content are organically related, as we sense the approach taken for each fight derives from, then helps us understand, the collaborators' interpretation of La Motta's mind-set during that particular bout. If it's one where time seemed to stop, then time does visually stop for us as we look at powerful still images. During the bout in which La Motta throws the fight, there is none of this stylization—only simple, flat filming to convey that the fight contains none of the grandeur and craziness of the other bouts.

Likewise, the bright lights of the flashbulbs in the fight scenes are portrayed as glaring white-hot explosions, far more intense than they could ever be in real life—but precisely as a fighter would recall them. The justifiably famous Steadicam shot—in which Scorsese follows De Niro from the bowels of the basement all the way up into the ring, accomplished without a cut—is one of the great moments in the movie. Yet it is not what Scorsese wanted it to be: his favorite take of the shot was damaged and had to be scrapped, leaving him with what he considered the second best—yet brilliant enough to dazzle movie lovers. The fight in which La Motta is defeated by Sugar Ray has all the trappings of realism. Vicki's reactions are precise duplications of photographs from *Life* magazine, the image is as grainy as in the TV broadcast, even including the old Pabst Blue Ribbon logo superimposed over the intermissions, while the announcer's voice is supplied by the very same person who actually announced the fight. Yet achieving his characteristic balance of realism and stylization, Scorsese insisted on editing the sequence in an unrealistic, heightened manner—he and editor Thelma Schoonmaker basing their pattern of cutting on the famous shower sequence in Alfred Hitchcock's *Psycho.*

Steeped in documentary tradition (he worked on *Woodstock,* among other films), Scorsese strove for heightened realism in many places. For Jake's home movies, which are in color, it was necessary to first desaturate the modern film colors, then scratch the negatives to make them look precisely as home movies taken in the early fifties would when viewed in 1964. Yet for the black-and-white New York scenes, Scorsese and his collaborators did not redo entire city streets for a period look, taking a less expensive, more suggestive, just as effective approach: going for specific details rather than an overview, adding the desired textures through clothing, cars, even the popular music playing on the sound track.

Music is the key to Scorsese's approach in all his films.

An overweight, aged Jake turns night club performer.

Colleagues insist he vividly remembers the first time he heard any pop song, storing this information away for as long as twenty years, sensing—during the preplanning of a movie scene—that here is a movie moment which emotionally correlates to that experience, using it at this juncture because of the perfect emotional fit. Even the scenes in which the sound seems to be "real"—Jake and Vicki alone in their apartment, with seemingly random street sounds, voices, and music leaking in—was actually planned out completely. What we experience is the illusion of reality, not simple realism.

But for Bobby, the role didn't completely fall into place until he found a black-and-white thrift-shop jacket he sensed was exactly what Jake would perceive as "stylish." Once he put it on, his characterization was virtually complete—and the jacket quickly became a basic part of the movie. De Niro perfectly incarnates a man who fights like hell to win, then believes he doesn't deserve what he achieves. His self-loathing is evident in the fight that he throws. Rather than work hard—"act," if you will—to convey a sincere bout to the public and effectively cover up his corruption, De Niro's La Motta looks bored and facetious as he grins cockily at the opposing fighter, who appears inept even when Jake leaves every avenue open for him to win.

Fellow director Jonathan Demme gave Scorsese a painting of La Motta he found, under which was the inscription: "Jake fought like he didn't believe he deserved to live." That proved a key to unlocking the story's meaning for Scorsese, helping him focus on what he most wanted to say—about self-loathing, raw ambition, obsessive behavior, paranoid jealousy—through the story. When up against the great Sugar Ray Robinson in a bout that costs La Motta the title, Jake—sensing he's lost—stands against the ropes, opening himself up totally to the blows, inviting his opponent to hit him while taunting Ray to try to knock him out. When Robinson tries—and cannot—Jake's cruel smile makes clear that this is the inverse of that famous final fight scene in the first *Rocky,* about a man who wins if only on his own terms. Here, La Motta instead loses on his own terms, by making clear to Sugar Ray that even though the magnificent young fighter can defeat La Motta technically, he cannot win by a KO because La Motta is too subhuman to allow himself the luxury of falling down. "Ya never knocked me down, Ray!" he jeers, laughing in the victor's face.

Jake's point of view is suggested through occasional POV shots that, at key moments, let us share Jake's unique take on reality. Mostly, this is achieved through slow-motion photography. If Jake's wife, Vicki, receives an innocent kiss good-bye from a male acquaintance, Scorsese first shows them moving toward one another from a relatively objective angle, then cuts to a reaction shot of La Motta/De Niro as his eyes glare, then finally to a subjective shot from his perspective in ever-so-slight slow motion. When viewed this way, the innocent kiss seems lingering and therefore less innocent. During shooting, these takes were done at three separate slow-motion speeds—ranging from a distortion so slight it's almost impossible to notice, to the other extreme of full, obvious slow motion—so that, in the editing room, Scorsese and his editor could try the sequence at each speed, then decide which worked best.

Most critics wrote ecstatically of Bobby's work. Jack Kroll, *Newsweek:* "De Niro's great performance captures the humanity in the bull and the tragic excitement in his rage. . . . There is terror, irony, and a grim humor in De Niro's depiction." Likewise, Richard Corliss of *Time:* "De Niro is always absorbing and credible, even when his character isn't." Bea Rothenbuecher of *Christian Century:* "As La Motta, Robert De Niro gives the performance of his already notable career." However, this was the film that solidified Pauline Kael's souring on De Niro. Belittling the remarkable completeness of characterization that so impressed others and eventually won Bobby his much-deserved Best Actor Oscar, the critic who had earlier been one of his strongest supporters complained in *The New Yorker:* "De Niro wears scar tissue and a big, bent nose that deform his face. It's a miracle that he didn't grow them—he grew everything else. He developed a thick muscled neck and a fighter's body, and for the scenes of the broken, drunken La Motta he put on so much weight that he seems to have sunk in the fat with hardly a trace of himself left. What De Niro does in this picture isn't acting, exactly. I'm not sure what it is. Though it may at some level be awesome, it definitely isn't pleasurable. . . . He has so little expressive spark that what I found myself thinking about wasn't La Motta or the movie but the metamorphosis of De Niro."

A fascinating view, certainly, but one few agreed with. Stanley Kauffmann of *The New Republic* wrote: "Obviously the whole enterprise was built around him. Previously De Niro played demented animalistic characters for Scorsese. . . . Here they have found the best beast for De Niro in La Motta, best because free of patent psychopathy, a 'normal' man capable of overpowering fury but still answerable to some social canons and therefore accessible to pathos rather than to clinical category. . . . Behind his false nose, he assaults us with force, engulfing force so sheer that it achieves a kind of aesthetic stature. Whatever subtlety is in the performance comes from De Niro rather than the role." Still, Kauffmann felt the need to add: "I have to hope that De Niro will make more films with other directors: though he and Scorsese clearly work well together, they stay within a relatively narrow spectrum, and the limits are demonstrably Scorsese's, not De Niro's."

Other critics praised the refusal to offer a pat psychoanalytic portrait. In *The Nation,* Robert Hatch: "No one concerned with the picture (director, writers, and most of all the actor, De Niro) attempts to explain Jake La Motta, and that may be felt as a lack. On the other hand, they make as palpable as one's own flesh the blind, destructive, self-punishing force of the man, and that may make up in large part for what they cannot tell us because they do not know." On the other hand, Diane Jacobs was one of those who did indeed feel "the lack," stating in her *Horizon* review: "Scorsese's decision to not humanize La Motta is courageous—to a point. My problem with *Raging Bull* and, to a lesser degree, with *Taxi Driver* and *New York, New York* is not with the elusiveness of the unpleasant protagonist or with the preeminence of the director's style, but rather with the director's attempt to redeem his unpleasant character through style. And, specifically, with an unspoken justification of violence." That justification was in fact spoken by Scorsese in another context: referring to the late-forties film noir *I Walk Alone* with great affection, Scorsese said of the Burt Lancaster character: "He has only one way to deal with his problems: brute force." Significantly, Jacobs noted that while non–De Niro heroes in Scorsese films (Harvey Keitel's Charlie in *Mean Streets,* Ellen Burstyn's title character in *Alice*) are engaged on moral "missions" (Charlie to save a childhood chum played by De Niro, Alice to save her little girl from the craziness of contemporary life), the heroes of the De Niro movies are progressively less interested in such idealistic quests. Travis, in *Taxi Driver,* does initially set off on a twisted variation of Alice's save-the-child trek, trying to save a child prostitute, becoming hysterically violent only when that proves impossible. Jimmy in *New York, New York* is interested only in developing the technical beauty of his jazz skills, becoming progressively more brutal in his dealings with his wife. Jake is that same character taken to the extreme, believing only in the skill and beauty of his work in the ring. Likewise, Scorsese himself concentrates, with each successive picture, more on the cinematic skill than the moral purpose—he is at one with his characters.

It's doubtful any other boxer would have appealed to the De Niro/Scorsese shared sensibility. Whereas other fighters moved about like lithe, crafty animals—avoiding taking a punch whenever possible—La Motta would stand still, absorbing everything the opponent had to throw. Then, when the man had exhausted himself, Jake would move in, with hideous snarl in place, to bludgeon the man into oblivion. It was as if he entered the ring in

Jake, victorious.

part because some self-loathing, coupled with guilt and a basic sense of worthlessness growing out of his Catholic-inspired ideals as opposed to his Mafia-taught street smarts, made this the perfect place to absorb the terrible punishment he felt due him. Only after suffering through the pain could he then claim the victory that, on some primitive level, he believed he'd earned through this cruel catharsis. Scorsese would say about the boxing scenes: "The fight reduces life down to its most basic element—it's as primitive as you can get in our 'civilized' world." There is certainly a basis in the actual Jake La Motta for this approach, but it is more a case of the character on-screen, called Jake La Motta, emerging as a collage of collaborators De Niro, Scorsese, Schrader, and Martin—an objective correlative portrait of themselves, or at least their worst-case scenarios about the sides of themselves they liked the least and wanted to objectify in art in the most honest and analytic way they could.

Therefore, the filmmakers found situations in their own lives that emotionally paralleled the events in the story. For instance, the scene in which Joey explains to Jake how he will win the title worked only when Scorsese explained to his two performers that they should play it as though Joey were a Hollywood agent, trying to explain to star De Niro how the deal for a proposed new movie would go, in terms of points and other financial arrangements.

Another key theme of the film is the concept of romanticism. Jake's tendency in this direction is made clear when he first tells Joey that he wants to be a heavyweight but will always be a middleweight—even if he becomes a champion. Joey, the realist, can make no sense of this at all; in his mind, Jake should be happy that he'll probably be the top in his league. Jake—a true romantic idealist, even though he never heard that term—is miserable. "I ain't never gonna get a chance to fight Joe Louis," he wails. "He's the best there is—and I'm better than him." This sets up the major romantic plot, involving Vicki. Jake is smitten at first sight by an image of a beautiful woman, a luscious girl in a white bathing suit; but Jake—animal that he is—does not merely lust after her. She is his romantic ideal. Conquering Vicki sexually is never an issue. In the movie, as in real life, La Motta initiates sex with his wife shortly before fights, backing off before consummation. The denial of pleasure and fulfillment to toughen himself up may be all the actual La Motta was doing, but in the film this ties in with the character's romanticism: the most precious fruit is that nearly but never tasted. In the words of the poet Keats, "Heard melodies are sweet, but those unheard, sweeter."

Jake perceives Vicki as something spiritual, magical, beyond the realm of normal life. Early on, he believes that if she will only agree to marry him, then that will justify his existence, as she is the one good, clean thing in the tawdry world around him. But as we know—and as Vicki knows—she is only a person. She does not understand the unarticulated agenda Jake brings to loving her; she thinks only that a successful athlete is proposing, and that he will probably be a good catch. The self-despising Jake is even more frustrated after winning Vicki than if he'd failed. In his mind, Vicki is too good for him. Jake can't believe a woman of her "class" (with her guttural voice, she is "classy" only in comparison to Jake) could possibly remain true to him. She must see his defects, must seek solace elsewhere—or so he believes. Some critics complained that the film never lets us know for certain whether Vicki cheated on Jake or not, but that's not a flaw; since the film shows events only as Jake sees them, the ambiguity is necessary.

"A slob Othello," Kael called Jake, adding: "He's a doomed strong man—doomed by his love for his wife and by his ability to fight. . . . It's a fall from grace; he has given up the only thing that counts," that being his integrity in the ring. His rage, then, is understandably (if mistakenly) directed toward his brother, the person who insisted he throw the fight on instructions from the Mob, and the only other man around to possibly compete for Vicki.

One way of understanding *Raging Bull* as a tragedy is to see Jake as a man torn between the Little Italy contradictions of the violent Mafia and the sexually repressive Catholic Church, suffering from the hypocrisy—moral schizophrenia, even—that develops as a means of dealing with the two opposing value systems. Another way is to see him as suffering from a form of tragic blindness, unable to distinguish between the ring and real life. To convey this without heavy-handedly putting it into words, Scorsese cuts from a shot of De Niro screaming at Moriarty or Pesci to a shot of him in the ring punching an opponent with such swiftness that we can barely tell where one punch ends and the other begins—that, of course, being the point.

This, then, is the essence of the full tragic catharsis: a fear experienced while watching that our own lives could go as awry as that of the character we are viewing, a sense of pity for that character despite the horrible things he has done. The opening sequence of the film, showing the young La Motta like a sleek jungle cat, contrasts strikingly with the image that immediately follows of the bloated La Motta, reeling incoherently as he again warms up, only this time for a tawdry self-effacing monologue. We can hardly help but react with the ultimate tragic epithet, "Oh, how the mighty have fallen!" The film that follows those two opening images

Jake, crucified.

recounts slowly, and painfully, the whys and the hows of that fall from grace, and the desperate but sincere attempt to regain something of what had been lost.

Jake's final monologue raises another fascinating theme, one that relates to other De Niro/Scorsese movies, most notably *Mean Streets*. The idea is that the movie we are watching is a movie about movies, the impact movies have not only on the characters in this particular film but also on all of us, providing the public with ideals we attempt to live up to, along with an image of life that is powerful and convincing but stylized—precipitating disaster when we attempt to lead our lives trusting that things will work out for us as they do in films. This is most strikingly obvious in *Raging Bull* when the bloated older La Motta rehearses his pathetic club routine, interspersing bits and pieces from his life with dramatic recitations. Scorsese focuses on Jake's rehearsal of the famed Brando-Steiger taxicab scene from *On the Waterfront*, in which Terry (Brando) tells his brother Charley (Steiger) he threw a fight only because Charley insisted he ought to, insuring Terry he'd get a shot at the title, though the compromise has cost him dearly in life: "I coulda been a contenda, Charley, instead of a bum—which is what I yam!" As La Motta recites the lines, we can't help but recall that the actor playing him, who achieved fame by assuming Brando's role for *Godfather II*, has constantly been compared to the young Brando, especially Brando in *Waterfront*. Also, La Motta threw the fight only when his brother requested that he do so. Did La Motta agree in part because he'd seen *On the Waterfront* and imitated, in real life, what had happened in the movie? Is De Niro

Jake, the victor once again.

playing La Motta imitating Brando, or is De Niro self-consciously using the scene as a means to comment on the parallels drawn between himself and the previous acting legend? The point is, in this more "realistic" modern movie, things do not work out happily for the main character, as they did for Brando's Terry in the supposedly realistic but ultimately dishonest *Waterfront*, with its contemporary fairy-tale ending of triumph. Here, the hero is left in a mire—yet still spouting the words of a previous movie hero who overcame his own corruption and compromise in a way the hero of *Raging Bull* cannot.

When Pauline Kael snarled that "Scorsese is trying to purify forties style by using the conventions in new ways," she inadvertently put her finger on his moviemaking sensibility. True, that's precisely what he's doing—and precisely what he ought to be doing. For, as La Motta said in the opening of his book, he saw his life as a movie, and "not a good movie, either, jerky, with gaps in it, a string of poorly lit sequences, some of them with no beginning and some with no end." In borrowing setups from past pictures, Scorsese visually fashioned the film La Motta verbally requested.

The decision to use black and white was also based on the opening line of his autobiography: "Now, when I think back, I feel like I'm looking at an old black-and-white movie of myself. Why it should be black and white I don't know, but it is." A film based on a book ought to be as true as possible not to the letter of the book but to its spirit, which is why the black and white here never seems an affectation but is dictated by the material itself.

Cathy Moriarty's character, so basic to the romantic theme, is also essential to the movie-about-movies concept. She is Jake's ideal, and this near-illiterate would draw his romantic images not from painting or poetry but popular films. Vicki, when first glimpsed, looks like a goddess plopped down in the Bronx—plucked from one of those late-1940s film noirs La Motta would surely have seen. Vicki is half Lana Turner from *The Postman Always Rings Twice*, half Rita Hayworth in *The Lady From Shanghai*. To have modeled her look on either one of those icons would have been wrongheaded; Scorsese makes her a mélange of the era's slut-goddesses, representing Jake's strong if imprecise memories of irresistible femme fatales in numerous then-recent movies.

By pursuing Vicki, Jake can feel, as every moviegoing American wants to feel, that his life is turning into a movie. Jake, likening himself to the tough-guy heroes in his favorite films, can't help but respond to a woman who is a living incarnation of a Hollywood dream girl. To be involved with a woman who looks like Lana Turner is to become John Garfield. Also, it's inevitable that he'll become jealous, suspecting her of the same kind of infidelities Turner was guilty of in her film. Once he's become Garfield by winning a woman who looks like Lana, he must go through the same turmoil Garfield suffered in *Postman*. Though many critics argued that in the film, La Motta's jealous rages are unmotivated, his outbursts are totally understandable if one approaches *Raging Bull* as less a movie about La Motta than a movie about movies.

Scorsese would, a few years later, fashion a film from the novel *Last Temptation of Christ*, originally hoping to persuade De Niro to play Jesus. Like that period piece, his more contemporary films have also been about the Catholic concepts of redemption and salvation. John Simon could complain that "putting a prestigious but irrelevant biblical quotation on a final title card is merely a hollow gesture," but in fact, it was another of those keys to *Raging Bull*'s meaning. More than a simple biographical film, *Raging Bull* is a movie about the least civilized man we have ever met—at least in the leading role of a major film—dealing with his need to come to terms with the pain he has caused, both psychological and physical, before he meets his maker. Understandably, then, Richard A. Blake of *America* wrote: "Religion, ever present in the film's imagery, merely portrays a boxer's prerational, and implicitly subhuman, world."

Jake's boxing dance appears so involved that he almost seems to be performing religious rituals before entering the ring. The Catholic/religious aspect is clear in those scenes showing De Niro/La Motta backed into the ropes, being pummeled as he extends his arms outward and upward as if hoping for a full crucifixion. The most highly symbolic religious moment occurs in an image that Scorsese recalled from one of the few real fights he witnessed in his youth (he is not a sports fan in general or a boxing fan in particular): a fighter, being sponge-bathed between rounds, was washed in his own blood. Though the moment may be drawn from real life, in the context of the movie it takes on a symbolic nature that could be lifted from a passion play—precisely what *Raging Bull*, on one of its many levels, is.

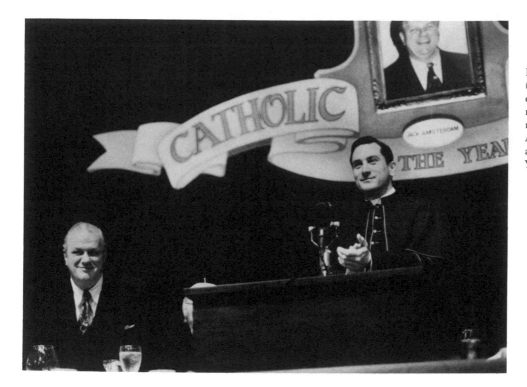

Monsignor Desmond Spellacy (Robert De Niro), unknowingly corrupted by power and money, smilingly introduces the morally monstrous Jack Amsterdam (Charles Durning) as Catholic Layman of the Year.

True Confessions

(1981)

A United Artists Release

CAST:

Robert De Niro (*Des Spellacy*); Robert Duvall (*Tom Spellacy*); Burgess Meredith (*Seamus Fargo*); Charles Durning (*Jack Amsterdam*); Ed Flanders (*Dan T. Campion*); Cyril Cusack (*Cardinal Danaher*); Kenneth McMillan (*Frank Crotty*); Dan Hedaya (*Howard Terkel*); Rose Gregorio (*Brenda Samuels*); Louisa Moritz (*Whore*); Jeanette Nolan (*Mom Spellacy*); Amanda Cleveland (*Lois Fazenda*); Pat Corley (*Sonny Mc-Donough*).

CREDITS:

Director, Ulu Grosbard; producers, Irwin Winkler and Robert Chartoff; screenplay, John Gregory Dunne and Joan Didion, from the novel by Dunne; photography, Owen Roizman; production designer, Stephen S. Grimes; costume designer, Joe I. Tompkins; editor, Lynzee Klingman; music, Georges Delerue; running time, 108 minutes; rating: R.

Male bonding, this time in the context of a literal brotherhood, was the subject for De Niro's next. *True Confessions* teamed him with another highly respected emerging actor, Robert Duvall, for the first time; though both appeared in *The Godfather II*, they shared no screen time. Additionally, *True Confessions* confronted De Niro with two major challenges. The first was to play a compassionate priest, a refreshing change of pace for a performer associated with tough-guy roles. In fact, Bobby was originally approached to play the part of the detective brother, seeming more naturally suited for Tom. Second, there was the opportunity to play an Irish American, necessitating the mastery of unique vocal patterns.

De Niro's character is Desmond Spellacy, a priest who—at the movie's beginning, in 1962—serves with humility and dedication at a minuscule parish somewhere in the deserts of southern California. His brother,

As Travis Bickle in *Taxi Driver* (1976)

In *Bang the Drum Slowly* (1973) with
Michael Moriarty

With Cyril Cusack in *True
Confessions* (1981)

With Meryl Streep in *Falling in Love* (1984)

As Rodrigo Mendoza in *The Mission* (1986)

With Mickey Rourke in *Angel Heart* (1987)

With Charles Grodin in
Midnight Run (1988)

With Robin Williams in
Awakenings (1990)

With Annette Bening in *Guilty by
Suspicion* (1991)

With director Ron Howard on the set
of *Backdraft* (1991)

With Donald Sutherland
and director Ron Howard
on the set of *Backdraft*
(1991)

On TV with Arsenio Hall

With very good friend Toukie Smith

As Max Cady in *Cape Fear* (1991)

In *GoodFellas* (1990)

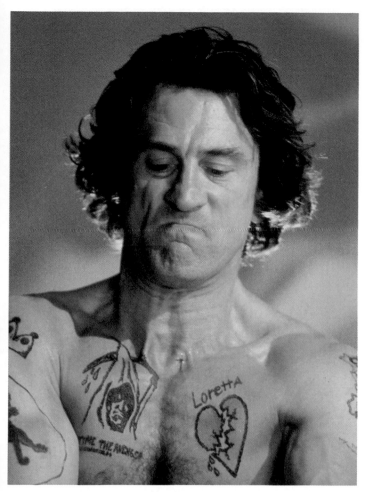

In *Stanley and Iris* (1990)

In *Falling in Love* (1984)

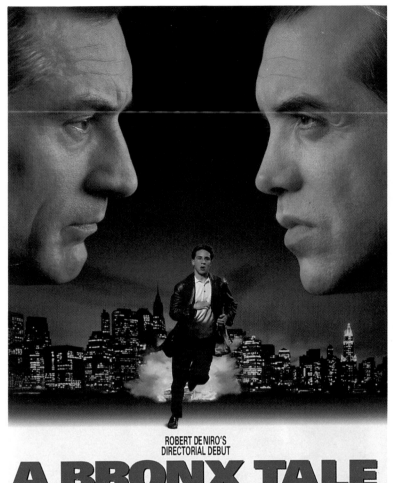

Advertising art for *A Bronx Tale* made clear how gracious and generous De Niro could be, allowing a virtual unknown to share top billing with him.

De Niro as the Frankenstein "Creature" in *Mary Shelley's Frankenstein*.

The Creature confronts his maker (Kenneth Branagh).

De Niro's status was by this time so significant that he was chosen for the cover of *Entertainment Weekly*'s special Holiday Movie Preview in the fall of 1995.

The good life: husband and
wife enjoy the calm before the
storm in *Casino*.

Lording it over his casino, Robert
De Niro in a masterful pose.

De Niro as the Gambling Man.

Sly and Arnold, move over: De Niro as an action-film star in *Heat*.

De Niro helps a fallen gang member (Val Kilmer) struggle to safety.

Al Pacino, De Niro's leading competitor as heavyweight actor of their time, plays his archenemy in *Heat*.

Det. Tom Spellacy, arrives, confronting Des for the first time in years; they are bitter men, each deeply disappointed with life. The brothers are together now only because Des is dying of cancer. Reconciliation is not easy, though, considering the source of their rift.

In flashback, we see the incident that drove them apart. Years earlier, a prostitute named Lois Fazenda was murdered. In seamy 1940s Hollywood, that hardly rated as a significant event, but the investigating officer was Tom. His chief suspect was Jack Amsterdam (Charles Durning), a former lowlife who rose to status in the Los Angeles community owing to great wealth. Courting not only politicians but also priests to attain respectability, Amsterdam showered money on the young, charismatic Monsignor Spellacy, who was transformed into something of a celebrity within the church establishment owing to his impressive ability to raise large sums—and who, like the hero of a Greek tragedy, suffered from hubris when he began believing his own legend. Des was therefore embarrassed when his detective brother relentlessly hounded Amsterdam, who was peripherally linked to the brutal sex murder.

Des hears the confession of his detective brother, Tom (Robert Duvall), who is going after Amsterdam.

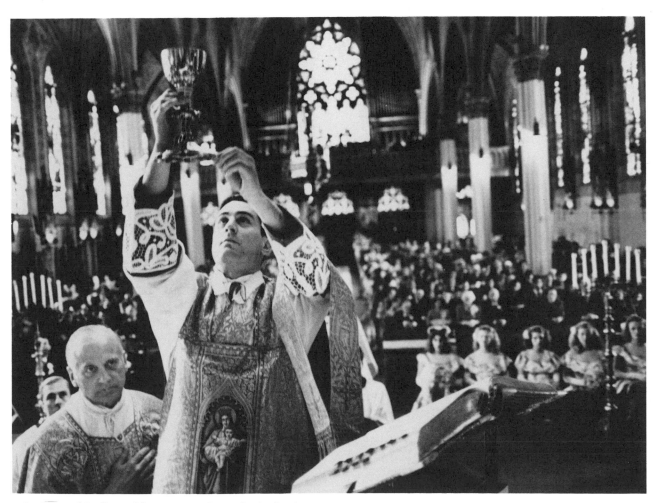

Right Reverend Spellacy celebrates a nuptial mass for the daughter of his most wealthy parishioner.

139

Tom admits to Des that he is going after Amsterdam in the Black Dahlia murder case, even though what he finds may implicate his own brother.

Also, the harrowing investigation was pursued at least in part because Tom harbored a personal grudge against Amsterdam dating back to even earlier days, when Tom's lover Brenda Samuels (Rose Gregorio) was forced, as one of Amsterdam's working girls, to take a fall, spending time in jail so Amsterdam could walk free. Des also felt, not entirely incorrectly, that Tom's getting Amsterdam (and tainting Des, guilty by association) might be an act of revenge on Des for having been considered, in their youth, the fair-haired boy. Tom was stunned to realize Des perceived it this way, insisting he continued the case only because, as a detective, it was the right thing to do. For Tom and Des, it ultimately did not matter how the case came out; the already tenuous relationship between the two would be destroyed by the police examination.

The John Gregory Dunne novel from which the film was adapted (by Dunne and his screenwriter wife, Joan Didion) was itself taken from a real-life case: the notorious, celebrated Black Dahlia murder, in which an ambitious prostitute and sometime movie extra named Elizabeth Short was abducted, tortured at length, then killed and dumped in a vacant lot. Though the police embarked on a massive search, no one was ever brought to justice; that the crime was unsolved has always been basic to its lingering fascination. Understandably, the story has inspired numerous novels and films.

Yet director Ulu Grosbard has claimed that his version "is not a detective story," but "a story about two brothers

Des brings unhappy tidings to elderly Monsignor Seamus Fargo (Burgess Meredith).

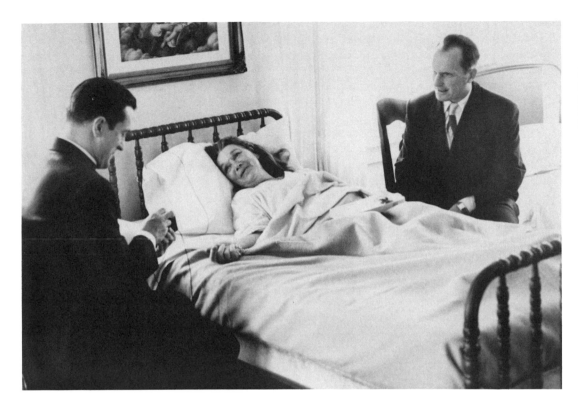

Des and Tom briefly reconcile in order to visit their dying mother (Jeanette Nolan) in her nursing home.

. . . we were more concerned about relationships," less a genre piece than an ambitious "serious" drama. While that may be admirable, it's also basic to why *True Confessions* failed to click. To be successful, it needed to work as a detective story first, then transcend such limitations—as, say, Alfred Hitchcock and Roman Polanski fulfilled the conventions of the thriller, then transcended them, in *Vertigo* and *Chinatown*. In trying to skirt those conventions completely, Grosbard turned out a film that refuses to engage its audience, going directly for something of higher importance, too often seeming nothing more than a thriller without thrills, burdened by its sense of self-importance.

"Oh, you find out who done it," Grosbard has said, "but it doesn't really make any difference." Inherent in that attitude—striving for art, condescending to entertainment—is the basis for failure. A few critics praised the picture, such as Jack Kroll of *Newsweek*, who hailed it as a "tense, tough blend of the whodunit and morality play." Far more would agree with Richard Corliss of *Time* when he noted that "this could have been a bitterly raucous movie, if only the artists involved hadn't confused seriousness with solemnity," placing the blame squarely on the shoulders of Didion, the "Empress of Angst," creator of "characters who should percolate with rage" but "simply simmer."

Part of the problem is that director Grosbard has never been able to make a completely successful American movie. *The Subject Was Roses, Who Is Harry Kellerman and Why Is He Saying Those Terrible Things About Me?* and *Straight Time* are generally viewed as interesting failures. Hailing from Antwerp, Belgium, Grosbard is a first-rate director of actors; the performances in his films—including *True Confessions*—are uniformly fine. But there's always a sense that he has no unique attitude toward the material at hand, no cinematic vision or artistic point of view (on the level of a Scorsese or Coppola) toward the story he's telling, much less any sense for the American scene in which the tale takes place. Grosbard understandably missed the novel's uniquely ethnic Irish American humor and overall anecdotal quality (the very elements that sustained the book through even its most harrowing moments), remaining true to the letter of the original but not its spirit.

The movie is almost unrelentingly grim. Though it's often difficult to point one's finger at what's wrong—as at any one juncture, we are confronting a serious, well-performed melodrama—the mind nonetheless wanders, the emotions are never fully engaged. There's no doubt, from the lurid but passionless beginning, that this is a "quality" item—hollow, heartless, and handsome—bolstered by a dream team of acclaimed actors. Yet midway through, most viewers find the film becoming too studied, sluggish, even sanctimonious; meticulous; the film is oblique, obscure, and off-putting. Would that this were the very kind of solid, involving detective story Grosbard consciously wanted to avoid!

Naturally, the one aspect of the film that won raves

was the acting, with many critics judging the two leads in tandem rather than individually. In the *New York Times,* Vincent Canby wrote that De Niro and Duvall "play together with an intensity and intelligence that illuminates the film . . . here, truly, is the kind of film for which there should be a collective award for the performances." Stanley Kauffmann of *The New Republic* took time out in his negative review to single out De Niro's acting as the most impressive thing on view: "De Niro's performance is almost one of his best. I think he relies a bit too much on his difference from Duvall's push and bite to help delineate his own character, a man with more of the wheeler-dealer in him than he cares to acknowledge. At the end De Niro tells his brother that he's grateful because the result of Duvall's investigations

was to get the monsignor off the ambition track and back into his vocation; this comment would ring a tone truer if we could sniff the ambition in him a bit more strongly when he's on the way up. But, as usual, De Niro has begun his performance with an idea about his body. This was overwhelmingly clear in *Raging Bull,* more subtly pervasive in *The Last Tycoon.* The way De Niro bears himself, walks, and gestures as the priest is his primary act of transformation." Likewise, James M. Wall of *Christian Century* insisted that with "his cool manner in carefully maneuvering through the intricacies of city politics and the church's material growth, [De Niro] is just about perfect."

Kroll added that "in his last few films Robert De Niro has changed his jawline more than the shapeshifting Lon

In the film's framing device, Tom and Des meet one final time, in hopes of reconciling at last.

Chaney himself. In *New York, New York,* De Niro's chops had the cocky thrust of the swing musician. In *Raging Bull* he showed us the iron jaw of the young Jake La Motta and the pathetic puffiness of the washed-up fighter. In *True Confessions* his eloquent mandible has undergone its most subtle metamorphosis: De Niro has taken on just enough flesh so that his face seems plump with spiritual pride, the willful set of the jaw cushioned with complacency. This sensitive sculpting of his face is part of the strategy that makes Des one of De Niro's most fascinating performances. The strategy is to under-play the character from beginning to end. But under-playing with De Niro is not a matter of surface effects and mere technique. With exquisite economy he shows you the tension between hypocrisy and honor in the young priest who is on the way up and on the make."

However, Michael Sragow of *Rolling Stone* tempered his admiration for De Niro's work, finding it technically masterful but somewhat lifeless: "As Des, De Niro gives off the quiet hum of intelligent calculation. Everything about him is measured, from his calm, unhurried speech to his gently rolling walk. . . . Again and again, De Niro has shown the ability to complete roles left unfinished by his collaborators, but *True Confessions* stops short when his character just begins to get complex." In the *National Review,* William F. Buckley, Jr., complained that "Robert De Niro is badly miscast. He is never entirely convincing." And Pauline Kael—an early, enthusiastic De Niro supporter—did not approve of his approach at all; in *The New Yorker,* she complained that "something has gone wrong with Robert De Niro's acting. In *The Godfather II,* he was so intense that he seemed in danger of imploding. Now, in *True Confessions,* when he's quiet and almost expressionless, there's no intensity—there's nothing. He could be a potato, except that he's thoroughly absorbed in the process of doing nothing. It may be that De Niro took up an intellectual puzzle in 1976 on the set of *The Last Tycoon:* How do you act without doing anything? In *True Confessions,* he has carried it so far that he's not in the movie. . . . De Niro's role is so underwritten that Des doesn't particularly react to Tom, or anything else. De Niro is in his chameleon trance; there's no light in Des's eyes—he seems flaccid, preoccupied, mourning his lost innocence." However, in the *Village Voice,* Andrew Sarris praised the very elements that Kael attacked: "De Niro's careerist priest here is controlled in much the same manner as his controversial Irving G. Thalberg in *The Last Tycoon.* I happen to admire bottled-up De Niro, but many of his most ardent champions prefer the free-flowing, gut-spilling De Niro on display in *The Deer Hunter, Taxi Driver,* and *Raging Bull.*"

De Niro's already famous predilection for lengthy, intense, and specific preparation began the moment he learned he'd be playing a monsignor. The first subject for study was the liturgy of the Catholic Mass itself, which Bobby learned in the original Latin, as the 1940s setting of the film's lengthy flashbacks necessitated his character take a conservative and orthodox approach to the Mass. The religious technical adviser on the film was Father Henry Fehren, who taught De Niro not only the precise words and proper pronunciation, but also, just as important, the meaning, symbolism, and interpretation of the dogma, so that Bobby's mind-set—as well as his manner—would be completely correct for that of an Irish Catholic. Father Fehren was impressed enough by De Niro's desire for total authenticity that he later reflected, "He may be the most authentic priest ever seen on the screen."

In addition to the acting challenges, one element that must have drawn De Niro to the project was its attitude toward money—the very kind of big money that some-how eluded Bobby's parents, despite their obvious talents. Most of his movies from this period—*1900, The Last Tycoon*—contain, among their diverse themes, a criticism of capitalism and its too-often-concurring side-light of money as an end that justifies any means. As De Niro biographer Keith McKay noted: "[Desmond's] business dealings with construction mogul Amsterdam have contributed to his becoming a man of nearly blind ambition—more an accountant than a priest . . . his dilemma is [that of] a church that has strayed from its flock, [placing] material gain before" the spiritual. And there is the theme of the Catholic code, which the De Niro character tries without success to live up to. Though De Niro may not direct or even (officially) help write his projects, he does choose them carefully enough that a certain autobiographical element can be discerned in the material.

Jerry Langford (Jerry Lewis) and Rupert share a glass of champagne, and a laugh; but their relationship will be no laughing matter.

The King of Comedy

(1983)

A Twentieth Century-Fox Release

CAST:

Robert De Niro (*Rupert Pupkin*); Jerry Lewis (*Jerry Langford*); Diahnne Abbott (*Rita*); Sandra Bernhard (*Masha*); Whitey Ryan (*Stage Door Guard*); Catherine Scorsese (*Mom Pupkin*); Fred de Cordova (*Bert Thomas*); Shelley Hack (*Cathy Long*); Edgar J. Scherick (*Wilson Crockett*); Martin Scorsese (*TV Director*); Cathy Scorsese (*Dolores*); Charles Scorsese, Mardik Martin (*Men at Bar*); and Ed Herlihy, Tony Randall, Dr. Joyce Brothers, and Victor Borge playing themselves.

CREDITS:

Director, Martin Scorsese; producer, Arnon Milchan; screenplay, Paul D. Zimmerman; photography, Fred Schuler; production designer, Boris Leven; costume designer, Richard Bruno; editor, Thelma Schoonmaker; music, Robbie Robertson; running time, 108 minutes; rating: PG.

De Niro next chose *King of Comedy*, working again for Scorsese and creating yet another unique character, this one more cartoonish than anything he had done since *The Gang That Couldn't Shoot Straight*. He plays Rupert Pupkin, a midthirties loser who ekes out a living as a New York City messenger by day, returning at twilight to the Hoboken home he shares with his nagging mother. There, Rupert slips down to the basement, where he lives out a rich fantasy life, one so densely textured it's downright chilling. On a precise re-creation of the *Tonight* show set, Rupert spends his evenings pretending to guest-host for "pal" Jerry Langford (Jerry Lewis), talking to "guest" Liza Minnelli, represented by a cardboard mock-up. But the closest Rupert ever comes to the real Jerry occurs when, like dozens of other fans, he crowds around the stage door as the star slips out of the studio and into his waiting limo.

One day, Rupert gets lucky: he helps Jerry escape from a particularly threatening crowd, receiving a quick, casual word of thanks. In Rupert's mind, this marks the beginning of a friendship. Jerry, after being rescued by Rupert only to be besieged for a spot on the show, brusquely tells him, "Call my office." Lewis delivers the line brilliantly, with that glib old show-business attitude: accepting public adulation unless there's the slightest hint of an appeal to share his success, at which point the persona turns sneering, snarling, superior.

The role was obviously created with Johnny Carson in mind, and Scorsese offered it to the real-life king of late night. Carson turned it down for two reasons. First, his only previous film appearances (in 1964's *Looking for Love,* with Connie Francis and in a guest bit in *Cancel My Reservation*) had convinced Carson that TV, not movies, was his natural medium. So loose and relaxed on the *Tonight* show, Carson nonetheless came off as uptight, jittery, and uncomfortable on film. More significant, Johnny feared that if he played himself here, frightening events like those in the film might actually follow its release.

What at first seemed a disappointment actually worked to the film's advantage. Playing himself, Carson would have wanted to be seen in a positive light, but with the fictional Langford, Scorsese and Lewis were able to create a complex, morally ambiguous, multidimensional character. In short, by pretending to create fiction, the filmmakers were able to come far closer to the truth. As Jack Kroll noted in *Newsweek,* "Lewis catches something dark and disturbing as he projects the overweening ego, the exhaustion and vulnerability of the superstar who needs and fears the gigantic fix of the worshiping millions." Rupert represents those millions, and Langford's glib phrase—"Call my office!"—is, of course, intended dismissively; Jerry is semipolitely telling Rupert he isn't going to be allowed "in." Rupert, however, accepts the phrase at face value, absolutely refusing to hear the not-so-hidden meaning.

Upon arriving at the office, Rupert perceives Jerry's cold secretary (Shelley Hack) as a misguided soul—failing to understand this woman is paid to keep people like himself as far away from Jerry as possible. Rupert then convinces a barmaid and sometime girlfriend, Rita (Diahnne Abbott), to join him on a visit to Jerry's country home for the weekend, leading to an ugly confrontation in which Jerry insists they leave. At this point, the reality of the situation and Rupert's subjective vision of it crash head-on, leaving him bitter and resentful. In the company of Masha (Sandra Bernhard), an upscale Langford junkie, Rupert kidnaps Jerry. His demand is to be allowed a spot on the live TV show, Rupert being the first screen character to live out that Andy Warhol

dictate about everyone in our time being famous for fifteen minutes.

However, this is followed by a postscript informing us that Rupert wrote a book about the experience while in jail, becoming a true celebrity and TV talk-show host

Robert De Niro as Rupert Pupkin.

Rupert and rich but deranged Masha (Sandra Bernhard) mistrust each other, but conspire to kidnap Jerry.

Jerry is not amused when Rupert and his friend Rita (Diahnne Abbott) invade Jerry's home without invitation.

Rupert desperately attempts to convince Cathy Long (Shelley Hack) to let him see Jerry, not realizing that her job is to keep the nut-cases like himself as far away as possible.

upon release from prison. This coda—hastily devised by Scorsese while shooting—stretched the already tenuous premise (the *Tonight Show* is taped, making Rupert's live broadcast virtually impossible; it's hard to believe Jerry's suburban home would be without any security system) too far. David Denby of *New York* argued that "we feel cheated and betrayed—the filmmakers throw out everything they've established for a flip, cynical ending." Veronica Geng, in the *New York Review of Books*, commented: "Bloating a taut little movie with this fancy bummer that fills your head with clichés about Media Mythmaking is a ghastly mistake." Pupkin may have been the perfect symbol for Warhol's fifteen minutes, but there's nothing about him that suggests he could actually sustain stardom beyond that. However, Rex Reed defended the film's conclusion, arguing that it effectively illustrated the horrible reality that "crime not only pays, but has lasting benefits and annuities, like movie deals, book contracts, and magazine covers."

Discussing his script, former *Newsweek* critic turned screenwriter Paul Zimmerman said, *"The King of Comedy* is about the desperate need to exist publicly, which is so American." Zimmerman had seen a David Susskind

Rupert initially makes contact with Jerry by rescuing the TV talk show host from adoring fans.

Rupert wanders around the set of Jerry's show, so near and yet so far to the fame he covets.

TV talk show about autograph hounds, and halfway through the program he was struck with the thought that such people were "just like assassins except that one carries a pen instead of a gun." The film Scorsese would eventually fashion from that script is thematically a variation on *Taxi Driver*, the tone comic (if the darkest of comedy) rather than edgily, anxiously dramatic. Scorsese later recalled that he darkened Zimmerman's script considerably during the shooting to make this a movie about "what it's like to want something so badly you'd kill for it." Though Rupert never commits physical violence, there's always the unstated sense that, if things went slightly awry, something brutal might transpire.

Perhaps because he was working in a genre far removed from what he does best, as well as with a first-time screenwriter, Scorsese included few of his distinctive visual touches. Whereas his other films are effectively florid, *Comedy* is surprisingly flat. The film does feature the "family" approach: in addition to showcasing De Niro's then-wife Diahnne Abbott (smashing as Rita), the regulars in Rupert's neighborhood bar included Martin's father, Charles Scorsese, and also screenwriter Mardik Martin, who had collaborated with them earlier. Still, watching *Comedy*, one gets little sense of the Scorsese personality behind the camera, in the way one feels his strong presence in every shot of previous pictures. Simply, *King of Comedy* does not look

Rupert convinces Rita (Diahnne Abbott) that he and Jerry are friends.

like a Martin Scorsese film; in truth, it might have been better directed by Jonathan Demme (*Something Wild*).

Reviews were tepid. Lawrence O'Toole of *MacLean's* dismissed this as "a sour meditation on [our] mania for celebrity," while Michael Sragow of *Rolling Stone* complained that "Scorsese, an unabashedly Catholic artist, can't get a grip on the predominantly Jewish milieu of the mass American comedy." Other critics killed the film with halfhearted kindness, such as Denby: "A clever, sometimes brilliant movie, but ice-cold and not really likable . . . it produces, at best, a nervous giggle—too bitter, too angry to make anyone laugh." Others, though, praised it highly: Jack Kroll of *Newsweek* insisted that *Comedy* "takes a hard, sharp look at the American obsession with fame, the celebrity as savior, the fan as both worshiper and menace [and] shows us the reciprocal pathology that infects a world of stars and star lovers."

Reflecting on the mixed critical reaction and box-office failure of *King,* De Niro would later conclude, "I think maybe the reason [the film] wasn't well received was that [it] gave off an aura of something people didn't want to look at or know." In part, that something was the false intimacy audiences feel with TV personalities, who enter your home at your whim. Also, De Niro—and to a lesser degree Scorsese—could understand the plight of the characters. Though a decade earlier each had been a Pupkin—desperately, hungrily stalking the borders of show business, hoping to make it big—theirs were the rare dreams that came true. With success came an about-face in sympathies. They fashioned a film in which Rupert and Jerry are not so much diametrically opposed characters as the opposite sides of a single coin. Rupert is Scorsese/De Niro before success; Jerry is either one afterward.

De Niro prepared by visiting various clubs and listening to the monologues of aspiring comedians. As always, he took a Method approach to the role, staying in character from the moment the film went into preproduction until long after it was over. The difference between the Method and Jerry Lewis's old-fashioned Hollywood approach was obvious when Lewis—thinking it would be pleasant to get to know his costar better—invited Bobby over for dinner. De Niro sensed this would lead to a pleasant rapport between them. Lewis was going to play his character; De Niro was becoming his character. "I wanna blow your head off," he said in reply to the invitation, "so how can we have dinner?" "I" meaning, of course, Rupert—and the actor who was temporarily turning into Rupert.

De Niro then devised an effective way to turn Jerry Lewis into a Method actor. One element of the Method is emotional substitution , in which the performers draw on their life experiences to make the fictional exploits of the on-screen characters totally real. Which is why in a

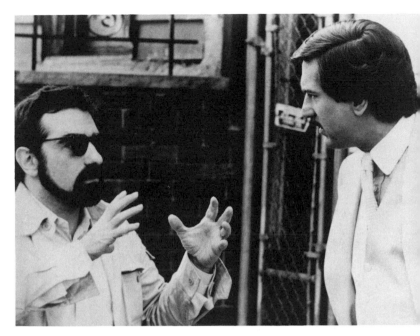

Martin Scorsese confers with De Niro on a key scene.

scene that called for Langford to grow angry at Pupkin, De Niro—just before the filming began—suddenly started shouting anti-Semitic comments at Jerry. Forgetting that the cameras were there, Lewis furiously turned on De Niro, so the anger we see him unleash is real. As compared to his usually calculated performances, Lewis here acts on a level he never achieved before or since.

Critics assessing De Niro's performance had to deal with how different Rupert was from any other role the actor had tackled. Understandably, then, Denby wrote that "in the past, De Niro has played punks, killers, and furiously alienated outsiders, so it's a shock at first to see him as a thoroughly mediocre person," adding that the role nonetheless fits into the De Niro canon, since Rupert is "not just mediocre, he's demonically mediocre—a De Niro character after all." Denby's assessment was cool and noncommittal: "Smiling fatuously, eyebrows curled in cartoon merriment, De Niro forces his voice into its most nauseatingly unctuous registers. Intentionally, he keeps the performance at the level of a loathsome caricature: he makes Rupert a man with fantasies but no unconscious, no depths—we're held by the outrageousness of his quest without ever liking him or rooting for him." Vincent Canby wrote, in the *New York Times,* that Rupert Pupkin was "one of the best, most complex and flamboyant performances of [De Niro's] career." Likewise, Richard Schickel of *Time* praised the performance: "Robert De Niro's Rupert has a cheerfully deranged imperviousness to traditional class distinctions and psychological boundary lines that makes

149

you laugh even as it makes you cringe for him—the beamy-faced lunatic who transcends the traditional boundaries of fandom, a national lunacy Rupert personifies." *Newsweek's* Kroll claimed this added "another indelible portrait to his growing gallery . . . Pupkin is a funny and frightening creature of our time. He's the nice nut, the dangerous devotee, the logical loony who can pop up at any moment with a grin, a gag, or a gun." Molly Haskell of *Vogue* insisted: "If there was any doubt that Robert De Niro is the greatest and most unsettling actor in movies today . . . then *The King of Comedy* should dispel it. . . . This is another of his characters we wouldn't bear to watch if we didn't know De Niro is inside, implying a necessary distance between real and artistically shaped mediocrity. Pupkin seems the furthest of any De Niro character from the actor's own moody, creative temperament, yet there is something uncannily familiar about him. Every time Rupert opens his mouth, it is like turning a corner and seeing someone we know, and want desperately to avoid."

On the other hand, Stanley Kauffmann of *The New Republic* complained: "De Niro seems somewhat hamstrung by the pasteboard ninny he consented to play. De Niro doesn't need violence in order to be excellent: remember his performance in *The Last Tycoon* (under another director). But basically he, like Scorsese, seems to have been partly anesthetized by infatuation with the idea of the script and hasn't perceived that the protagonist as written is only an arrangement of actions to make that idea possible. . . . De Niro does his extraordinary best to transform the mechanics into a man. He gets Rupert's requisite basic hearing block; the man never really hears the denials, rejections, put offs that come his way. De Niro tells us this with half-smile, with glinting eyes, with assumed svelte superiority. He also gets the unrhythmical quality of Rupert's movement and gesture, epitomized in that one TV appearance. De Niro knows that Rupert has studied Langford and other comics, that he thinks he has learned how to do the stuff. But all Rupert has acquired is some of the mannerisms—the Bob Hope run-on, for instance. He doesn't have the central ease, his delivery is a collection of remembered inflections, he hasn't a clue about what to do with his arms. Because that scene is the best in the script, De Niro, one of our best film actors, is able to blend Rupert's imitations of professionals and his residual amateurishness into a spot of horror. But the rest of the script, with its faked characterization and flabby dialogue, its unrealized insanity, gives De Niro troubles."

Robert De Niro and Jerry Lewis.

Noodles Aaronson is released from prison, after covering for his friends.

Once Upon a Time in America

(1984)

The Ladd Company/Embassy International/PSO International
A Warner Brothers Release

CAST:

Robert De Niro (*David "Noodles" Aaronson*); James Woods (*Max*); Elizabeth McGovern (*Deborah*); Treat Williams (*Jimmy O'Donnell*); Tuesday Weld (*Carol*); Burt Young (*Joey*); Joe Pesci (*Frankie*); Danny Aiello (*Police Chief*); William Forsythe (*Cockeye*); James Hayden (*Patsy*); Darlanne Fleugel (*Eve*); Larry Rapp (*Fat Moe*); Amy Ryder (*Peggy*); Scott Tiler (*Young Noodles*); Jennifer Connelly (*Young Deborah*); James Russo (*Bugsy*); Richard Bright (*Chicken Joe*).

CREDITS:

Director, Sergio Leone; producer, Arnon Milchan; screenplay, Leone, Leonardo Benvenuti, Piero De Bernardo, Enrico Medioli, Franco Arcalli, Franco Ferrini, and Stuart Kaminsky, based on the novel *The Hoods* by Harry Grey; photography, Tonino Delli Colli; art direction, Carlo Simi and James Singelis (New York); costume designer, Gabriella Pescucci and Richard Bruno; editor, Nino Baragli; music, Ennio Morricone;

running times (various): 265 minutes (Italian-TV version); 227 minutes (European release print); 143½ minutes (American theatrical release); rating: R.

Once again, De Niro would find himself headlining a film of too enormous a length for normal American distribution, with the question of cutting it down to size turning into a major source of irritation and controversy among the filmmakers. This time, though, the situation proved far more tragic than in the case of *1900*, for director Sergio Leone's longer cut of *Once Upon a Time in America* remains, for those lucky enough to have seen it, a true masterpiece, while the shorter version—though containing moments that are memorable, even brilliant—ultimately rates as little more than a routine gangster story.

Certainly, "routine" is something Leone's film was never meant to be. The director's cut begins in 1933, as hit men kill Eve (Darlanne Fleugel), girlfriend of gangster "Noodles" (De Niro), while searching for him. Noodles escapes, and the action then leaps across the decades to 1968, when Noodles—now an old man—returns to New York after a lifetime on the lam, visiting old pal Fat Moe (Larry Rapp), inadvertently discovering what Hitchcock would have called the MacGuffin—a briefcase filled with money, the key to the past. The film then traces Noodles' memory of 1922, and how he and his friends, while small children, adapted to the fierce climate of New York's Lower East Side by committing petty crimes. In this flashback, they also experience their initiation into sexuality with various neighborhood girls, though Noodles (played, as a child, by Scott Tiler) falls madly, romantically, idealistically in love with Moe's sister, Deborah (Jennifer Connelly as a child, later played as an adult by Elizabeth McGovern). In time, the

Robert De Niro as Noodles and James Woods as Max, childhood friends locked in a power struggle over their mob.

Like so many of the other characters De Niro has chosen to play, Noodles is something of a closet romantic, harboring a lifetime obsession for Deborah (Elizabeth McGovern) and using his money and power to create the perfect situation for their moment of love; tragically, everything goes all wrong.

young "musketeers of the street" eliminate the local gangster Bugsy (James Russo) and take over the entire area, with the loss of the youngest boy, Dominic (Noah Moazezi). Noodles, the triggerman who shoots Bugsy, accidentally kills a local cop in the process and does hard time in jail, eventually returning to his cohorts, now Prohibition-era mobsters.

Significantly, the boys decide early on to pool half the profits of their crimes and stuff the money into that suitcase, kept in a railroad station locker. The key to that suitcase (and, however unwittingly, to their lives) will be hidden in the grandfather clock in Moe's saloon. Noodles and Max (James Woods) argue over whether or not the gang should rob the Federal Reserve Bank. Max suffers from full-blown hubris: the gang has been so successful that he's apparently lost touch with reality, no longer grasping there are indeed limitations to what they can pull off. Hoping to avoid a bloodbath, Noodles informs the police, but his convoluted plan to save Max

Noodles meets the nymphomaniac Carol (Tuesday Weld) during a robbery, and allows her to become a gun moll for the gang.

by betraying him backfires. There's a horrible shoot-out, and Noodles' friends are all butchered, Max himself apparently, though not clearly, dead.

Noodles runs away from this unintended fiasco; he's also horrified by his treatment of Deborah, whom he sweetly courted, then suddenly raped. The courtship represented his romantic side, that part of him which sincerely wants to remain idealistic; the rape—as much a surprise to him as to the woman—is his realistic side, wherein his animal/street instincts for survival and conquest cause him to violate his better, finer aspirations.

Thirty-five years later, Noodles—living in Buffalo, New York—receives a cryptic unsigned letter, returning to find Max still alive, as Noodles had always secretly feared and believed. The two confront one another, each feeling he is the innocent who was betrayed, each perceiving the other as evil incarnate. At the end of Leone's version, Noodles exits Max's mansion; we understand that neither man has been able to force the other to accept his version of the truth. Each of them—like all of us—creates a personal reality, living inside that subjective, self-serving version of events. At the end of the truncated version, however, Noodles hears a shot—presumably Max's suicide—allowing a closure to the story Leone did not intend or want.

The shorter version is indeed a "story" in the most simplistic sense of the term. The flipping back and forth across the decades, as we do in our minds when memories of one incident cause us to consider a related event from years later or earlier, was eliminated entirely, the film restructured as a straight narrative line, with much sex and violence (and especially the sexual violence) removed. In the truncated version, the rape of Deborah is brief, as are the other graphic scenes, most of them involving Tuesday Weld as a masochistic robbery victim who begs the thieves to rape her before leaving. De Niro's visits to an opium den, and his eventual reunion with McGovern, were both excised. Essentially, the recut film was an ordinary gangster movie with several extraordinary touches, quickly failing at the box office. Leone's cut is a four-hour movie about the complex and intertwined memories set off in a singular man's mind, during an opium-induced state, by the ringing of a telephone—the call that he has regretted making all his life.

Director Leone felt that the Prohibition era was "the second frontier in American history," a twentieth-century equivalent to the lawless post–Civil War period. In order to make his operatic epic a tribute to the movies that mythologized the era in larger-than-life images, rather than remain slavishly true to historical accuracy, Leone planned to use various American superstars from the past, all closely associated with the tough-guy movies this was to be the apotheosis of, in supporting roles: such film noir veterans as Glenn Ford, George Raft, and Henry Fonda all agreed to play parts, along with France's Jean Gabin, the Gallic equivalent to Spencer Tracy. Significantly, Leone planned to use three different actors for each of the leading characters at the key junctures in the story: 1922, 1933, and 1968. Leone explained (through an interpreter) his choice of De Niro for Noodles this way: "In six months of casting the film, I saw so many great actors. I was embarrassed when I finally had to make a choice. I find great spontaneity in American performers—no one is better than De Niro at being studied and spontaneous at the same time."

But deals that appeared to be written in cement somehow turned to sludge, and after nearly twelve difficult, strained years of planning, Leone came to America to personally pitch the project to American distributors. This led to a deal in which the Ladd Company would put up $10 million of the final budget, which has been estimated at between 28 and 40 million dollars, with Ladd distributing the film in America through Warner Brothers.

After the filming, Leone explained his concept for the movie as being a study of people who "remain bound to the past, and to the people they knew and were." However hard they may try to re-create themselves during their lifetimes, or deny their origins, they are always—as F. Scott Fitzgerald put it in *The Great Gatsby*—"like boats against the current, born back ceaselessly into the past." Coscreenwriter Enrico Medioli later reflected, "The real protagonist of the film is

Noodles realizes that his enemies are closing in; his latest girlfriend is Eve (Darlanne Fluegel).

always offscreen—time itself! Everyone is bound to a common past, to the people they knew and were. No matter what happens to them in the course of their widely different experiences [after they leave one another], they are at last reunited by the same force that drove them apart." In Leone's words, the film was meant to be experienced as "a mélange of memories, impressions, and fantasies"—real events that take on a dreamlike quality when relived through memory.

Audiences may have laughed out loud at the scene in which Noodles encounters Deborah thirty-five years after their last meeting, complaining that while De Niro is in heavy makeup to allow for an aged look, she appears the same as in the earlier sequence. They failed to grasp that Leone, showing us the event as it appears to Noodles, was visually stating that the man does not see the woman as she now appears, but as she remains

Deborah—the dream girl he has worshiped all his life and has been romancing so elegantly—when she leans forward and kisses him. The problem is that she reacts exactly as Weld's nymphomaniacal Carol character did earlier. Noodles misunderstood the gesture; as David Denby of *New York* put it: "Leone has emphasized the white-hot connection between violence and sexual feeling more explicitly than earlier directors of gangster movies have; some of this movie pushes beyond the forbidden into areas that are both funny and lewd." Noodles is as wrong with Deborah as he was with Max—tragically wrong—and will have to live out the rest of his life with the consequences of each mistake.

At any rate, to satisfy the demands of Warner Brothers, the Ladd Company cut *America* to less than two and a half hours, rearranging the incidents into a neat, nonconfusing tale. No one was very happy with the results, *Variety* reporting that "the anonymous cutters have made the picture more playable and palatable, but they have also steamrolled it toward a normalcy and tidiness it was probably never intended to possess. . . . Director's own cut resembles an immensely ambitious but failed epic poem, while the American version is more akin to a condensation of an overwritten novel." Reviews of the truncated version tended toward the paradoxical: David Ansen of *Newsweek* tagged it "shamefully entertaining" in its "baroque craziness." *Time*'s Richard Corliss called it a "flawed, fascinating epic," while David Chute of the *Los Angeles Herald-Examiner* claimed it was "a fascinating, infuriating movie" and "a god-awful mess . . . despite its great visual beauty." Those who chose to review it again, in the

forever frozen in his mind. However, the Reagan-era American audiences of 1984 did not like their movies complex or demanding. Likewise, theater owners wanted films to be short so that they could fit in more showings and make more money. Executives of the Ladd Company explained they felt "compelled" to trim the movie after a disastrous February 17, 1984, screening in Boston, at which mainstream moviegoers were angered at their inability to easily grasp what was going on, while feminists in the audience became livid at the rape scenes—failing to understand that this was a movie about (and critical of) macho behavior rather than a superficial exploitation of it.

The point is that Noodles—a noble fool of the type found in classical literature from Spain's *Don Quixote* to England's *Môrte D'Arthur* to America's *The Great Gatsby*—means well but does wrong; this is a movie about the evil that good men do. He betrays his best friend professionally, attempting to save Max from a mistake but destroying them both. Likewise, he rapes

Noodles (second from left) listens attentively as Max deals with some gangsters, including Joe (Burt Young, second from right).

Director Sergio Leone, once more working in an epic mode, caught the teeming reality of turn-of-the-century Lower East Side streets.

156

longer form screened at Cannes and at the New York Film Festival, often changed their opinions: Arthur Knight of the *Hollywood Reporter*, who expressed "a notable lack of enthusiasm" for the short version, admitted that "each restored foot of film reveals the intricacies and resonances so sorely missed in the original."

"Cart." of *Variety* wrote: "Quiet and subtle throughout, De Niro and his charisma rep the backbone of the picture, but despite frequent threats to become engaging, Noodles remains essentially unpalatable. . . . The characters, including lead Robert De Niro, are so brutal and essentially unsympathetic [they] will undoubtedly put mass audiences off." The fact that the public stayed away in droves is perhaps proof of that. American audiences, hungry in the post-*Rocky* era for easily accessible and completely cuddly heroes, could not lock into Noodles or Max. European audiences, however, who ironically had far more respect for the postwar film noirs that this movie is an extended homage to (De Niro and Woods are essentially playing variations on the characters incarnated by Burt Lancaster and Kirk Douglas in *I Walk Alone* or Robert Mitchum and Kirk Douglas in *Out of the Past*), found this a remarkable and important picture. About the shorter American release print,

"Cart." later wrote: "Cutting has made Noodles a more palatable character for the audience, but it has also rendered him a great deal more bland and shifts the weight of the drama more in the direction of James Woods's Max."

Pauline Kael, who in *The New Yorker* found the truncated version to be "incoherently bad," praised the "dreamy obsessiveness" of the full-length version, arguing that "in its full length, the movie has a tidal pull back toward the earliest memories, and an elegaic tone. Partly, I think, this is the result of De Niro's measured performance. He makes you feel the weight of Noodles' early experiences and his disappointment in himself. He makes you feel that Noodles never forgets the past, and it's his all-emcompassing guilt that holds the film's different sections together. De Niro was offered his choice of the two leading roles. . . . I respect De Niro's decision [to play Noodles] because he may have thought that the passive [character], whose urges explode in bursts of aggression against women, would be a reach, would test him. . . . In the full version, De Niro gives the film its dimensions. He keeps a tiny flame alive in his eyes, and his performance builds."

The Lords of the Lower East Side: Noodles and Max.

Robert De Niro as Frank Raftis.

Falling in Love

(1984)

A Paramount Picture

CAST:

Robert De Niro (*Frank Raftis*); Meryl Streep (*Molly Gilmore*); Jane Kaczmarek (*Ann Raftis*); George Martin (*John Trainer*); David Clennon (*Brian Gilmore*); Dianne Wiest (*Isabelle*); Harvey Keitel (*Ed Lasky*); Victor Argo (*Victor Rawlins*); Wiley Earl (*Mike Raftis*); Jesse Bradford (*Joe Raftis*).

CREDITS:

Director, Ulu Grosbard; producer, Marvin Worth; screenplay, Michael Cristofer; photography, Peter Suschitzky; production designer, Santo Loquasto; costume designer, Richard Bruno; editor, Michael Kahn; music, Dave Grusin; running time, 106 minutes; rating: PG-13.

"The nice thing about it, the whole point: the nonconsummating part. I mean, sex in a movie—isn't that the easiest thing to do?" So spoke Robert De Niro about his participation in *Falling in Love*, which was very much a love story for the mideighties, when the return of conservative values—along with the growing fear of mainstream AIDS—brought to an end the sexual revolution that had flourished during the 1970s, as well as the demise of screen love stories filled with casual sex. No question about it, *Falling in Love*—despite some serious limitations on a dramatic level—deserves time-capsule status as the most telling romantic film of its era. As its central characters attempt an extramarital affair, then find themselves unable to complete sex, they represent an entire generation that had stepped back to more traditional values.

Frank Raftis (De Niro) works as an architectural engineer in New York City, commuting by train every day from the upscale suburbs of Westchester County, where he lives with his wife, Ann (Jane Kaczmarek), and their two children. Molly Gilmore (Meryl Streep) is employed as a graphic artist, also comfortable in her marriage to Brian (David Clennon). Though they meet while Christmas shopping in the chic Rizzoli bookstore and are immediately attracted to one another, each is straight enough to mentally rule out an affair. Frank is particularly offended by the indiscriminate attitude taken toward sex by his friend Ed (Harvey Keitel). But Molly's confidante Isabelle (Dianne Wiest) senses that Molly's emotions go far deeper than Molly realizes, and that Molly's comfortable but cool marriage leaves her vaguely unsatisfied in ways she has never come to grips with.

It is Frank who arranges another "accidental" meeting, and though Molly attempts to avoid him, she can't deny that she's attracted. The two try an afternoon tryst, but neither can go through with sex; they leave each other feeling guilty but unsatisfied, the worst of all possible situations. Meanwhile, their respective spouses sense that something is going on, and on an emotional (if not sexual) level, Frank and Molly are certainly adulterous. They break it off until they happen across each other one year later, on the commuter train, each discovering the other has ended his/her marriage.

Falling in Love might have been a full-blown domestic tragedy, as was the case with Jack Lemmon in *Save the Tiger*, or a realistic case study of a little guy in love, as with *Marty* starring Ernest Borgnine. What author Michael Cristofer (the flavor-of-the-month writer, having recently won a Pulitzer for his play *The Shadow Box*) opted for was a high-level soap opera, employing all sorts of melodramatic flourishes that trivialized the important issues. When Molly, desperately driving through a rainstorm to see Frank, finds her car stalled on the railroad

Robert De Niro and Meryl Streep, united for the first time since *The Deer Hunter*.

Molly Gilmore (Meryl Streep) strikes up a conversation with Frank while riding on the commuter train.

As the relationship becomes more serious, Molly and Frank must find ever more desperate ways to communicate.

De Niro, so often associated with mentally aberrant tough guy roles, was completely convincing as the extremely normal, soft-spoken, sophisticated suburbanite, Frank Raftis.

tracks as a train approaches, it's clear that the plot is padded with clunky dramatic conventions that were timeworn and threadbare even when people were still making silent movies. So that we don't become too sympathetic toward the quietly appealing spouses, Cristofer has Molly's husband tell a bold-faced lie, while Frank's wife dumps her children rather than, as would be far more likely, fight to keep them.

Perhaps Cristofer hoped his remarkable leading actors would prove dynamic enough to make the old clichés, and a situation left over from the 1946 British classic *Brief Encounter*, seem fresh again. Perhaps he hoped critics and audiences would be so overwhelmed by the chance to see De Niro and Streep together again on-screen (their first pairing since *The Deer Hunter*) that we wouldn't notice the writing failed to support the acting. But people did notice and, in fact, resented that such exquisitely wrought performances were lavished on what seemed nothing more than a routine romance. But how could any fan of serious drama forgive the film's happy, sappy ending, in which De Niro and Streep darted to each other from the far ends of a crowded train, as the syrupy pseudosymphonic music rose around them?

"What a waste of talent," Stanley Kauffmann complained in *The New Republic*. "The best passages of dialogue are those that, apparently, [Michael Cristofer] didn't write—the imprecise, half-expressed fumblings at tense moments that the leading actors improvised."

Pauline Kael of *The New Yorker* was likewise unmoved by what she saw: "Can a vacuum love another vacuum? That's the question posed by *Falling in Love,* a piece of big-star packaging. . . . They have nothing to say; each stares past the other into a separate space. The most compelling thing about them is the beauty-spot wart on De Niro's cheekbone: it has three dimensions—one more than anything else in the movie."

The film allowed De Niro one of his rare "normal" roles, as a quietly attractive suburban man of middle-class values. On the set, director Ulu Grosbard ecstatically exclaimed, "*Falling in Love* has a new De Niro. Nobody's ever seen this De Niro before. He's funny. He's tender!" De Niro added, "I thought I could concentrate on things other than what I usually concentrate on—makeup, or whatever. I don't always have to do high-risk parts. I thought it was something different than I've done before, and for that reason alone it was good to do it." But if playing a regular guy might strike some as an easier job than, say, the weight-gain challenges of *Raging Bull,* they are naive about the most difficult task for an actor, which is making the everyday and ordinary seem worthy of attention. "It only appeared to be easier" than a Jake La Motta type role, De Niro rightly insisted.

For an actor who wants to bring the part vividly to life, De Niro grasped that "you always have to worry, always have to concentrate—it's just more deceptive when you work on the surface." Frank is one more mask to try on; since Frank features none of the obvious elements of fascination De Niro's freak-show escapees all display—drastically different from one another, yet alike in their "otherness"—he is more difficult to make specific. The challenge to doing Frank well came in creating a delicate balance between the universal and the unique, between creating a character all upper-middle-class male movie-goers could associate with and a fully realized, three-dimensional, totally singular human being who—despite being a recognizable type—was true, vivid, and believable as an individual. To draw a metaphor from De Niro, Sr.'s profession, Bobby had been able to paint his previous characters in daringly colorful strokes; now, he was forced to work in a far more subtle form of portraiture.

As always, Bobby prepared meticulously so he would be perceived as living rather than playing the part. He had elegant business cards made up with the name *Frank Raftis,* carrying them everywhere—knowing, as a good Method actor would, that their presence in his pocket helped him lock completely into the identity of Frank as a man who would never have left the house without his cards.

Most critics looked on the results with favor. In London's *Financial Times,* Nigel Andrews noted: "De Niro's crinkly grin, irrepressible Italian hand-weave gestures, and vast ironic pauses with cocked head (no other actor skates so close to making you think he's forgotten his lines) spirit a character into being where

Frank and Molly grow concerned about the effect of their affair—however platonic—on their home lives.

161

Frank suggests they turn to a fortune-telling machine in order to determine what they ought to do next.

and anguish, De Niro is merely empty—a darkly handsome young man with an oddly scary smile." Kauffmann complained a bit, too, though finding the overall characterization to be successful: "De Niro, dealing with a . . . stock character, works to realize it as if it had never before been seen. My one complaint is that he insists on a thuggish accent. In this successful architectural engineer, with a solid, middle-class, college-grad wife—why? His speech makes it just a shade harder for Streep to convince us that she is stricken by him. But she does; and so does he convince us in return—of the reluctant but invincible love, the buried heartache."

If the overall film proved wanting, *Falling in Love* still served Bobby's purposes, allowing him to prove he could indeed play Mr. Normal. In fact, De Niro is so convincing as Raftis that his performance actually surprised some viewers who thought that such a middle-of-the-road characterization was out of his range, which ran to extremes on either side. By convincingly delivering such a performance, De Niro managed to change the public's perception of him, eliminating what many saw as a key limiting factor in his possible casting.

De Niro's own comments suggest he understands it was anything but a heavyweight project: "I was tired [from doing physically demanding roles], this script came along. It was a nice story, set here in New York." Indeed, the loving portrait of New York locations, sweetly captured by director Grosbard, was one of the chief virtues of this film. Christmas in New York is convincingly captured here, even though *Love* was shot in mid-April. The film company took over Saks Fifth Avenue on a Friday night just after closing, immediately set about putting all the holiday decorations in place, then shot the necessary scenes during the wee hours, finishing just in time to take down the decorations moments before customers began trickling in for the Saturday sales. Ultimately, though, even this aspect of the film led to an overall sense of insincerity: Grand Central station and the various commuter trains looked far too scrubbed-clean to be quite believed.

nothing was before." British critic James Cameron-Wilson admired Bobby's performance, claiming that "it is a difficult part to play, the role of a commonplace man in love. Frank Raftis is no smooth-talking lothario, like Jimmy Doyle in *New York, New York;* or the devastatingly romantic and proper Monroe Stahr in *The Last Tycoon.* As Raftis, De Niro has to convey the conventional sex appeal of an Everyman." A few critics, however, were so unawed by the movie that they were unable even to enjoy De Niro. Denby complained that "De Niro . . . can't find anything to play in this solid-citizen businessman-architect, and he goes flat. He lacks the charm, the ease to appear even minimally convincing as Mr. Right, and without his (usual) rage, his mockery

The relationship, which began on a train, develops further during another trip.

Robert De Niro as Harry Tuttle.

Brazil

(1985)

A Universal Pictures Release

CAST:

Jonathan Pryce (*Sam Lowry*); Robert De Niro (*Archibald "Harry" Tuttle*); Michael Palin (*Jack Lint*); Kim Greist (*Jill Layton*); Katherine Helmond (*Ida Lowry*); Ian Holm (*Kurtzmann*); Ian Richardson (*Warren*); Peter Vaughan (*Eugene Helpmann*); Bob Hoskins (*Spoor*); Derrick O'Connor (*Dowser*); Charles McKeown (*Lime*); Barbara Hicks (*Mrs. Terrain*); Sheila Reid (*Mrs. Buttle*); Kathryn Pogson (*Shirley*).

CREDITS:

Director, Terry Gilliam; producer, Arnon Milchan; screenplay, Gilliam, Tom Stoppard, and Charles McKeown; photography, Roger Pratt; production designer, Norman Garwood; costume designer, Jim Acheson and Ray Scott; editor, Julian Doyle; music, Michael Kamen; running time, 131 minutes; rating: R.

An Orwellian vision of the future as a negative utopia—laced with touches of Swiftian satire and Kafkaesque surrealism—was the basis for *Brazil*, Terry Gilliam's bizarre and highly controversial work in which De Niro chose to appear briefly, less for the acting challenge (which was minimal), more for the opportunity to work with the eccentric, iconoclastic filmmaker.

The focus is on Sam Lowry, an ordinary fellow who, like the hero of *1984*, spends his time doing drudge work in an automated future world, though he knows in his imagination that there must be something more to life. Our first image is of this ordinary man enjoying an extraordinary experience, in which he soars out of his workaday world up into the heavens, sporting actual wings, reaching the clouds, and there joining his dream girl (Kim Greist). Then, he snaps out of his fantasy, returning to his lowly job as a petty bureaucrat, trudging around the edges of a gray universe—a land in which paperwork dominates everyone's daily existence, computers constantly print out incorrect information as-

Harry, who may be a government agent, an anti-government revolutionary, or an air-conditioning repairman (or, for that matter, all three) convinces Sam Lowry (Jonathan Pryce) that they are in mortal danger.

sumed to be true, and every conceivable device from air conditioners to elevators constantly breaks down. Until, one day, he spots a woman who looks amazingly like the fantasy lady in his dreams and wonders if he can perhaps turn dream into reality.

Sam uses his family connections (his mother, played by Katherine Helmond, is a superficial socialite who undergoes plastic surgery on a daily basis) to get himself transferred to another office where he's able to check up on Jill's identity. This allows him to meet her, but when he does, Jill has recently witnessed one of life's horrors, as yet another of those computer errors informed the police that her neighbor, who did nothing wrong, should be arrested. As a favor to the now-deceased man's widow, she is trying to learn the actual reason for his arrest—and the method of his death. However, such individual initiative is not tolerated by the state, so Jill has been placed on an enemies list of suspect people. Evidence does suggest she actually belongs to a secret terrorist group. Still, she's Sam's dream girl, so he can't resist pursuing the romance—and aiding Jill in her quest. That, of course, makes him suspect, as do his periodical run-ins with Harry Tuttle (De Niro), who claims to be into "free-lance refrigeration" (whatever that means). Tuttle is so bizarre, so ambiguous, so obscure that it's impossible to grasp whether he is what he claims to be, works for the government in some surveillance job, or is an antigovernment agent. In the end, though, Sam finds himself being prepared for official government torture by Jack (Michael Palin), who was his best friend and coworker. As Jack smilingly

prepares the torture devices, he coos, "Nothing personal."

Brazil is a brilliant film on a technical level, with grotesque sets and remarkable production design, all photographed in the most strikingly offbeat manner. The edgy editing and innovative musical score also add to the success in creating a viable future world on-screen. As Arthur Knight wrote in the *Hollywood Reporter*, "like the labyrinthine halls and passageways of its futuristic skyscrapers and shopping malls, the plotting seems to intersect itself, coming back to the same place to start over, or bumping into obstacles that send it flying in new directions. . . . The settings have an eerie strangeness: a dingy stairway leads to an [elegantly] appointed Victorian flat . . . half dream, half nightmare, the projection of a world which may have already begun sprouting around us." Yet the effectiveness of all this is undercut by a sense we've already seen and heard everything Gilliam wants to tell us many times over. The script is little more than a collage of trendy cautionary-fable clichés, culled from the aforementioned *1984,* Kafka's *The Trial* (and Orson Welles's striking film version of it), as well as Aldous Huxley's *Brave New World.* The more one has read (or watched) previously, the less impressive *Brazil* seems. Gilliam himself referred to the film as "Walter Mitty meets Franz Kafka," though it often plays as a Monty Python riff on *1984.*

Amazingly, Gilliam said at the time that he had never read the Orwell book. At any rate, Universal did not originally schedule a 1985 release, though they had $9 million invested in the $15-million movie, rumor having it that Sidney J. Sheinberg, president of MCA, wanted to trim the two-hour-eleven-minute movie down to under two hours and tack on a happier ending—despite the ecstatic reaction at Cannes. Gilliam (who achieved fame as the only American member of the otherwise British Monty Python group) offered to fly American critics to other countries where the film was playing (20th Century-Fox International released the uncut version overseas) so they could write about it when Universal canceled all critics screenings. Desperate, Gilliam even took

out ads in trade papers asking: "Dear Sid Sheinberg—When are you going to release my film *Brazil?*" The Los Angeles Film Critics screened the movie by slipping into a USC cinema class where it was being shown to the students, then named *Brazil* the Best Picture of the Year (perhaps out of respect for Gilliam's integrity and concern for his awful plight). Universal then hurriedly booked it into selected theaters so *Brazil* might qualify for the upcoming Oscar nominations. "*Brazil* may not be the best film of the year," Janet Maslin wrote in the *New*

Sam's Grand Guignol mother, Mrs. Ida Lowry (Katherine Helmond), takes him on a tour of a surreal salon in this futuristic cautionary fable.

York Times, "but it's a remarkable accomplishment." She pointed out that the movie was not named for the country, but for the once-popular song, and the dream of impossible romance that it allows every listener, both in the radio days when it was released and as a refrain in Gilliam's film: "The gaiety of the music stands in ironic contrast to the oppressive, totalitarian society in which the story is set." David Denby of *New York* commented: "Everyone is stoned on popular culture—Hollywood movies of the thirties and forties and sugary songs like 'Brazil'—which seems to represent the population's lost hopes, its nostalgia and desire."

By the end, we grasp that the hapless Mr. Buttle (Brian Miller) was arrested in his living room (and his wife [Sheila Reid] politely handed a receipt for the husband she would never see again) because a large bug happened to drop into a computer, causing a typographical error. The man whom the police should have arrested is in fact Harry Tuttle, who, Maslin noted, "is played by Robert De Niro as a combination repairman and commando. Mr. De Niro has only the briefest of roles here, but he makes a lot of it." Indeed, the appearance was so brief that many critics failed to analyze it at all, merely mentioning Bobby in passing. "Robert De Niro shows up," Denby wrote, "with a black hood and a cigar, as some sort of rebel leader who swings in and out of buildings on a rope." In her lengthy review of the film, Sheila Benson of the *Los Angeles Times* praised "Robert De Niro, in a small but crucial role as a laconic, stogie-chewing, commando type." Interestingly enough, Pauline Kael—who had recently been ripping each successive De Niro performance in her *New Yorker* reviews—found his character far preferable to the purposefully dull one played by Pryce: "The marginal characters—especially Robert De Niro as Tuttle—are far more entertaining. I hate to think what the movie would be like without them. . . . De Niro's role is no more than a cameo—but, all revved up and chomping on a cigar, he's a prankster-daredevil, a comic-strip hero, high-spirited and the life of the party. He even has a healthy color. Tuttle repairs heating systems illicitly (he doesn't have a license), and when he's in danger of being caught, he slides down a rope as if he were jet-propelled, dropping down from the top of an astoundingly tall skyscraper to street level in the blink of an eye. Tuttle must be the first kinetic Underground Man in the movies."

That he was, though the role remains part of an awkward period for Bobby, who was busying himself with interesting little roles rather than seeking out the more demanding parts that his talent deserved.

Early in the story, Mendoza—self-interested slave trader—returns with a bounty of freshly captured Guarani Indians he will soon sell to the highest bidder.

The Mission

(1986)

A Warner Brothers Release

CAST:

Robert De Niro (*Mendoza*); Jeremy Irons (*Gabriel*); Cherie Lunghi (*Carlotta*); Ray McAnally (*Altamirano*); Aidan Quinn (*Felipe*); Liam Neeson (*Fielding*); Ronald Pickup (*Hontar*); Monirak Sisowath (*Ibaye*); Daniel Berrigan (*Sebastian*); Charles Low (*Cabeza*); Tony Lawn (*Father Provincial*); Rafael Camerano (*Spanish Commander*).

CREDITS:

Director, Roland Joffe; producers, Fernando Ghia and David Puttnam; story and screenplay, Robert Bolt; photography, Chris Menges; production designer, Stuart Craig; costume designer, Enrico Sabbatini; editor, Jim Clark; music, Ennio Morricone; running time, 128 minutes; rating: PG.

The Mission is to South America and Catholicism what *1900* had been to Italy and communism: a huge historical epic of ideas in which two very different men,

initially on opposite sides of an issue, come to symbolize the political, social, and moral conflicts inherent in the story. At least this time, though, De Niro did not have the problem of being cast against type. He played Rodrigo Mendoza, a man of adventure who mindlessly makes a fortune as a mid-eighteenth-century slave trader, capturing Guarani Indians in Paraguay, selling them for a fat profit to the local governor. Mendoza's life is so comfortable that he believes the city of Asunción exists for his immediate gratification of animal urges, expressed in fierce hunting with his younger brother Felipe (Aidan Quinn) or treating the attractive, wealthy widow Carlotta (Cherie Lunghi) as if she were his personal possession.

Carlotta, however, has fallen in love with the handsome, sensitive Felipe. When she tries explaining this to Mendoza, his temper rages out of control; Mendoza kills his brother along with a passerby. Afterward, Mendoza

During the following years, Mendoza and Gabriel become close if wary companions, running the mission in tandem while allowing each other wide berth. Everything changes, however, when in 1750 Spain and Portugal sign the Treaty of Madrid, redefining their territorial borders in the Americas. Spain (which has forsaken slavery) delivers the Indian land to Portugal (where it remains legal). To avoid the expulsion of the Jesuit order from Portugal, all the Jesuit missions in South America are ordered closed by the Pope, the Indians living there abandoned to the slave traders. The Guarani Indians intend to stay and fight for the mission they have come to love, causing conflict for Mendoza. On the one hand, he has taken the Jesuit vow, binding him to obey this and all other papal edicts while continuing to practice nonviolence; on the other, he still possesses the skills of a master fighting man, realizing that he and he alone can attend to the task of teaching the Guaranis proper

Robert De Niro as Rodrigo Mendoza, the mercenary.

suffers extreme guilt, becoming a Jesuit postulant. Father Gabriel (Jeremy Irons), who has always cared for the natives in the gentlest manner and resented the encroaching slave traders, at first is unsure if Mendoza's desire to do penance and achieve redemption is sincere. But Mendoza—pulling a netful of his now-forsaken armor along behind him, like Sisyphus encumbered by his stone—proves himself by first making the arduous journey up to the isolated mission above Iguaçu Falls, then assisting the pacifist Gabriel as he teaches the Indians to appreciate the joys of music through handmade violins, as an introduction to the values of Christianity.

Mendoza and his younger brother Felipe (Aidan Quinn) find themselves in conflict over the beautiful courtesan, Carlotta (Cherie Lunghi).

self-defense, even as his cohort Gabriel sees to the final salvation of their souls.

Though *The Mission* is different from the films made by Martin Scorsese, it is, like them, a study of Catholic ideals in conflict with the practical prerogatives of the real world. The film also allowed De Niro to play once again a character torn between his learned duties as a priest and his personality as a man, a motif he has returned to again and again, from the flimsy *The Gang That Couldn't Shoot Straight* (in which, at one point, he played an apocryphal padre) to the far more ambitious *True Confessions* (in which his priest fell victim to the secular pangs of mammon and ambition). There has always been something of the spoiled priest about De Niro, which he comes to terms with when tackling such roles.

This marked the first time in his career that De Niro was ever directed by an Englishman, Roland Joffe, a

Consumed with guilt after killing his own brother, Mendoza is comforted by the kindly Father Gabriel (Jeremy Irons).

former theater and upscale-TV director in London, who had recently earned a reputation as a heavyweight thanks to *The Killing Fields*. *The Mission* script, by Sir Robert Bolt, was a throwback to the kind of thinking person's epics Bolt had penned during the 1960s (*Lawrence of Arabia, A Man for All Seasons*). Bolt had written *The Mission* in 1978 at the request of Italian producer Fernando Ghia, who had seen a play on the same subject, *The Strong Are Lonely* by Austrian dramatist Fritz Hochwalder. Rather than optioning it, Ghia commissioned Bolt to create a totally original screenplay emphasizing the relationship of the Jesuits to the Indians, rather than the inner workings of the political and papal elements. Ghia searched for financial backing until he attracted interest in America from David Puttnam, then in a position to make pretty much any movie he chose, following his success with the Oscar-winner *Chariots of Fire* but before his debacle as head of Columbia Pictures.

Additionally, *The Mission* marked Bobby's first appearance in a period-piece part that preceded our century. Even before filming began, some critics wondered if De Niro could successfully incarnate a historical character, or if his ultramodern demeanor and vocal inflections would reveal his contemporaneity immediately. Joffe, for one, expressed no nervousness about casting De Niro, insisting that "*The Mission* was a very courageous step for Bobby to take, a very proper one—I'm glad he's done it. Mendoza was a classical role, and nobody until now had had the balls and size to tackle it. But I felt Bobby could rise to that." Knowing that he and

169

Puttnam needed a man who was not only a fine actor but also a superstar to headline the $23-million project, thereby making it commercially viable, Joffe invited De Niro down to the Colombian locations even as he was doing his initial preparations of the film's sets, including historically accurate reproductions of the mission. "Let me have a chance to look at you in that world," he wired De Niro.

De Niro accepted the challenge. Together, they explored the villages in Argentina, the jungles outside of Santa Marta in Colombia, and Colombia's walled city-fort of Cartagena, which had been founded in 1533, along the way casting local Wuanana Indians as the films' Guaranis. "Once I decided he was the man I wanted," Joffe would later reflect, everything fell into place, because "it [is] important to realize that your leading actor is a keystone. If the director is an architect, then he has to choose his keystone very carefully, because everything comes to rest on that in terms of performance, the spirit of the crew . . . [absolutely] everything." Joffe realized immediately, though, that Bobby—used to working with the ultracontemporary Scorsese—tended to improvise his lines, employing the script as a mere starting point, whereas the more traditional writing style of Robert Bolt tends to be "set"—intended to be played precisely as written.

According to Joffe, this conflict was happily resolved: "Bobby did improvise initially, to find his character's expression, but essentially he had to deal with the text as it was." Joffe did note, though, that De Niro's character—though top-billed—actually has far less dialogue than Irons's Gabriel, a highly articulate man, one who expresses himself best in words, rather than through actions. De Niro's performance was therefore based on his remarkable screen presence, along with the kinds of ideas and emotions he can express through body language—completely in keeping with the personality of the man he plays. Acknowledging the classic/contemporary question, Joffe would say only that "the important thing for Bobby was to find a level where he had to infer period but remain modern."

There was even the possibility that a touch of anachronism might serve the film well, as Joffe has always insisted this story initially appealed to him not only as an opportunity to mount a historical epic but also because the horrid treatment of the South American natives in 1750 struck him as "the root of much of what is happening now." An actor with Bobby's contemporary qualities could serve to remind viewers that this was not a waxworks history lesson so much as a true story from the past, here told to remind us of what is in fact still happening today. Ultimately, critics took Joffe at his word, judging the success or failure of the film's "archi-

Giving up his slave-trading ways, Mendoza does penance by dragging his armor over miles of impassable terrain.

tecture" on whether or not they could accept De Niro in the part. Certainly, he stretched here as never before; in the eyes of some, he failed resoundingly for the first time. "Sege" of *Variety* wrote that "*The Mission* is probably the first film in which De Niro gives a bland, uninteresting performance."

He was not alone in this judgment. James M. Wall of *Christian Century* described *The Mission* as "a fumbled attempt to project liberation theology into the eighteenth century," suggesting that the movie was both revisionist and politically correct. "The 'perfect' Indians and the 'pure' Jesuits are finally too good to be true [while] the insensitivity of the papal representative is portrayed without sufficient attention to the church's need to satisfy the political goals of Spain and Portugal." Numerous critics noted a naïveté at the heart of the

entire conception: though the papacy is taken to task for succumbing to political pressure and abandoning the Indian converts, there is no sense whatever that the very work of the missionaries—here presented as being every bit as pure as the unspoiled Indians—may have been intrusive and fundamentally wrong.

However, other critics lauded the work. Tom O'Brien of *Commonweal* insisted that while Irons's performance was "sublimely restrained," De Niro's was "even better," the film working primarily because of his ability to project a man torn asunder when "his vows of obedience and nonviolence cannot outlast the threat of genocide to the Indians he has come to love. De Niro deserves an Oscar nomination for facial acting, concentrating the pain and irony of his position into eyes and cheek muscles." O'Brien appreciated the movie in large part because it forced the audience to face, in historical context, an issue that was more relevant than ever in the mid-1980s: "The end raises the issue of violent resistance to evil in a brutally powerful, provocative way. Joffe's cool camera style and evenhanded treatment of Irons's pacifism and de Niro's [*sic*] resort to 'just war' avoids a simple judgment. As an epigraph about current Jesuit activities among the Indians notes, the issue of violence in defense of the powerless is still painfully relevant. *The Mission* will not be comforting to those who dismiss liberation theology or ignore the murder of Latin American archbishops and nuns when committed by right-wing fanatics."

Like most other reviewers, Wall and O'Brien each noted the stunning cinematography of Chris Menges (all but lost when the film is viewed on video, though

Having staged his very own Calvary, Mendoza—now transformed from a killer into a Christ figure—weeps with joy as Father Gabriel happily tells Mendoza that he has redeemed his soul.

Mendoza leads his native warriors on an attack against the invading whites.

Mendoza realizes that to protect the natives he now loves and cares for, he must once again return to the ways of the sword; an adoring child (Bercelio Moya) comforts him in his decision.

memorably impressive for those lucky enough to have seen *The Mission* in a 70mm print) of the breathtakingly immense Iguaçu Falls, accompanied by Ennio Morricone's music, which effectively mixes the liturgical sounds of the Jesuits with basic native rhythms to convey, through the score, the basic theme: the mixing of two distinct cultures, one sophisticated and complex, the other sweetly primitive. However, even reviewers who, such as O'Brien, marveled at the movie could not help pointing out certain sore points: "*The Mission* has the common weakness of all films about the third world: undo attention to the outsiders . . . there should have been more climactic focus on what the Indians, not merely the Jesuits, were thinking."

Though O'Brien mentioned this in passing, presenting the problem as a minor flaw in an otherwise fine film, those reviewers who did not appreciate *The Mission* seized on this issue, making it the basis for their attacks. David Denby, of *New York,* complained that "Joffe has committed the unspeakable error of patronizing the Guarani, of letting them come off as smiling children. . . . There isn't a single Indian who steps forward and becomes a real character in the movie. . . . In all

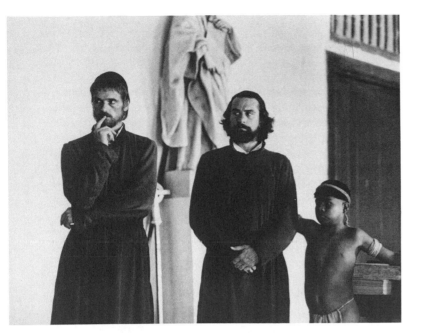

Now a Jesuit priest himself, Mendoza ponders the problems besetting the mission with his friend Gabriel (Jeremy Irons) and the Guarani Indian convert-child (Bercelio Moya).

Felipe (Aidan Quinn), younger brother of Mendoza, in an early, reflective moment.

Robert De Niro as Mendoza.

innocence, the moviemakers repeat the same inhuman mistakes as the eighteenth-century colonials," by suggesting the Guarani cannot care for themselves, but must be protected from bad whites by good whites. Denby added that "the style of *The Mission* salutes its own high-mindedness; the movie's failure is encased in ethnographic purity."

Not surprisingly, then, Denby did not care for De Niro's performance: "As a 'hot-blooded' Spaniard with shoulder-length hair, De Niro gets to stride around furiously with his rapier and deliver such lines as 'So, me you do not love?' The period role doesn't suit him at all . . . once De Niro kills his brother (in a love quarrel) and seeks absolution among the savages, he's finished as an actor. He smiles at the Guarani and they smile back." In fact, Puttnam always saw the movie as an exciting combination of the 1980s fashion for action-adventure on a big scale and the insightful, thought-provoking pictures that had flourished several decades earlier. "*The Mission* is a Clint Eastwood version of *Becket*," he claimed, featuring "an intellectual theme treated with guts." But whereas Puttnam perceived this paradox as the essential genius of the project, critic Denby scoffed at the irony between high-mindedness and commercial consideration: "The most nobly intentioned movie in years. Bravely done, boys! Bravely done! And now, the body count . . ." Stanley Kauffmann of *The New Republic,* who complained that Bolt had "slimmed down the political-social aspects of the subject [and] puffed up the religious aspect into movie pietism," wrote that "Robert De Niro plays Mendoza—just about perceptibly. The role is no better written than Gabriel, but Irons at least tries. The volcanically talented De Niro has never given such a perfunctory performance, full of long 'meaningful' stares that are meant to supply content to a vacuous character. De Niro has accepted some parts he ought to have left alone, but not since *1900* has he given such depressing proof of that fact."

Jeremy Irons as the gentle man of the cloth, who proves that music really does have charm to soothe the savage beast.

I AM A CAMEO:

Robert De Niro as Louis Cyphre, alias Lucifer.

Angel Heart

(1987)

A Tri-Star Pictures Release

CAST:

Mickey Rourke (*Harry Angel*); Robert De Niro (*Lou Cyphre*); Lisa Bonet (*Epiphany Proudfoot*); Charlotte Rampling (*Margaret Krusemark*); Stocker Fontelieu (*Ethan*); Brownie McGhee (*Toots Sweet*); Michael Higgins (*Dr. Fowler*); Elizabeth Whitcraft (*Connie*); Elliott Keener (*Sterne*); Charles Gordone (*Spider Simpson*); Dann Florek (*Winesap*).

CREDITS:

Director, Alan Parker; producers, Alan Marshall and Elliott Kastner; screenplay, Parker, from the novel *Falling Angel* by William Hjortsberg; photography, Michael Seresin; production designer, Brian Morris; editor, Gerry Hambling; music, Trevor Jones; running time, 113 minutes; rating: R.

A major trap for serious actors who have become superstars is to slip into the "I Am a Cameo" syndrome. Having asserted themselves as talented young comers, then proven their gifts in strong roles, such actors sometimes glide while approaching the "mature" phases of their careers. Even Marlon Brando, the actor/star to whom De Niro has most often been compared, did precisely this. So when De Niro—whose painstaking preparation for complex roles is all but legendary—began drifting in this direction, fans and critics took note. Was it possible that he had already reached—and passed—his peak?

First, Bobby did a brief bit in *Brazil*, and few complained; but when he followed that up shortly after with another "phoned-in" performance, this time in a gimmicky piece, it stood to reason that those who had long since accepted De Niro as the new Brando feared that, like his predecessor, the actor was now entering that fading-superstar walk-on phase of his career. The film was *Angel Heart*, a work by Alan Parker—hardly the sort

Harry Angel (Mickey Rourke) approaches Lou Cyphre about a private-eye job.

of director one readily thinks of as a collaborator for De Niro.

The British Parker began his career as a director of TV commercials. His films—*Midnight Express, Fame, Shoot the Moon, Come See the Paradise*—are marvelous looking, boasting detailed attention to production design, cinematography, and editing. Also, Parker is a strong director of actors. Unfortunately, his films tend to be as facile as they are forceful, designed for immediacy of impact, though the more one thinks about them afterward, the less impressive they seem—as thematically specious as they are visually stylish. Also, Parker's pictures tend to start strong, then grow tiresome, even silly, as they approach their denouements.

Angel Heart begins as a genre piece, then turns into an utter embarrassment when it opts for a contrived metaphysical solution, featuring an ever more baroque plot

and an outrageous ending. The opening moments of this dark, murky movie (the carefully desaturated colors create an effectively monochromatic palette on-screen) seem to be setting up a film noir, with Mickey Rourke playing a 1955 Mike Hammerish slob/hero private eye named Harry. He's summoned to a dilapidated Harlem club where a mysterious client named Lou Cyphre (De Niro, ponytailed and with extraordinarily long fingernails) offers Harry a huge fee to take on a missing-person case. With a commanding though creepy voice, a cynical smirk on his face, and a devilish twinkle in his eyes, Lou explains that he wants Harry to locate a popular singer from a decade earlier named Johnny Favorite; the man disappeared without paying Lou an important (though unspecified) debt. Searching for him, Harry wanders from Coney Island to New Orleans, becomes involved with various shady ladies (including Charlotte Rampling

Harry Angel finds himself searching for a onetime big band singer who has disappeared after being hired by Cyphre.

as a Lauren Bacall–ish sophisticate and Lisa Bonet as a voodoo princess who likes to make love while rolling in chicken blood), ultimately realizing he himself is Johnny Favorite. Years ago, he sold his soul to the devil (Lou Cyphre, alias Lucifer) for show business success, then ran away (repressing his identity) to avoid paying the debt.

The most notable element about the film was the flap over a hot lovemaking sequence between Rourke and Bonet (owing in part to her having endeared herself to mainstream America by playing Bill Cosby's super-straight TV daughter), ten seconds of which was excised before the film's initial X rating could be modified to an R for theatrical release. The videocassette release does contain the entire scene, which is not noticeably more volatile or graphic than the footage that was allowed. Today, the film would probably receive a rating of NC-17 without the raising of an eyebrow, but the movie benefited from the ratings controversy. Otherwise, it seemed little more than an overly elaborate lead-up to a contrived finale, the ending a dishonest trick rather than a satisfying twist. Watching De Niro suddenly turn into Satan did offer audiences a thrill, though a cheap one.

Also lacking was the sense of ironic humor that made the book work in a way the movie doesn't. Noting this, Vincent Canby of the *New York Times* claimed that "the only wit is supplied by Mr. De Niro, who delivers his lines, some of which are genuinely funny, with a comic daintiness that gives firm style to the otherwise pointless narrative." Pauline Kael of *The New Yorker,* no longer the unabashed De Niro supporter she had once been, wrote that "De Niro drops in from time to time; it's the sort of guest appearance that lazy big actors delight in—they can show up the local talent. God knows he's

welcome, but he isn't quite the comic-strip life of the party that he was in his cameo in *Brazil,* and this picture's no party." *Variety* noted: "De Niro, who has four major scenes, sports elegant attire, a beautiful cane, and ever-growing manicured fingernails to offset his equally anachronistic big beard and long hair left over from *The Mission.* His character, which he plays with great precision and economy, and also as if in on a joke of which nobody else in the cast is aware, is so weird, however, that the offbeat look seems acceptable."

Unquestionably, De Niro gave Parker precisely what he needed for the film. Thankfully, De Niro would shortly move away from the clever-cameo trap and back into the kind of leading roles and substantive supporting parts that his talent both deserved and demanded. His trilogy of baroque bits—*Brazil, Angel Heart,* and *The Untouchables*—are best viewed, in retrospect, as a time of treading water for the actor, undertaken as an entertainment for himself as well as for us, even as he searched for new artistic directions.

During his search for the elusive singer, Harry finds himself involved with Epiphany Proudfoot (Lisa Bonet), daughter of a voodoo priestess; their sex scenes together caused a controversy since Bonet had been playing Bill Cosby's prim and proper TV daughter.

Robert De Niro as Al Capone.

The Untouchables

(1987)

A Paramount Picture

CAST:

Kevin Costner (*Eliot Ness*); Sean Connery (*Jim Malone*); Charles Martin Smith (*Oscar Wallace*); Andy Garcia (*George Stone*); Robert De Niro (*Al Capone*); Richard Bradford (*Mike*); Jack Kehoe (*Payne*); Brad Sullivan (*George*); Billy Drago (*Frank Nitti*); Patricia Clarkson (*Ness's Wife*).

CREDITS:

Director, Brian De Palma; producer, Art Linson; screenplay, David Mamet; photography, Stephen H. Burum; visual consultant, Patrizia Von Brandenstein; wardrobe, Giorgio Armani; costume designer, Marilyn Vance-Straker; editors, Jerry Greenberg and Bill Pankow; music, Ennio Morricone; running time, 119 minutes; rating: R.

Originally, *The Untouchables* had been the title of a book written by Eliot Ness with Oscar Fraley, chronicling how a government agency aided in the 1929 investigation of mob boss Al Capone. It had been adapted, in 1959, as a two-part filmed episode for television's *Desilu Playhouse,* those broadcasts proving so unexpectedly popular that a weekly TV series, itself highly successful, played on ABC from 1959 to 1963, with Robert Stack as Ness. The shows provided shockingly violent entertainment for their time; it's worth noting, though, that while the public accepted what they saw at face value, the series was highly fictionalized. In virtually every episode, Ness shot it out with gangsters, though in his written account, there's no indication a single shot was ever exchanged. The Untouchables, who had mostly worked as desk cops, were mythologized by the television series into a 1930s equivalent of the two-gun marshals of cowboy lore—likewise more mythological than historical.

But when De Palma agreed to do a new film version, it was the myth, not the reality, he wanted to portray. To

Al Capone finds himself on trial, after Eliot Ness and his Untouchables amass evidence that the gangster has been involved with income tax evasion.

While watching an opera, Capone receives word from henchman Frank Nitti (Billy Drago) that problems have arisen in their brewery operation.

emphasize this, Brian and David Mamet (Pulitzer Prize–winning playwright of *Glengarry Glen Ross*, screenwriter for *The Verdict*) even included something that had never been done in the old series, much less reality: a shoot-out in which Ness, aided by red-coated Mounties, takes on the Capone gang along the Canadian border. At this moment, *The Untouchables* becomes less a gangster film than an updated western. As had been the case with the old television series, the Untouchables were here portrayed as a four-man team, with stalwart WASP family-man Ness (Kevin Costner) abetted by tough Irish cop Malone (Sean Connery, Oscar winner for Best Supporting Actor), nervous accountant Oscar Wallace (Charles Martin Smith), and cool, calculating Italian American sharpshooter George Stone (Andy Garcia). Other than Ness, their individual characterizations have absolutely no basis in fact; the Untouchables were actually a ten-man team. Though in the film both Malone and Wallace are killed by the criminals, no member of Ness's ten-man group ever died in the line of duty.

Bob Hoskins, riding high on the strong critical reception of *The Long Good Friday* and *Mona Lisa*, was signed by the studio to play Al Capone when De Niro, approached by De Palma, expressed interest but put off making a decision, owing to his commitment to complete the run of a Broadway play, *Cuba and His Teddy Bear*. But Brian relished the thought of working again with his former star, convincing producer Art Linson (*Melvin and Howard*) to go after De Niro anyway. In time, Bobby agreed to join the cast, in large part

because, in his words, "I had always wanted to play Al Capone." So Linson requested that Paramount buy out the disappointed Hoskins for his full $200,000 salary. De Niro was then signed for what has alternatively been reported as $1.5 and $2 million for the two weeks' work, while Hoskins went on to star in *Who Framed Roger Rabbit*.

Linson, meanwhile, was less than impressed when he met De Niro for the first time, later reflecting on the shock of encountering "this guy about one hundred and fifty pounds, with a ponytail, looked thirty, weird, barely articulate." Fearful they had made a disastrous mistake, Linson called De Palma in the middle of the night, wailing, "We're doomed. We gave up Hoskins for this guy? We're out of business." Calmly, De Palma assured him, "Wait. You'll see." Linson waited, and saw.

Upon agreeing to do the picture on relatively short notice, De Niro's challenge was once again to change his appearance (more than he had done for any film since *Raging Bull*) with as little resort to makeup as possible—thereby becoming, rather than playing, Capone. This

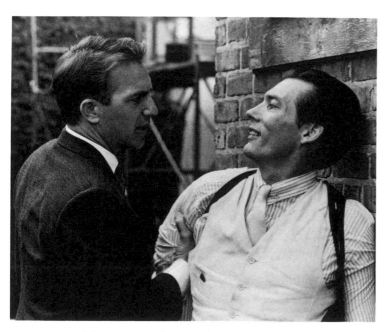

While Capone stands trial in the courtroom below, Ness (Kevin Costner) confronts Nitti on the roof.

The Untouchables: Andy Garcia, Sean Connery, Kevin Costner, and Charlie Martin Smith.

Eliot Ness raids a Chicago warehouse.

meant gaining twenty-five pounds in a mere five weeks, which Bobby achieved by devouring immense portions of pasta, potatoes, desserts, beer, and whole milk. Much of this was consumed in Italy, as he hastily went there to master the nuances of language. Since his participation was something of an afterthought—rather than the film's raison d'être, as had been the case with *Raging Bull*—De Niro was working under time pressure, and he himself was disappointed in what he was able to achieve, later insisting, "I wish I could have been heavier!" However, when it was over, he also said, "Gaining the weight was very hard, very, very depressing. It's the last time I'll ever do that."

Still, when shooting began, De Niro felt it necessary to add even more bulk to his body, borrowing a latex "body suit" that had allowed Treat Williams to believably play J. Edgar Hoover in a made-for-TV movie. As with *Raging Bull*, Bobby changed the shape of his nose, using a series of plugs that created a broader appearance while also having his entire head "relandscaped" so it more closely approximated the look of Capone in old photos and

newsreels. As the actor told critic Jack Kroll, "I had this ponytail I wore in *Angel Heart*. It sounds simple, but it took a week, sitting in a barber's chair for seven hours at a stretch while they snipped and shaved and tweezed, checking with photographs of Capone. It was incredible; if just one hair was off, it looked artificial."

Though De Niro had Armani as the studio-designated costume designer, he redesigned his wardrobe entirely, with the help of a tailor in New York's Little Italy, to conform more with the reality of Capone. When De Niro learned that Big Al had worn silk underwear, purchased only from a store called A. Sulka and Co., he immediately ordered silk underwear from that store, then wore it exclusively during filming. Little matter that there are no scenes allowing us to see De Niro/Capone in his underwear; this was one of those actor's keys that helped Bobby lock into the character.

In a scene derived from Eisenstein's 1925 classic *Battleship Potemkin*, Ness confronts the Capone gang in Union Station while a baby carriage somehow slips into the fray.

Diversity is, of course, a major factor in De Niro's choices, and he had already played the young Don Corleone. Was yet another gangster really worth his while? Bobby decided that the two characters being gangsters was a less significant similarity than it at first seems—given that these were very different men, in very different movies, filmed by very different directors. Even the backgrounds of the characters (which dictated the vocal inflections De Niro had to master) were dissimilar, as De Niro later reflected: *"The Godfather* characters were Sicilian, Capone was Neapolitan. The Sicilian is a darker personality, closer to Africa. The Neapolitans are more lively and flamboyant," which made playing Capone "fun" in a way the more intense and serious Don Corleone had not been.

For what would amount to six scenes, shot in a brief two weeks, De Niro had embarked on a full three months of painstaking preparation, spending long days in front of full-length mirrors, trying on different suits, ties, and the long coats that would cover them. Reportedly, he even spent several hours studying himself with different-sized cigars in his mouth, wanting to hone in on precisely the right one that would make his Capone vivid

and convincing—accurate to both the real Capone and De Palma's conception of him for the film. Producer Linson merely shrugged when asked about this exhausting, expensive, almost obsessive attention to detail on De Niro's part and said, "Bob has earned the right to do all that."

In addition to the physical, though, De Niro also achieves an even more important psychological parity with any character. So he not only studied every old photograph and scrap of newsreel film on Capone to insure that the look was right—from the natty clothing to the cocky walk—but also read everything he could get his hands on about Capone, especially articles and books that contradicted one another in their opinions, hoping a complex, rather than simplistic, characterization might jell. One little-known book that impressed him was by a man who had done odd jobs for Big Al and also played piano in one of Capone's clubs, eventually advising the inwardly troubled mobster to visit a psychiatrist. Capone had initially entered into therapy with much enthusiasm, pouring out his heart and soul to the doctor, then— suddenly becoming terrified about the person (helpful? curious? nosy?) to whom he had entrusted so much dangerous knowledge—ruthlessly ordered the shrink rubbed out. As *Newsweek*'s Kroll wrote: "The mind boggles at the thought—that might have made the greatest scene in the movie."

Those words are right on target, for a film about that relationship would certainly have been far more original and intriguing than anything we see here—allowing Bobby the chance to create the kind of Capone characterization he wanted to achieve, but does not. The many fine qualities here include the handsome period design, the evocative Ennio Morricone music, and of course De Niro as Capone. The movie's memorable moments are those focusing on him: the opening, in which Capone sits on a barber's chair as if it were a throne, luxuriating in simultaneously being shaved and sharing his philosophy on life with gathered reporters who hang on his every word; one marvelous bit in the middle, when he marches ceremoniously down his staircase, looking in his incongruously elegant clothes (camel's hair coat, cashmere suit, natty fedora) like a Jake La Motta with brains and style but not a whit more compassion. Or, best of all, weeping at the melodramatic complications of an opera, only to be interrupted by a henchman who reports an enemy has been bloodily dispatched, eliciting a cruel grin. As Stanley Kauffmann wrote in *The New Republic:* "Robert De Niro . . . gives Capone the clumsy theatricality of a barbarian who wants to be a ham."

The baseball-bat scene, in which Capone initially speaks charmingly at a testimonial tuxedo dinner for a colleague, then uses the bat to violently beat the man to death, is a virtual replaying of a scene in Billy Wilder's 1959 comedy *Some Like It Hot.* That scene was played as a burlesque of similar scenes from serious gangster movies (notably, Nicholas Ray's 1958 *Party Girl*), while here it is all but impossible to tell whether the filmmakers are resurrecting the clichés at face value or doing yet another parody that doesn't quite come off. The weakest scene occurs earlier, when a furious Ness bursts into the baronial hotel where Capone maintains his headquarters. So overwhelmed is the film's wimpish Ness by De Niro's vibrantly menacing Capone that Big Al's words momentarily recall those of La Motta. "You wanna do it now?" De Niro shrieks at this lame interloper. "Wanna go to the mat?" If *The Untouchables* was intended as an epic duel between good and evil, it fails if only because Kevin Costner seems so pathetically inadequate to his antagonist.

Still, *The Untouchables* proved a considerable box-office success, costing $25 million to make and bringing in $15.9 million in its first week alone, remaining a solid draw throughout the summer of 1987. Most critics were positive, too: Terrence Rafferty of *The Nation* admired the film as "a clean, uncomplicated piece of Hollywood entertainment," while Richard Schickel of *Time* went over the top, heedily hailing this as "a masterpiece of idiomatic American moviemaking." Tom O'Brien of *Commonweal* was one of the few who demurred, dismissing it as "an evil film—exquisite-looking schlock." In *The Humanist,* Prof. Harry M. Geduld rightly described De Niro's performance as "florid, almost operatic"; David Ansen of *Newsweek* similarly called it "a bravura cameo . . . flamboyantly entertaining." Schickel: "In Robert De Niro's grandly scaled performance he is demonically expansive, our first thug celebrity." Even Pauline Kael in *The New Yorker* had uncharacteristically (for this period) kind words: "The magnificent widescreen vistas require a villain on a grand scale, and Robert De Niro's Alphonse Capone is a plump peacock. . . . De Niro isn't in many scenes, but his impact is so strong that we wouldn't want more of him."

But De Niro could not even begin to approximate his lofty ambitions for the piece. He once said, "I've never seen [Capone] done the way I think it should be done. Capone wasn't just pure evil. He had to be a politician, an administrator. He had to have something going for him other than just fear." Compare that statement with the following line from Schickel's rave: "What [De Niro/Capone] evokes, finally, is pure horror . . . the film is rigorous on this point—no sympathy." De Niro had intended to do the most intricate Capone ever, yet what emerges has more in common with Neville Brand's delightfully over-the-top cartoon performance as Capone in TV's *The Untouchables.*

Still, De Niro appears to be having great fun with it all: cynically informing reporters that he's not a criminal but a public-spirited citizen, responding to community needs and the will of the people by providing the liquor they want during Prohibition, gleefully explaining that he learned in his old neighborhood "you can get further with a kind word—and a gun—than you can with just a kind word"; telling an avid listener that he's against violence "because it's bad for business"; finally exploding with rage when harassed by Ness and informing his henchmen that "I want him dead, I want his family dead, I want to go there in the middle of the night and piss on the ashes." Little wonder that David Denby exclaimed in *New York:* "De Niro, so often chary of words, digs into Capone's self-serving rant with evident pleasure. He's always been a great actor; this is the first time he's seemed an exuberant one."

A WOLF CAPTURED IN A COMEDY:

Jack Walsh attempts to bring The Duke (Charles Grodin) in, despite competition from the FBI, the mob, and a fellow bounty hunter.

Midnight Run

(1988)

A Universal Film

CAST:

Robert De Niro (*Jack Walsh*); Charles Grodin (*Jonathan Mardukas*); Yaphet Kotto (*Alonzo Mosely*); John Ashton (*Marvin Dorfler*); Dennis Farina (*Jimmy Serrano*); Joe Pantoliano (*Eddie Moscone*); Richard Foronjy (*Tony Darvo*); Robert Miranda (*Joey*); Jack Kehoe (*Jerry Geisler*); Wendy Phillips (*Gail*); Danielle DuClos (*Denise*).

CREDITS:

Producer and director, Martin Brest; executive producer, William S. Gilmore; screenplay, George Gallo; photography, Donald Thorin; production designer, Angelo Graham; costume designer, Gloria Gresham; editors, Billy Weber, Chris Lebenzon and Michael Tronick; music, Danny Elfman; running time, 122 minutes; rating: R.

Midnight Run stands out in the canon of De Niro films as the most clearly commercial venture he has ever appeared in, a marvelously crafted work of popular buddy-buddy entertainment without any of the substance De Niro ordinarily goes for in his projects. Perhaps he had been without a major hit for so long (he has, in fact, never consistently been a box-office attraction) that it seemed a wise career move to get into a film with commerciality written all over it. Perhaps he thought it would be fun to try a more relaxed, less intense performance, just to show the public (and perhaps himself) that he can let down his hair and have a good time, working in an upscale action-comedy rather than in ultraserious art. At any rate, *Midnight Run* performed precisely as it was supposed to.

Brian D. Johnson of *MacLean's* noted that the secret of success was "an ingenious script [that] transcends a familiar formula." Nicely put, and right on target: De Niro is cast as Jack Walsh, a onetime cop—rough around the edges but as honest as the day is long—who, after losing his position on the Chicago police force, survives as a modern-day bounty hunter. He's hired by a sleazy, weaselly bail bondsman (Joe Pantoliano), for a hefty $100,000, to run down an eccentric embezzler who jumped bail and is currently in New York. Jack has but four days (before the bail bondsman loses his investment) to bring this fugitive back to Los Angeles and hand him over to the authorities. Picking up Jonathan Mardukas (Grodin) in Brooklyn is easy enough to do, though the moment Jack meets the soft-spoken and appealingly wimpish family man, Jack realizes he's not dealing with your common white-collar criminal. True, Jonathan embezzled $15 million—but rather than a selfish yuppie, Jon turns out to be an accountant who, without his knowledge, was hired to work for an organized-crime boss (Dennis Farina). Upon realizing the corruption he'd inadvertently become involved with, Jon lifted the gangster's money, then—a contemporary Robin Hood—gave it away to charity.

Jack handcuffs himself to Jonathan and they start west, though their simple trek—a plane trip—doesn't work out owing to Jonathan's phobia about flying (it is one of his endless array of quirks). Essentially, Jon is Felix Unger while Jack is Oscar Madison, and this is *The Odd Couple* reconceived as an action-road flick rather than a situation comedy. Their expulsion from the plane (Jon purposefully lapses into loud convulsions) causes the two to travel by train, bus, and car (then train again, as freight hoppers) in what becomes an exciting though funny odyssey—part violent-chase thriller, part charac-

Robert De Niro as Jack Walsh, ex-Chicago cop turned bounty hunter.

Special Agent Alonzo Mosely (Yaphet Kotto, right) and his men
interrogate Jack during a stopover in Chicago.

ter comedy—as they are pursued (and attacked) not only
by henchmen of that mobster who wants Jonathan dead
before he can testify (and who coincidentally was the
man who caused Jack to get bounced from the force),
but also by a rival bounty hunter (John Ashton) eager to
be the one who turns the fugitive in and collects that fat
reward, as well as an FBI agent (Yaphet Kotto) hoping to
persuade Jonathan to testify for him.

The plot of George Gallo's script is intriguingly complicated, the action complex and marvelously staged.
One extended chase sequence involving all the princi-
pals tearing through mountain passages, firing back and
forth from cars to helicopters, is perhaps the best thing
ever done of this type. Better still, for a work of this
genre, the emotions run surprisingly deep, as Jack and
Jonathan, who initially irritate each other so, come to
care deeply for one another. The droll, condescending
Jon develops a sincere concern over Jack's indulgence in
alcohol, tobacco, and cholesterol-laden foods. The sensitive inner-Jack slips out from behind the tough-guy
facade, admitting he only wants to open a little restaurant with his profits from this job.

Johnson, of *MacLean's*, wrote: "His face creased with
shifting currents of anxiety and rage, De Niro is utterly
believable as the working stiff desperately trying to do
his job. And Grodin, as the white-collar criminal who

chides his captor about the dangers of smoking, serves as
his deadpan foil." Richard Schickel of *Time:* "It is De
Niro's work that redeems an inherently improbable plot.
He handles guns, quips, and tight spots with the requisite élan. He brings something else to the part, too: a
deftly imagined sense of hard roads traveled before he
hit this one, of a past lived, not just alluded to. When you
root for him, you root for a man, not a killing machine."

John Simon of *National Review* wrote: "De Niro has a
marvelous way of scrunching up his face into a smile of
agony, as well as of exploding on the installment plan,
and he somehow manages to play his part to the hilt even
while faintly suggesting that he is kidding it. He oozes
canniness and determination along with a lot of repressed decency, as his compact, streamlined frame
races ahead on unleaded nervous energy." David Ansen
of *Newsweek* found Bobby "overqualified" for the modest demands made on him here, while Terrence Rafferty
of *The New Yorker* noted that "his gestures, especially
the movements of his head, are hilarious, because he
looks as if he were trying so hard not to make them. It's as
if the actor were afraid that he'd overwhelm his slender
role by using the full range of his expressive gifts." Also,
Stanley Kauffmann of *The New Republic* noted that De
Niro seemed to be "a wolf captured in a comedy,
twisting, snarling, snapping, lunging, kept from the

As helicopters swirl overhead, rival bounty hunter Marvin Dorfler (John Ashton) temporarily halts his friendly-enemy competition with Jack in order to help him defend the Duke from enemies who descend from the sky.

Walsh forces The Duke to verify their whereabouts to a bail bondsman.

purely feral by his sense of humor and by the cool professionalism at the root of his behavior."

Action fans of course recall the big chase scene, while lovers of comedy remember the humorous give-and-take as Jon first warns Jack about the financial dangers of starting a restaurant, then suggests gourmet dishes (such as lyonnaise potatoes) he might serve. But for fans of movie characterization, perhaps the most touching moment occurs when the two make a side trip to visit the home of Jack's ex-wife (Wendy Phillips), now remarried, borrowing her car so that they can get away. Just before Jack shuts the door on Jon, he tucks the man's coat in, and the brief bit (blink and you'll miss it) adds a wealth of texture and humanity, suggesting the nature of the relationship between Jack and his wife (clearly, he habitually did this for her) before the breakup, making this a moving human story rather than one more kiss-kiss/bang-bang pyrotechnical exercise in superficial shoot 'em up. No wonder, then, that David Blum of *New York* neatly tagged it "the *My Dinner With Andre* of action movies."

Though the genre limitations did not allow for the kind of soul-searching work that's at the base of most De

Mobsters Tony (Richard Foronjy) and Joey (Robert Miranda) try and take The Duke away from Jack.

The situation grows ever more desperate for Jack and The Duke.

would not hear of anyone else, however lofty a box-office draw that person might be. Owing to that, Paramount dropped the picture and Universal picked it up. Though with a bigger name in the costarring role this might have been a blockbuster, Brest's integrity is to be admired, for it could not possibly have been a better film.

After meeting for the first time for a reading at the Sherry Netherland Hotel, De Niro and Grodin initially sensed (just as their characters do) how very different they were. Then, like Jack and Jon, they slowly, cautiously developed a warm relationship that, by movie's end, left them close friends. Afterward, Grodin recalled that De Niro, such a bug for authenticity, insisted on doing his own stunt driving for all the zany chase sequences. "Who the hell knows what kind of a driver Robert De Niro is?" he later wailed. "All you know is he's a guy who'll gain a lot of weight or lose a lot of weight. He's Mr. Realism. So he's going to drive that thing full out. I don't know what his skills are. So a lot of what you see [on-screen] is actually happening" (in terms of Grodin's horrified expression). He also insisted that now, whenever the two friends drive anywhere, Grodin always takes the wheel, never De Niro: "I ain't going anywhere with him driving!"

Niro performances, some improvisation did lead to quality results. Chief among them is the scene on a train in which Jack first confesses his desire to open a restaurant, at which point his prisoner disagrees: "As your accountant, I'd have to recommend against that." In Gallo's script, the rather flat line had been: "As an accountant . . . " Grodin changed the single word, subtly altering the situation as the seemingly soft Jon is, in a quiet kind of way, assuming power and control in the relationship. De Niro, knowing that once a single improvisation has happened it's impossible to stick with the script as written, then responded as his character logically would, trying to regain dominance: "Well, you're not my accountant." Grodin then naturally has to improvise once again: "I know, I'm only saying, if I *were* your accountant." The appealing, understated argument—in which they sound like a pair of grannies grumbling—goes on for a full minute; though they don't receive screen credit, Grodin and De Niro were responsible for this telling "writing."

Originally, the notion had been to team De Niro with another full-fledged superstar; Paramount executives agreed to take on the project with that concept in mind. Various big names were mentioned, among them Cher! But the superstar who actively campaigned for the part was Robin Williams (he would have to wait three years to work with Bobby, in *Awakenings*). Williams went so far as to audition for the role, all but unheard of for a star of his stature. Director Brest, meanwhile, had come to believe Grodin was the only person to play the part and

The cast of characters, clockwise, from top left, includes: Yaphet Kotto as the FBI agent, John Ashton as a rival bounty hunter, Dennis Farina as the mob boss, and Joe Pantoliano as the bail bondsman.

Megs attempts to help his friend Dave (Ed Harris).

Jacknife

(1989)

Cineplex Odeon Films/Kings Road Entertainment

CAST:

Robert De Niro (*Joseph "Megs" Megessey*); Ed Harris (*Dave*); Kathy Baker (*Martha*); Charles Dutton (*Jake*); Loudon Wainwright III (*Ferretti*); Tom Isbell (*Bobby*); Elizabeth Franz (*Pru*).

CREDITS:

Director, David Jones; producers, Robert Schaffel and Carol Baum; screenplay, Stephen Metcalfe, from his play *Strange Snow*; photography, Brian West; production designer, Edward Pisoni; editor, John Bloom; music, Bruce Broughton; running time, 102 minutes; rating: R.

De Niro returned to *Deer Hunter* territory, for a similar characterization but not, alas, the same commercial and critical success, in *Jacknife*. This was clearly an attempt to tell a small, serious story, doing so in a restrained, intelligent way, with an emphasis on charac-

terization and the complex tension between people in a close relationship. Occasionally, the film does succeed on that level; mostly, though, *Jacknife* rates as lukewarm, due to second-rate melodramatic writing.

De Niro is cast as Joseph Megessey, known as Megs to most everyone, though he has another, more private nickname. His best buddy, Bobby, always called him Jacknife, though Megs has not been referred to as that since Bobby perished during the Vietnam War. Megs survived combat and returned; now, he is one of the walking wounded, a slightly deranged vet (suffering from "post-Vietnam stress syndrome") who cannot quite fit in with society. Referred to as a burnout, he at least is able to make a living as a car repairman, though another wartime comrade is not so fortunate. Dave (Ed Harris), a drunken truck driver, has all but retreated from life during the decade and a half that followed their return, so Megs takes on the responsibility of drawing Dave out of his shell by coaxing him to enjoy life again, also urging Dave to face up to some of the darker memories, thereby hopefully setting them aside. While accomplishing this, Megs also falls in love with Dave's sister, Martha, a schoolteacher.

One problem with the script by playwright Stephen Metcalfe is that it doesn't provide the audience with what we most need near the beginning: a sense of past closeness between Megs and Dave that would help us understand why Megs becomes so dedicated to solving Dave's problems now, even at the cost of giving up what little happiness he's found for himself. There's no sense of what drew Megs to the small Connecticut town where Dave and Martha live, whether Megs consciously sought Dave out or if it was coincidental. Yet we do get the feeling that Dave is none too thrilled about having Megs

show up at his house ("He was not my friend, just a guy I was in the war with," he tells his sister) with the excuse that they once planned (while in Nam) to spend the first day of the fishing season together. Therefore, the "bond" that causes them to tolerate each other, no matter what, is apparently nothing more than that they were in the same outfit during the war—and it is not enough to sustain our belief.

Toward the end, we finally get a sense that Dave's catharsis can only grow out of his first acknowledging, then accepting responsibility for the death of the unseen though much-discussed Bobby. As that character was Megs's best friend, we finally grasp that that's the reason why Megs chose to look up Dave at this late date. But rather than a moment-of-truth revelation, the information arrives much too late, leaving us wishing that the

Robert De Niro as Megs.

191

One of the walking-wounded left over from Vietnam, Megs finds himself attracted to Dave's sister, Martha (Kathy Baker).

film had allowed us more of a sense of this earlier, so we could have better understood the drama as it was unfolding. Worse, what's never comprehensible, even after the movie is over, is why Megs would show up after fifteen years, rather than on the first day of the fishing season following their return home. Apparently, he has been haunted by ghosts of Nam all along, and they finally catch up with him, but we nonetheless need and never get some sense of the trigger that finally sets him off.

The love story, though a bit contrived, is far superior to the postwar angst, which is respectably done but seemed, arriving on-screen in 1989, awfully familiar, with the words about the inability of onetime combatants to adjust echoing *Distant Thunder* and a dozen other films that had appeared since *The Deer Hunter* and *Coming Home*. The best moments in the romantic plot are, conversely, those that were most original, such as the scruffy De Niro trying to clean up his act, shaving and putting on a suit so he could accompany the straitlaced teacher to a prom she's scheduled to chaperon. Moments like this are tender as well as unique, though even they are underdeveloped. One gets the sense that there was supposed to be more to it than there is, not only in terms of plot but also emotional resonance.

Fireworks do happen when Dave crashes the prom and makes an embarrassing scene, but even this is far too easy to see coming. The film is also theatrical—based on a play, developing its story line less as cinematic narrative than as a drama, statically bound to a single place, a feeling director David Jones (*Betrayal, 84 Charing Cross Road*) was unable to alleviate. Even the best dialogue sounds more stagy than cinematic, as when the

repressed if flustered Martha, describing her relationship with the distant Dave to concerned Megs, says, "Sometimes I eat with David; David, however, eats alone."

A number of critics felt *Jacknife* appeared in the wrong medium. In the *Village Voice*, Renee Tajima pointed out that "*Jacknife* is reminiscent of television's golden age, when stellar acting, direction, and a powerhouse cast—not glittering images—made the drama." Kevin Thomas of the *Los Angeles Times* tagged *Jacknife* "a small independent film, more suited to television in its scale. . . . As admirable and affecting as it is, you cannot help but feel it would have more impact as a Hallmark Hall of Fame presentation." Less kind was David Ehrenstein of the *Los Angeles Herald-Examiner*, who dismissed *Jacknife* as being no better than an ordinary made-for-TV problem picture that pretends to seriousness while ducking any in-depth portrayal of the issues: "When a film features actors of the caliber of Robert De Niro, Ed Harris, and Kathy Baker, a minimal level of dramatic interest is guaranteed. But in *Jacknife*, that minimum barely registers. While the stars do their best, they can't hide the fact that this melodrama about emotionally scarred Vietnam veterans is thin, listless, and trite."

Generally, De Niro received good reviews even when the film was being panned. *Variety* stated that "Robert De Niro's tour-de-force turn as a feisty Vietnam vet fails to save *Jacknife*, a poorly scripted three-character drama." Similarly, Thomas commented that while *Jacknife* is "a work of standard kitchen-sink realism that cries for a more boldly cinematic" presentation, "there's absolutely nothing pedestrian about Robert De Niro, Ed Harris, and Kathy Baker." Not everyone agreed; De Niro did something here he had not done before, which is to repeat himself. The role is essentially the same character he played in *The Deer Hunter,* so much so that the film practically plays as a sequel to that movie—without any of the raw power or cinematic brilliance. Which helps explain Janet Maslin's less-than-thrilled reaction in the *New York Times:* "There may be no such thing as a typical Robert De Niro film, but certainly *Jacknife* is atypical, since it gives Mr. De Niro so little chance to shine. . . . De Niro gives Megs the kind of rollicking, good-old-boy manner that, in this sort of fiction, always masks a heart of gold." Stanley Kauffmann of *The New Republic* likewise found this an awfully easy role for Bobby to play: "Though De Niro is certainly good, his vigor and explosiveness seem old reliable De Niro qualities rather than the specifics that the other two bring to their performances." No one was doubting that De Niro remained our most gifted and remarkable actor; however, Pauline Kael was no longer alone in finding things to criticize in his work. The question now was raised: Had De Niro, in his brilliant earlier work, already given us the best of what he had to offer?

Megs cleans up his act for the sake of Martha, a respectable professional woman.

Megs courts Martha as best he can.

Sean Penn and Robert De Niro as the convicts who pretend to be priests.

We're No Angels

(1989)

A Paramount Release

CAST:

Robert De Niro (*Ned*); Sean Penn (*Jim*); Demi Moore (*Molly*); Hoyt Axton (*Father Levesque*); Bruno Kirby (*Deputy*); Ray McAnally (*Warden*); James Russo (*Bobby*); Wallace Shawn (*Translator*); Jessica Jickels (*Rosie*); John C. Reilly (*Young Monk*); Elizabeth Lawrence (*Mrs. Blair*).

CREDITS:

Director, Neil Jordan; producer, Art Linson; executive producer, Robert De Niro; screenplay, David Mamet from the 1955 screenplay by Ranald MacDougall, adapted from the play by Sam and Bella Spewak, based on *La Cuisine de Anges* by Albert Husson; photography, Philippe Rousselot; production designer, Wolf Kroeger; costume designer, Theoni V. Aldredge; editors, Mick Audsley and Joke Van Wijk; music, George Fenton; running time, 108 minutes; rating: PG-13.

Listed in the credits as "executive producer," De Niro began his move to behind-the-camera involvement with this remake of a one time Humphrey Bogart vehicle. The 1955 *We're No Angels* was no great shakes of a movie, by any means. Concerning three Devil's Island escapees (Bogart, Peter Ustinov, and Aldo Ray) who hide out in the home of a family on Christmas Eve only to change those people's lives for the better, redeeming themselves in the process, it offered a strange combination of moral fable and black humor. Director Michael Curtiz couldn't disguise the fact that the project was based on a popular Broadway play, *My Three Angels* (itself taken from a French farce), so the film remains stage-bound throughout: simple camera setups photographing actors on a single set. The worst thing you can say about the 1955 version is that it's less a movie than a filmed play.

Ironically, that's the one and only negative thing that can't be said about the 1989 version. Producer Art Linson announced from the outset that this was only

Jim (Sean Penn) and Ned (Robert De Niro) escape from jail . . .

. . . and disguise themselves as priests. De Niro has often played criminals or men of the cloth; here he had the opportunity to play both.

"very loosely based on some of the ideas" found in the original. Set along the U.S./Canadian border, it concerns the attempts of two dim-witted Depression-era New England jailbirds, Ned (De Niro) and Jim (Sean Penn), to cross over into Canada, where U.S. lawmen will not be able to retrieve them. A third, murderously inclined prisoner (James Russo) is also skulking about the border town, having escaped with them at the moment he was supposed to have been dispatched in the electric chair, though he is alien to the duo. The two heroes, meanwhile, disguise themselves as priests in hope of crossing over the bridge to freedom during the local religious pageant. The key conceit in David Mamet's screenplay is that they make it halfway across only to be turned back, time and time again, for some new and supposedly funny reason.

The images of De Niro and Penn, in costume, nervously approaching the bridge—cutting from them to their point-of-view shots—are, as rendered by director Neil Jordan (*The Company of Wolves, Mona Lisa*), completely cinematic. There is nothing whatsoever like this in the older version, in which the lovable criminals simply sat around in the living room of bourgeois home, talking endlessly (if appealingly.) Then again, there is in the new version none of the cleverness, the charm, and the brittle humor of the original. As Vincent Canby claimed in the *New York Times,* "the movie proceeds at the pace of a child reluctant to go to bed. It dawdles over irrelevant details and grows sleepier and sleepier until it seems to be snoozing, though still standing up."

Hot-tempered Molly (Demi Moore) teaches Ned what Women's Lib is all about.

A tough frontierswoman, Mrs. Blair (Elizabeth Lawrence) holds the boys at gunpoint.

Though disguised as a priest, Ned finds himself highly attracted to Molly.

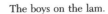
The boys on the lam.

What attracted De Niro to the material? Most likely, the Catholic concept of redemption. Initially, Ned and Jim take on the garb of priests only to make their escape that much easier. But the border town is famed for its shrine of the Weeping Madonna, a statue of the Virgin Mary believed to excrete actual tears; in fact, the roof simply leaks over the statue's head. The two men, meanwhile, are mistaken for visiting ecclesiastical scholars, their every word treated by the locals as fraught with wisdom. For a while, it's humorous to hear the ignorant, near-illiterate criminals improvising ideas, and to watch the crowd beam with admiration at what they believe to be the gems of spiritual knowledge. Ultimately, then, *We're No Angels* is meant as a religious parable; posing as priests, the tough guys gradually find themselves transforming into priestlike people.

There is another link to previous De Niro pictures. Bobby has been fond of playing characters who, though not professional actors, find themselves acting a role in life. His parts in such diverse movies as *Greetings, Taxi Driver, King of Comedy, Brazil, Raging Bull, Angel Heart, Stanley and Iris,* and *Cape Fear* are all people whose strategy in life is to perform at being something totally different from what they actually are. It's fascinating to note how many De Niro films are, at least by implication, actually about the business of acting.

It was De Niro who instigated the project. He and the then-twenty-eight-year-old enfant terrible Sean Penn had become close friends and were looking for a project to do together. When they approached Linson, De Niro's producer on *The Untouchables*, he recalled that

Ned converses with a Yugoslavian bishop (Wallace Shawn).

197

Jim sneaks a cigarette.

Director Neil Jordan (left) confers with De Niro, Penn, and producer Art Linson on location.

198

Paramount owned the rights to *Angels,* phoning David Mamet (who had penned the *Untouchables* script), suggesting Mamet take a stab at the screenplay. Though not at first thrilled with the idea, Mamet gave it a shot; but the actor was less than overawed with what Mamet wrote. De Niro admitted while on a break during the filming, "That sometimes happens. But I read it again, and the more I read it, the more I liked it. Now I see more in the script every day. This is not just a story about escaped convicts. It has a lot of levels to it." That only proves the old adage about how important it is to trust one's first reaction to anything.

Some of the problems were due to the highly talented but incongruously chosen crew—U.S., Canadian, English, Irish, a few assorted Europeans—each member of the group being an expert in his field, be it costume design or cinematography, but each committed to an artistic vision that had little in common with the vision of anyone else on the project. Mamet's terse Chicago-esque prose was not only all wrong for what should have been breezy material, but also was particularly unsuited to the fairy-tale approach ordinarily taken by Irish-born director Jordan. He, working on his first American film, and for the first time directing a script he had not written himself, was less than comfortable directing Method actors. "The internal logic of a character, what he does and why, is very important to American actors," he sighed on the set. "But English actors coming from a theatrical background don't need to examine the psychological realism of their parts." If nothing else, *We're No Angels* offers proof that a film cannot succeed on the basis of the sum of its collaborators; their collective talent is not enough if there is no sense of community tying those talents together into a single artistic knot.

The film, budgeted at $20 million, was shot on a lake approximately fifty miles east of Vancouver. The set designers built all twenty-three of the border town's buildings, from the huge hotel to the little blacksmith's shop, from scratch at a cost of $2.5 million, resulting in the largest single film set ever constructed in Canada. Demi Moore literally fought for the right to be in the picture, playing the part of a single mother who helps convert De Niro's Ned to true Christian thinking, and she does bring a conviction to the character that helps make this flawed, foolish work at least bearable.

As for reviews of De Niro's work, most critics were tougher than ever before. Georgia Brown of *The Village Voice* wrote that "De Niro plays the more earthbound 'Father Reilly' by screwing up his face and bobbing as if he's doing an 'oriental gentleman,'" while David Ansen of *Newsweek* bemoaned "a heavily mugging De Niro." David Brooks of the *Wall Street Journal* similarly noted that "Mr. DeNiro [*sic*] is surprisingly inept, mugging throughout the movie with what he seems to think is a comic expression."

More charitable was Michael Wilmongton of the *Los Angeles Times,* who wrote that "De Niro takes the gruff, embittered, knit-eyebrows stance he used for his bounty hunter in *Midnight Run* and takes it further. He digs himself in, plants his face like a clenched fist, and works up four or five comic glowers and variations on wary, disguised hostility." Even this kind review, however, pointed out that Bobby was at last repeating himself.

A MODERN RIP VAN WINKLE:

Robert De Niro as
Leonard Lowe, modern
Rip Van Winkle.

Awakenings

(1990)

A Columbia Pictures Presentation

CAST:

Robert De Niro (*Leonard Lowe*); Robin Williams (*Dr. Malcolm Sayer*); Julie Kavner (*Eleanor Costello*); Ruth Nelson (*Mrs. Lowe*); John Heard (*Dr. Kaufman*); Penelope Ann Miller (*Paula*); Alice Drummond (*Lucy*); Judith Malina (*Rose*); Anne Meara (*Miriam*); Richard Libertini (*Sidney*); Dexter Gordon (*Rolando*); Max Von Sydow (*Dr. Ingham*).

CREDITS:

Director, Penny Marshall; producers, Walter F. Parkes and Lawrence Lasker; screenplay, Steven Zaillian; based on the book by Oliver Sacks, M.D.; photography, Miroslav Ondricek; production designer, Anton Furst; costume designer, Cynthia Flynt; editors, Jerry Greenberg and Battle Davis; music, Randy Newman; running time, 121 minutes; rating: PG-13.

Awakenings seemed an unlikely choice for De Niro, if somewhat less so than *Midnight Run* because of the

remarkable acting challenge it offered. Still, the film—for all its considerable qualities, De Niro chief among them—looked suspiciously like an A-movie equivalent of the made-for-TV disease-of-the-week flick, though done with a panache for sweet/sad sentimentality that director Penny Marshall had previously revealed in *Big*.

The film was based on a 1973 book by Dr. Oliver Sacks, in which the nonconformist/neurologist recounted his experience of some five years earlier. A researcher with little practice dealing with people, he was hired by a Bronx hospital for his first hands-on job, conducting a controversial experiment with a number of catatonic patients. Dr. Sacks notices that the seeming vegetables were capable of a lucidity other medical people had overlooked, responding to selective stimuli. A dropped card would make the frozen cardplayers slap their own cards down violently; each responded to the sort of music he or she had most enjoyed before becom-

Dr. Malcolm Sayer (Robin Williams) helps Leonard readjust to the real
world.

Leonard finds himself falling in love with pretty Paula (Penelope Ann Miller) when she visits her father in the same hospital where Leonard has been sleeping his life away.

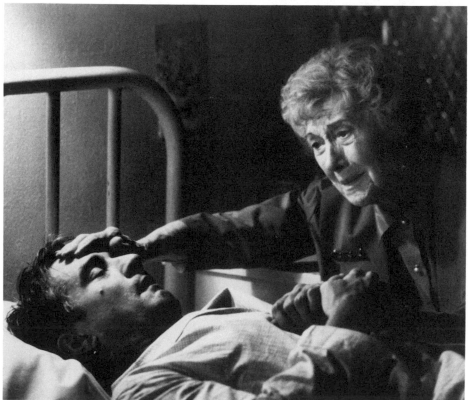

Mrs. Lowe (Ruth Nelson) comforts and cares for her sleeping-sickness son throughout his long illness.

The hospital staff and fellow patients gather around Leonard, as he attempts to stave off a relapse into his post-encephalitic state.

ing a virtual somnambulist. One, Leonard Lowe (in the movie, De Niro), even employed an Ouija board Sacks gave him to spell out a reference to the poet Rilke's lines about being a caged panther. That caused Sacks to understand these people were not, as had been assumed, brain-dead and beyond help, but rather "alive inside"—so he began searching for the key that might unlock them.

What he discovered was that these diverse patients from drastically different backgrounds all had a single thing in common. During the epidemic of sleeping sickness that spread around the world between 1916 and 1927, every one had been stricken by encephalitis, then had seemingly recovered—not falling into the catatonic state until years later. This is why no one had diagnosed the current vegetablelike existence as being related to the earlier, long-forgotten sickness. Convinced that was indeed the cause of the stasislike (and supposedly inexplicable) problem, Sacks—over rigorous medical opposition—administered a new and virtually untested "miracle drug" (L-dopa), which did indeed bring the patients back into the everyday world for a few months. Yet the

period of elation, in which they transformed into modern-day Rip Van Winkles wandering out to explore a brave new world, was short-lived. When the effects of the drug wore off, they gradually reverted to catatonia.

In the script by Steven Zaillian (*Falcon and the Snowman*), the events were fictionalized, even the name of Dr. Sacks being changed to Malcolm Sayer so Robin Williams would enjoy a certain freedom in playing him. Williams did not receive a much-deserved Best Actor Oscar nomination for this role; however, De Niro did receive a nomination for his work as Leonard, the first patient Dr. Sayer works with and, in the movie version, the focal one.

The two develop an intriguing odd-couple relationship, the brainy nerd that Williams plays beautifully complimented by the freewheeling, life-loving fellow De Niro so effectively (and affectionately) incarnates on-screen. When he did not win (Best Actor instead went to Jeremy Irons for *Reversal of Fortune*), most Hollywood insiders believed that the decision had nothing to do with the quality of his work (precisely what such decisions should be, but seldom are, based on), rather on

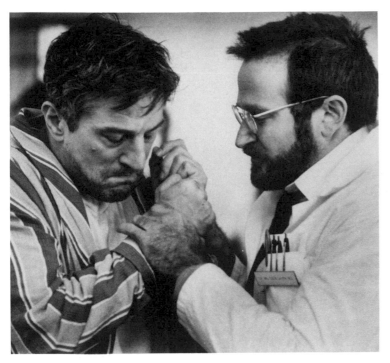

With the help of Dr. Sayer, Leonard attempts to live a normal life—or something approaching normalcy.

the fact that in the previous two years, Dustin Hoffman and Daniel Day-Lewis had won that statuette for *Rain Man* and *My Left Foot* playing similarly incapacitated characters. Academy voters were concerned that the Best Actor category could begin to look like a patient-of-the-year award, with anyone playing a "normal" man (however brilliantly) deemed out of the running.

Still, it was obvious that De Niro had done his homework thoroughly (the real Dr. Sacks, who admitted to being "in awe" of the actor's talent, made sure Bobby visited the right hospitals to observe patients with similar disabilities). The reviews were, understandably, mostly raves. David Denby of *New York* wrote that "his limbs and face, tilted, askew, like a ship listing badly, attain something like normality [after the drug]. . . . The most wonderful and frightening thing about De Niro's performance is the way, despite several paranoid outbreaks, he remains generally lucid throughout Leonard's increasing physical disarray, commenting bitterly on each defection of his body as it occurs [when the drug's effect wears off]. The process of alienation from one's own body—what we all go through as we age—has never been made so vivid [on-screen]." David Ansen of *Newsweek* concurred: "De Niro's role demands, and gets, a virtuoso performance—he goes from catatonia to elation and (finally) into states of paranoid megalomania and despair. He's superb." Ralph Novak, in *People,* relished the film's melodramatic flourishes and Bobby's partici-

Dr. Sayer takes Leonard and other patients into the world on a bus trip.

pation in them: "If anyone in the theater has a dry eye when the awakened De Niro walks across a room to hug his mother . . . check them for a heartbeat. It's a beautifully staged sequence, full of too-good-to-be-true exhilaration subtly controlled by Marshall, De Niro, and [Ruth] Nelson [as his Mom]. You assume De Niro will be spectacular, and he is, delivering all the pain, confusion, and childish joy his character is entitled to."

Richard Corliss, in *Time,* appraised the film as little more than an "upscale heart-tugger," nonetheless conceding: "To watch De Niro shrink into the shadow of catatonia is to be made aware of his great gifts of body control, of withdrawing into character, of seeming to be. It's an awesome show that reveals more about De Niro than about the man he is playing." In the same vein but assuming a harsher tone, John Simon, who otherwise trashed the film in the *National Review* (insisting Sacks's book had been "oversimplified, falsified, romanticized"), reined in his rush of invectives to praise Bobby: "The film's glory is the Leonard of Robert De Niro [who] once again amazes us with his ability [for] total submersion in a role, no matter how different from or dangerously similar to his last. This Leonard is too harrowingly real for facile sympathy, too much like us to dismiss with a few uplifting tears. If only the entire picture had as much grit as his contribution—but then Hollywood would cease being Hollywood."

More negative was Pauline Kael in *The New Yorker,* lacing her mild put-down with occasional backhanded compliments: "As for De Niro—well, when you're playing a silent, somnolent person who wakes up and soon

afterward erupts into madness, you certainly give the impression that you're acting. Twitching and shaking (impressively), De Niro is upping the ante on Dustin Hoffman's autistic savant in *Rain Man*. . . . He's giving you an actor's idea of a decent guy who'll be appealing to people. . . . Mostly, this too-muchness is [director] Marshall's [fault], but sometimes it's clearly De Niro's. When he holds out his arms to his mother, he knows he's a poster boy."

Most critics noted that there were, throughout the film, concessions to commerciality that cut away from the potential power, even as they insured that *Awakenings* would work as a crowd-pleaser. The hospital administrators (especially the one played by John Heard) are depicted as insensitive, stereotypical snobs, the courageous intellectual-rebel doctor standing alone against them. In fact, that is a dubious rewriting of what Dr. Sacks described in his book. The administrators were actually of varied attitudes—some seeing merit in Sacks's approach, others objecting to it for sound reasons, including their fear that what eventually does happen would happen.

Likewise, in real life Leonard was not the lovely fellow we meet here (who enters into a sweet, contrived, predictable romance with a lovely lady, charmingly played by Penelope Ann Miller), but a hysterical (if brilliant and Harvard-educated), libidinous character who harassed the nurses and proved dangerous (masturbating in public, threatening to rape female passersby) when allowed out on the street. Including this would have made the film less appealing, less accessible as a

Leonard and Dr. Sayer become close friends.

work of middlebrow entertainment, but far more fascinating. Certainly, a demanding (rather than diverting) filmmaker with a Scorsese-like desire for complexity would have insisted the audience witness all the dark sides of Leonard. What we see is powerful and touching, effective enough on the level of polished showmanship to win (and deserve) our tears. Still, the truth—if the filmmakers had dared to show it—could have been more devastating.

Finally, there's a ridiculous romance tacked on for the doctor, in which a fictional nurse (Julie Kavner) loves him from afar throughout the film, apparently without his ever noticing. Then, when Leonard and the others have slipped back into catatonia (in real life, some patients remained alert, though for the film it was believed that to have some revert and others stay normal would prove too confusing), the doctor suddenly asks the nurse for a date, suggesting that as a result of his experience with Leonard and the others, the doctor has himself finally awakened. This was done to leave us with a happy finale (the last image is of Williams and Kavner walking off hand in hand.) Better to recall De Niro's last great moment when, facing the fate he knows cannot be avoided, he stares into Williams's eyes and mourns, "Learn from me! Learn from me!"

Iris (Jane Fonda) attempts to apologize to Stanley after realizing that she has inadvertantly cost the man his job by exposing his illiteracy.

Stanley and Iris

(1990)

An MGM/UA Release

CAST:

Jane Fonda (*Iris*); Robert De Niro (*Stanley*); Swoosie Kurtz (*Sharon*); Martha Plimpton (*Kelly*); Harley Cross (*Richard*); Jamey Sheridan (*Joe*); Feodor Chaliapin (*Leonides*).

CREDITS:

Director, Martin Ritt; producers, Arlene Sellers and Alex Winitsky; executive producer, Patrick Palmer; screenplay, Irving Ravetch and Harriet Frank Jr.; based on the novel *Union Street* by Pat Barker; photography, Donald McAlpine; production designer, Joel Schiller; costume designer, Theoni V. Aldredge; editor, Sidney Levin; music, John Williams; running time, 102 minutes; rating: PG-13.

Stanley and Iris is a film by Martin Ritt, the aging director of such sweet-spirited if sometimes cloying social documents as *The Molly Maguires, Conrack,* and *Norma Rae.* Ritt, who has since passed away, always

spoke disparagingly of his best movie, 1963's cynical *Hud,* featuring Paul Newman as a heel-as-hero not unlike the one later played by De Niro in *New York, New York.* Ritt's more characteristic work attempts to portray some serious issue through the entanglements of extremely likable people. *Stanley and Iris* was just such a picture, which is why it's a lukewarm drama, despite the expected excitement of a De Niro–Jane Fonda matchup.

The social issue here was the quiet, generally overlooked problem of those 32 million American adults who are "functionally illiterate." Before tackling this problem, though, *Stanley and Iris* addresses another one: those sad New England mill towns, which a decade ago drew young people into the blue-collar trap of menial assembly-line jobs, but more recently left them lost and out of work as the factories, one by one, closed down. Iris (Fonda) is the widow of just such a worker, and the sole support of not only her teenage daughter, Kelly (Martha

Plimpton), and younger son, Richard (Harley Cross), but also a sister (Swoosie Kurtz) and her husband (Jamey Sheridan), who are unable or unwilling to make lives for themselves. Iris finds employment at a large bakery, managing to hold the family together.

Jane Fonda plays the part of this blue-collar saint in a slumming, patronizing, mannered way. When a thief attempts to grab Iris's purse, Stanley (De Niro), a cafeteria cook at the bakery, intervenes. These two people who have been working near each other without ever really saying hello thus form a friendship of sorts. But Stanley loses his job when his boss, suffering from a headache, asks him to get him some aspirin; Stanley brings him the wrong bottle of pills. As Iris discovers, Stanley can't read or write, and he now drifts from one menial job to the next. Iris offers to teach him how, but Stanley initially refuses. Then, desperate, he overcomes his deep embarrassment—shame, really—and reapproaches Iris, explaining that as a child he traveled around so much with his father, he never settled down at any one school long enough to learn.

As she teaches him, Stanley has such difficult moments that he threatens to quit, referring to himself as a

Blue collar blues: Iris convinces Stanley that he must make a serious effort to learn how to read and write.

Robert De Niro as Stanley Cox, functional illiterate.

"big dummy," though he is in fact a brilliant man who has never mastered this skill. As he does, he also falls deeply in love with Iris, and she with him. *Stanley and Iris* plays like an "educational film" despite the star power of Fonda and De Niro; it exists mainly to teach us about illiteracy, eventually revealing that ignorance has nothing whatsoever to do with intelligence. As Stanley Kauffmann noted in *The New Republic,* "the film takes too long to get to its reason for being, Stanley's illiteracy: before that, and after, it's laden with family decor that is supposed to provide texture but seems like mere padding."

One failure of the film derives from an inconsistency in the writing of De Niro's character. Though we are asked to believe that this intelligent man has devised an elaborate series of strategies to get through the day while keeping his secret shame hidden from others, we're also asked to accept that he has never devised a method to tell aspirin from other pills, by the shape of the bottle or the colorings on the label—making the key plot pivot seem highly suspicious. Certainly, someone as clever as Stanley would have covered himself here.

This proved an impossible film to dislike. David Denby of *New York* tagged it as "pleasing in a mild sort of way . . . in the earthy-liberal-humanist mode" that

Martin Ritt was known for. Pamela Young of *MacLean's* described the film as "plucky" and "well-intentioned, awash in the positive thinking," and that pretty much sums up the movie. Ritt was the Norman Vincent Peale of contemporary cinema. Young felt the need to add, though, that the film "is really more of a predictable love story than a relevant social commentary," and that strikes to the very heart of what's wrong with *Stanley and Iris*. The characters are generic, despite the best efforts of the two powerhouse stars to make them appear as something more. Their romance works out in the most obvious and expected ways.

Everyone involved apparently felt the need to gild the lily. Rather than merely depicting Stanley, like the one-fifth of the public that the Department of Education

Convinced that Iris is right, Stanley allows her to teach him how to read . . .

. . . eventually realizing that, far from stupid, he may actually be something of a creative genius.

insists is functionally illiterate, as a person of normal intelligence, the filmmakers instead have him turn out to be a mechanical genius. Once his illiteracy is overcome, Stanley is well on his way to becoming a captain of industry and multimillionaire. How much more important a film this would have been were Stanley representative of the normally intelligent person who is secretly illiterate, showing him overcoming his disability and taking on some semblance of an ordinary life, rather than hitting the big time. When the monied Stanley returns and asks Iris to marry him, what we are watching is clearly a prefeminist fantasy and traditional Hollywood fairy tale for adults. He is the prince who was stuck inside a frog's body, returned to his proper form thanks to her kiss. She is the Cinderella princess without a throne; the promise of a wedding supposedly solves any and all problems still existing.

Reaction to Bobby's work was modestly positive. "De Niro's performance is the best thing about the movie," Young wrote, "With his homely-handsome palooka's mug and reticent but commanding presence, he is wonderfully convincing as an intelligent man trapped inside the disability that he refers to as his 'prison.'" Denby added: "Robert De Niro has a way of speaking very simply, as if he were confiding only the most important things to us. Fit and trim, De Niro, forty-six, is more handsome than he's ever been in his career, but he carries with him his aura of strangeness. He gives Stanley a slightly hesitant, almost recessive quality and an overall neutrality, showing us how this character, by an immense act of will, struggles to convince the world that he is a civilized man. It's a fine, light, unemphatic performance and might have been great if De Niro had been given more to do."

Jane Fonda, as Iris, learning to live and love again by helping her newfound friend, Stanley, learn how to read.

One of the most respected men in organized crime, Jimmy attempts to give some good advice to Henry Hill (Ray Liotta), who wants to be a wiseguy.

GoodFellas

(1990)

A Warner Brothers Release

CAST:

Robert De Niro (*James Conway*); Ray Liotta (*Henry Hill*); Joe Pesci (*Tommy DeVito*); Lorraine Bracco (*Karen Hill*); Paul Sorvino (*Paul Cicero*); Frank Sivero (*Frankie Carbone*); Tony Darrow (*Sonny Bunz*); Mike Starr (*Frenchy*); Gina Mastrogiacomo (*Janice Rossi*); Frank DiLeo (*Tuddy Cicero*); Frank Vincent (*Billy Batts*); Catherine Scorsese (*Tommy's mother*); Charles Scorsese (*Vinnie*); Julie Garfield (*Mickey Conway*); Henny Youngman (*Himself*); Jerry Vale (*Himself*).

CREDITS:

Director, Martin Scorsese; producer, Irwin Winkler; executive producer, Barbara De Fina; screenplay, Scorsese and Nicholas Pileggi; based on the book *Wiseguy* by Pileggi; photography, Michael Ballhaus; production designer, Kristi Zea; costume designer, Richard Bruno; editor, Thelma Schoonmaker; music, various recordings; running time, 146 minutes; rating: R.

In 1985, journalist Nicholas Pileggi had just completed and seen the publication of *Wiseguy*, an as-told-to biography of Henry Hill, a middle-level mafioso who had been up and down in organized crime, ratted on his best friends, and been given a new identity under the government's Witness Relocation Program. Like all writers, Pileggi hoped he might get lucky and have his book picked up for a motion picture. But success would occur beyond his wildest dreams. As Pileggi would later recall: "I got to the office [of *New York* magazine] one day, and there was a message: 'Call Martin Scorsese.' I thought someone was playing a joke on me. So I didn't return the call. But later in the week, the phone rang at home late at night, and a voice said, 'My name is Martin Scorsese. I'm a film director. I've been looking for this book for years.' And I said, 'I've been waiting for this phone call all my life.'"

Scorsese explained his attraction to *Wiseguy:* "I was drawn to the book because of the details—life—stuff that I remembered friends saying when I was growing up in Little Italy and that I had never seen written down before." Instead of merely buying the rights away from Pileggi, then closing him out as most filmmakers would do, Scorsese was generous enough to allow Pileggi full collaboration. The two would discuss potential scenes for the film, which Scorsese then worked out in cinematic terms, Pileggi all the while listening closely to Marty's descriptions; then, each would take a copy of what they had come up with together, go off separately, and hone the results. Lengthy discussions of any given scene would follow, after which—according to Pileggi's *New York* colleague David Denby—Pileggi would type out the version they had agreed on. This routine was repeated again and again, until the script had gone through eleven drafts in a period of five months. The movie was then shot in Queens and New Jersey at a cost of $25 million.

The name would eventually be changed from *Wiseguy* to *GoodFellas,* to avoid confusion with a then-current TV series, as well as the theatrical film *Wise*

Jimmy realizes that Henry has betrayed him.

Guys. But the film that emerged is more than just an inspired version of Pileggi's book. *GoodFellas* stands as Scorsese's variation on one of his favorite films from the past, Luchino Visconti's Italian neorealist classic *Rocco and His Brothers*—likewise an ensemble picture, marked by ferociously strong acting, also concerning relationships between men. *GoodFellas* covers a large canvas in terms of time, if not place, as the thirty years in the lives of these characters occur in a self-contained, hermetically sealed universe of their own making. Scorsese includes all the qualities that have always been the hallmark of his best collaborations with Robert De Niro, though too often these elements have not been present in the films he's done with different stars: a bizarre but effective combination of edgy comedy with tense drama; an ability to portray the most graphic violence without losing sense of the serious aesthetic ambitions and degenerating into superficial exploitation; richly detailed personalities and intricately textured settings that are completely convincing. This is at once a vivid recreation of actuality and a subjective, slightly surreal personal take on the milieu. On view are remarkable technical accomplishments in editing and sound dubbing, and best of all is the sense of being propelled into a world that is both frightful and fascinating.

In short, *GoodFellas* is a masterpiece. De Niro and Scorsese had opened the eighties with *Raging Bull,* the first great American film of the decade—and, in fact, the finest movie that would appear during that entire ten-year period. In 1990, they did much the same thing again. Though the decade is still too young to predict whether any domestic film might equal or even top *GoodFellas,* what's undeniably clear is that this will be the film to beat. Dazzling to look at while making major intellectual and emotional demands on the viewer, *GoodFellas* makes clear that studio-financed films can, at least on rare occasion, lead to the most highly personal and uncompromised work.

In *America,* Richard A. Blake hailed it as "Scorsese's brilliant, funny, violent, tragic, and disturbing look at the Mafia," while Denby of *New York* called it "the greatest film ever made about the sensual and monetary lure of crime," referring to the "whole perversely brilliant movie [as] an ambiguous celebration of murderous freedom." In *Newsweek,* David Ansen wrote that the collaborators "distill these four decades of larceny into the most abundantly detailed—and frequently hilarious—nuts-and-bolts account of organized crime ever put on-screen." In the film's first third, Scorsese took the point of view of a child to communicate something that has never been effectively shown: the reasons why a little boy would want to grow up and become a mobster. "I never wanted to be anything else," we hear the upwardly

Robert De Niro as Jimmy Conway, mobster and dog-lover.

A group portrait: Ray Liotta, Robert De Niro, Paul Sorvino, and Joe Pesci as the wiseguys.

Paul Cicero (Paul Sorvino), a Mafia kingpin, joins Jimmy in instructing young Henry as to the ways of organized crime.

mobile Hill (Ray Liotta), a virtual parody of the consumer-crazed public, admit on the sound track. The eleven-year-old child, running important errands for the local gangsters, is rewarded with money and the sense of security that grows from a friendship to raw power. How pathetic and powerless his Irish father seems in comparison to the man Henry adopts as a substitute father, the much-respected local mobster Paulie (Paul Sorvino), who is treated like a king. When the school sends letters home to Henry's parents, wanting to know why he hasn't been attending, Paulie merely has mobsters threaten the postman, frightening the poor fellow to the point where he agrees not to deliver any more letters from the principal. That's the kind of respect Henry wants, the kind of respect he gets after becoming a mobster—or, as they choose to call each other, a "good fella."

"Charting Hill's progress from the 1950s to the 1980s, from innocence to corruption, Scorsese mirrors the larger evolution of American culture," Brad D. Johnson claimed in *MacLean's*. "His movie is a slice of life—and death—from a criminal culture that seems an exaggerated version of the world outside. Funny and frightening, unpredictable and provocative, *GoodFellas* may be the most authentic Mafia picture ever made." A great part of this authenticity grows directly from the manner in which Scorsese tells the story. As Henry enters a neighborhood restaurant, a seemingly endless tracking shot allows us to share with him the experience of being treated with "respect," making the seductiveness of such a lifestyle completely comprehensible to the viewer without a single word of dialogue on the subject. The cinematic technique is dazzlingly done, yet there's a similar and even more spectacular shot, as Henry brings his girlfriend (and later wife) to the Copacabana. At the time, Karen (Lorraine Bracco) does not know what Henry does for a living, but she senses something strange is going on when, from her point of view, we are literally sucked into the scene as Henry drags her past the waiting crowd, down an endless set of stairs into the bowels of the club, past smiling faces of chefs and waiters in the kitchen, then up onto the main floor where a table is reserved with champagne waiting. At this point, Karen acknowledges that the man she's dating probably does not work construction.

But the sequence, like the preceding one in the neighborhood eatery, is more than just flashy technique, showing off a filmmaker's accomplished style to no particular purpose. The technique is inseparable from the meaning of the movie: we experience the rush with the characters so we can sense—without its ever having

Jimmy listens intently as fellow mobsters Henry and Frenchy (Mike Starr) suggest a daring plan.

to be explained to us in words—how a nice Jewish girl could be seduced into the lifestyle of organized crime. Scorsese does not need to explain how this could happen, as Pileggi did in his book. Instead, he makes us share her awe, exhilaration, and sense of being overpowered by the sudden rush—and while watching, we know she's been hooked on the cheap thrills of this lifestyle.

Though long since a full-fledged superstar, De Niro was completely comfortable in assuming the part of Jimmy Conway, essentially a supporting role. The focus remains on cocky, ambitious Henry, as he ascends to power within a Brooklyn Mafia family. Liotta's voice-over immediately makes clear that Henry Hill never really wanted to be anything other than a gangster, desiring since childhood the money, women, and prestige that went along with the "profession"—though he is less able to deal with the nonstop violence that comes with the territory than are many of his friends, Jimmy Conway included. Yet Henry's plan of ascendancy—hard work, natural talent, and pure luck—is, if not doomed, then certainly limited owing to the fact that he's Irish on his father's side and so will never be accepted fully into the highest reaches of the Sicilian-controlled "business." De Niro's character is likewise a hybrid of Irish and Italian lineage who feels hampered

by this, despite his great natural gifts as a gangster. Rounding out the Three Musketeers friendship is Tommy DeVito (Joe Pesci, Academy Award–winning Best Supporting Actor for the part), an emotionally unpredictable, psychologically unbalanced character who terrifies even close companions such as Henry Hill and Jimmy Conway.

In one of the film's most horrifying sequences, Tommy grows impatient when a waiter serves him too slowly, firing a gun at the young man and hitting him in the foot. Tommy is then stunned when Henry and Jimmy want to interrupt their card game to spirit the wounded man off to a doctor. When, a week or so later, the waiter again tries to serve Tommy—dragging a bandaged foot and moving like a mummy in an old Universal horror film—Tommy notices the man's sullen (though silent) resentment and pulls his gun again, this time killing the youth in cold blood. Tommy also kills a fellow gangster during an argument in a bar, and the extended sequence in which the members of the troika then dispose of the body late at night is a masterpiece of dark, edgy comedy—always on the edge of total tastelessness, but undeniably brilliant in its on-target portrait of totally amoral characters. The three are able to drive upstate to dispose of the body only after a Mafia matri-

215

Early in the story, Jimmy takes young Henry (Christopher Serrone, left) and young Tommy de Vito (Joseph D'Onofrio) under his wing.

Years later, the aging Jimmy realizes that Henry has turned on his old mentor.

arch (played by Scorsese's mother) serves them a huge meal. The irony of the film is that Tommy, so horribly inept at being a top "good fella," has a better shot at becoming one of the leading wiseguys than do his extremely clever, highly motivated friends—simply because he is pure-blooded Sicilian, and they are not.

Like Coppola's *The Godfather*, *GoodFellas* offers a contrast between the old gangsters (perceived as men of integrity because of their loyalty to the "code" of the gangster) and the new, amoral breed. While Henry's padrone Paulie is completely against a movement into the emerging drug trade, Henry goes that route anyway. When he makes the mistake of sampling his own wares, Henry begins to "disintegrate physically as well as spiritually," as Blake put it in *America:* "Like Michael Corleone in *The Godfather* series, Henry survives, but at the price of his own soul. In the end, he has no loyalties, no resources, and no values. His upward mobility has led to emptiness. He is a hollow man. He doesn't need a rival gang or the police to destroy him; he does the job himself."

Jimmy is a mentor to Henry, and it is from Jimmy that Henry learns the new gangster code, which is do it to the other guy before he can do it to you. Following a remarkable robbery at JFK airport—the $6-million Lufthansa heist, then the largest single robbery in U.S. history—it is Jimmy who cautions his colleagues that they must for the time being resist the temptation to show off their spoils. When his fellow thieves disregard his words of wisdom, Jimmy, as greedy as he is paranoid, has them murdered, confiscating their shares. Henry, afraid that he might be next, turns in both Jimmy and Paulie; he is incapable of loyalty, even to his best friends. With Jimmy trying to kill both Henry and his wife, Henry takes on a new personality under the government's Witness Relocation Program—and in real life, if not in the film, uses his new identity to start all over again as a criminal in his new location.

Johnson found the acting "superb, and so natural that no one—least of all De Niro—seems to be performing. Although he has top billing, De Niro plays a character so oblique that he almost escapes notice." Ralph Novak of *People*, who didn't care for the film, noted only that "De Niro is predictably convincing as a businesslike hit man." Denby found it impossible to separate the work by De Niro and Pesci, so closely linked are they in the film's fabric, insisting that the former *Raging Bull* costars "connect at some level below thought. De Niro's Jimmy, a cold, calculating killer, loves crazy Tommy, and De Niro selflessly keeps himself way under Pesci's gaudy excess, goading, remonstrating, observing, enjoying." However, several critics attacked Bobby's performance. Stanley Kauffmann of *The New Republic*, in an archly negative review, wrote that "most of the acting is, at best, facile. De Niro does absolutely nothing we haven't seen him do often before; he seems content to deliver predictable product." Stuart Klawans of *The Nation* complained that "Robert De Niro has been cast more for his name than his talent; his role might have been played by anybody."

That statement, though, goes against the grain of one of the oldest truisms of performance, that being, there are no small roles, only small actors. De Niro's willingness to take a supporting role, albeit a strong one, is indicative of his seriousness as an actor. The role of Jimmy is, though certainly not focal, vivid and unique. A demanding role, it is precisely the kind of work a superstar should do to prove he's comfortable working within the complex tapestry of an ambitious story without necessarily taking over the entire film.

When an interviewer pointed out to Scorsese that Tommy and Jimmy have much in common with the characters previously played by De Niro in *Taxi Driver*, *New York, New York* and *Raging Bull*, then asked why Scorsese was attracted to such paranoid, violent-prone characters, the filmmaker answered, "There are a thousand answers to that. It's good drama. You see part of yourself. I like to chart a character like that, see how far they go before they self-destruct. It's interesting how it starts to turn against them after a while, whether it's shooting people in the street or arguing in the home, in the kitchen or the bedroom. How after a while the breaking point comes when everything just explodes, and they're left alone." Scorsese noted that when Jimmy ends up in the slammer here, he's not so different from Jake (in *Raging Bull*), likewise imprisoned, and likewise finally forced to face his ultimate enemy, that being himself: "That's the one thing he's been paranoid about all along . . . he's got to battle it out in the ring. He's got to battle it out at home. He's got to battle it everywhere until finally everybody else has disappeared, and he's dealing with himself. And ultimately . . . ultimately it's you . . . the ring [from *Raging Bull*] becomes an allegory of whatever you do in life. You make movies, you're in the ring each time. People just living daily life—when you go to work, you're in the ring."

Jimmy reasons with a mob boss while Henry stands by, listening.

NAMING NAMES:

David Merrill (Robert De Niro) stands up to the House Un-American Activities Committee during its McCarthy-era witch-hunting heyday.

Guilty by Suspicion

(1991)

A Warner Brothers Release

CAST:

Robert De Niro (*David Merrill*); Annette Bening (*Ruth Merrill*); George Wendt (*Bunny Baxter*); Patricia Wettig (*Dorothy Nolan*); Sam Wanamaker (*Felix Graff*); Luke Edwards (*Paulie Merrill*); Chris Cooper (*Larry Nolan*); Ben Piazza (*Darryl F. Zanuck*); Martin Scorsese (*Joe Lesser*); Barry Primus (*Bert Alan*); Gailard Sartain (*Chairman Wood*).

CREDITS:

Director, Irwin Winkler; producer, Arnon Milchan; screenplay, Winkler; photography, Michael Ballhaus; production designer, Leslie Dilley; costume designer, Richard Bruno; editor, Priscilla Nedd; music, James Newton Howard; running time, 105 minutes; rating: PG-13.

For the first time since *The Last Tycoon*, De Niro played a Hollywood insider from the past, though this time the era was the fifties rather than the thirties. Once

more, he played an erudite, articulate, intelligent "suit" with a conscience and a code of conduct, one of those soft-spoken roles he does so well but that have never become associated with him in the way his recurring wild men have. And once more, De Niro provided a quality performance that, sadly, was not supported by the overall film. Though this case study of a McCarthy-era blacklistee is accurate in its portrayal of the witch-hunt era, and every technical aspect of the production was first class, *Guilty by Suspicion* seemed more an educational film, created for classroom purposes, than an entertainment with social comment. Serious to the point of being somber, *Guilty by Suspicion* is a film that's far easier to respect than to admire.

Originally it was to have been called *Fear No Evil*, then *Dark Shadow*, though both those titles were scrapped, sounding too much like conventional thrillers, something *Guilty by Suspicion* definitely was not. Well-

David confers with fellow filmmaker Joe Lesser (Martin Scorsese) before Joe slips off to England lest he be arrested for his Communist affiliations; the role of Lesser was based on real-life director Joseph Losey.

Accused of being a Communist sympathizer and unfit mother, Dorothy Nolan (Patricia Wettig, center) tearfully informs Ruth (Annette Bening, left) and David Merrill that her child has been legally taken away from her.

Big-time Hollywood producer Darryl Zanuck (Ben Piazza) attempts to convince David that he ought to name a few names to the committee, so that he can go on working.

known producer Irwin Winkler (*Rocky, Raging Bull*) turned first-time writer/director took over this earnest, well-intentioned project after the original writer, Abe Polonsky (a former blacklistee himself), left, demanding that his name not be listed anywhere in the credits; with him went director Bertrand Tavernier (*Round Midnight*). Their major complaint: the emerging movie was not what they had intended, a film about an American writer-director, once a member of the Communist Party, searching for work in Europe after being forced to leave his native land or face jail at the height of McCarthy-era madness.

Winkler wanted the story to take place in Hollywood and persuaded De Niro, a veteran of his past projects, to play the role of David Merrill, a successful writer-director employed by the legendary producer Darryl F. Zanuck (Ben Piazza). Since David has been working and living in Europe for most of 1950–51, he returns to America only dimly aware of the housecleaning fervor that has swept the industry since the creation of a Washington-based committee to study possible communist infiltration into Hollywood films, which right-wing politicians fear could be used as a conduit to spread leftish ideas. One way people are able to salvage their

suddenly shaky careers is by naming names, telling the representatives from HUAC—the House Committee on Un-American Activities—the names of people who might have ties to Soviet causes. David learns that some colleague has identified him; David laughs at the thought that someone claimed he was once a member of the Communist Party; he never was, though he did attend a few meetings in the 1930s just to learn what it was all about. However, Zanuck does not see this as a laughing matter, insisting David meet with a HUAC rep to clear himself. In a shabby hotel room, David explains that he was never a card-carrying Communist; but he balks after realizing he'll be let off the hook only after naming other people.

David believes he will be supported by the Hollywood community. Instead, he's dropped from his job at 20th Century-Fox, learns from his agent that he must return the $50,000 advance he has received for a new project, and soon is in danger of losing his house. No one will socialize with him, much less hire him for a film; he can't even find live-theater work back in New York. A director named Joe Lesser (based on the real-life blacklistee Joseph Losey, played here by Martin Scorsese) tells David, on the way to the airport where he's heading to

London in hopes of finding work, that the horror has just begun. Though David's ex-wife, Ruth (Annette Bening), stands by him (literally feeding and housing her onetime husband), and the two become closer than they have been in years, his best friend, Bunny (George Wendt) approaches David, begging for permission to name David when Bunny will shortly be called before the committee.

This is the case study of a Hollywood Everyman—very middle of the road, without political convictions—discovering the world going mad all around him. The situation is Kafka-esque, but the movie's style is pedantic and pedestrian. The characters never move us to any involvement with them on a human level, merely appearing as puppets in a political tableau out to make a point. The film failed at the box office, which should have come as no surprise: audiences will happily sit through the horrors of the blacklist, just so long as the film also offers the requisite entertainment, be it drama (*The Way We Were*) or comedy (*The Front*).

Philip French, in the *London Observer,* noted: "In making Merrill a high-minded liberal who never joined the Party, the audience is put in the comfortable position of identifying with a wholly innocent victim" rather than facing the more complex issue of whether such treatment would or would not have been legitimate if leveled at a true believer in communism, there having been many such in Hollywood. For all its dramatic weaknesses, however, the film did at least bring the madness of that era back into the public consciousness, with its image of FBI agents tailing a man who is absolutely harmless. David Denby made this point in *New York* when he wrote that "this is the kind of thesis movie in which each episode illustrates some moral point [but] familiar as the material is, [*Guilty by Suspicion*] has a kind of primal horror: I could feel the anger rising in the audience when Merrill finally appears before the committee."

In part, De Niro was attracted to the project's political message and its sense of substance. In addition, he was, like the character, a workaholic who had become estranged from his family owing to a primary dedication to his filmmaking. No wonder, then, that Winkler said, "The De Niro in this film is far closer to the Robert De Niro I know than any other role he has ever played." Also, now a highly successful member of the movie community, with his TriBeCa studio in New York, De Niro couldn't help but be personally moved by what happens to David in the story, as everything that a man has worked for all his life is taken away, his success and apparent power counting for nothing. "I could easily identify with David Merrill's situation," De Niro admit-

David and Ruth realize that their comfortable Hollywood lives are all over unless he testifies against his old friends.

Writer Bunny Baxter (George Wendt) asks his friend David for permission to name him as a Communist so that he (Bunny) can continue working.

"Are you now, or have you ever been, a member of the Communist Party . . . ?"

ted, "and understand what it might have been like to have suffered through that time. If you had achieved any semblance of recognition, then were blacklisted and forgotten, it must have been suffocating. You might as well have been dead."

Whatever limitations the film had as drama, it certainly showcased the actor in a soft-spoken mode. "Looking more raffish and trimmer than he has in a while," *Variety* noted, "De Niro perfectly conveys a charming, quiet confidence at the outset. After his character's protracted confusion, he distills his true feelings during the extraordinary appearance before HUAC, finally blossoming into a man of conviction and passion. The actor pulls off this last-minute transformation beautifully." David Denby felt that De Niro's genius overcame a dishonestly written role: "David Merrill is meant to be a driven artist who has sacrificed his family to his career; at the same time, he comes off as an utterly sane, regular sort of guy. Yet the two characteristics don't fit together. . . . Merrill isn't truly interesting, yet De Niro, with his reserve, his anger, saves him from banality." Stanley Kauffmann in *The New Republic* observed that "here, adorned with curly ringlets, De Niro works—and finds the right range of vivid colors. His courageous flare-up at the end is made more convincing by him than by the script." Janet Maslin of the *New York Times* noted that "the character's very humanity, fully captured in Mr. De Niro's fine and affecting performance, is what makes his crisis of conscience so compelling. The film's climactic scene, with the camera trained closely on the actor's face as he registers all of Merrill's conflicting emotions, manages to invest a potentially familiar event with enormous tension and surprise."

Rimgale at work, attempting to learn the identity of a serial pyromaniac.

Backdraft

(1991)

A Universal Release of an Imagine Entertainment Presentation

CAST:

Kurt Russell (*Stephen McCaffrey/Pop McCaffrey*); William Baldwin (*Brian McCaffrey*); Jennifer Jason Leigh (*Jennifer Vaitkus*); Scott Glenn (*John Adcox*); Rebecca De Mornay (*Helen McCaffrey*); Robert De Niro (*Donald Rimgale*); Donald Sutherland (*Ronald Bartel*); J. T. Walsh (*Martin Swayzak*); Jason Gedrick (*Tim Krizminski*); Tony Mockus, Sr. (*Chief John Fitzgerald*); Ryan Todd (*Brian, age seven*).

CREDITS:

Director, Ron Howard; produced by Richard B. Lewis, Pen Densham, and John Watson for Brian Grazer Productions; screenplay, George Widen; photography, Mikael Salomon; production designer, Albert Brenner; costume designer, Jodie Tillen; editors, Daniel Hanley and Michael Hill; music, Hans Zimmer; special effects and pyrotechnics, Allen Hall; running time, 136 minutes; rating: R.

This film—a solid box-office success when released in the early summer of 1991, just before the advent of the seasonal blockbusters—was burdened by an overly complicated story (with so many subplots that none were properly developed) and, conversely, an oversimplistic approach to characterizations and ideas. *Backdraft* concerned the McCaffrey brothers, a pair of Irish Americans from a family steeped in a tradition of professional firefighting; their father died in 1971 going up against a blaze. Twenty years after that accident, Stephen (Kurt Russell), known as the Bull, works as a rugged fire fighter out of the same Chicago station where his dad was once employed, much to the chagrin of wife Helen (Rebecca De Mornay), who daily fears for his life. Younger brother Brian (William Baldwin), recently returned to the neighborhood, has finally decided to likewise become a fire fighter, something he's avoided

223

The cast, clockwise from top left, included: Robert De Niro as real-life arson investigator Donald Rimgale, Scott Glenn as veteran Chicago firefighter Adcox, Jennifer Jason Leigh as political aide Jennifer, and Rebecca De Mornay as Helen, a fireman's estranged wife.

since that traumatic day when he witnessed his dad's death, afterward developing a fear of fire. But big brother Stephen, fearful of the danger a panicky Brian might pose to his men, tries to intimidate the youth into quitting: "In this job, there's no place to hide. You have a bad day here, and somebody dies."

Brian, meanwhile, rekindles a romance with his old flame Jennifer (Jennifer Jason Leigh), employed by a shady politician (J. T. Walsh) out to catch an arsonist/ murderer whose weapon is "back drafts," a sudden explosion that occurs when a door is opened to an oxygen-starved blaze. At Jennifer's suggestion, Brian is assigned to work with Donald Rimgale (De Niro), also known as the Shadow, a special investigator attempting to track down the culprit. With the help of a jailed arsonist named Ronald (Donald Sutherland, playing a counterpart to cannibal Hannibal Lecter in *Silence of the Lambs*), Rimgale and Brian eventually realize the man they're after is none other than John Adcox (Scott Glenn), Stephen's fire-fighting partner and best friend—who killed off various politicians, (along with, by accident, several of his own buddies) after they voted to cut city funds to the firehouses.

The big denouement, in which Adcox (while fighting a horrible blaze) suddenly confesses everything to Stephen, borders on the ludicrous. The rest of the drama is, at best, routine. "Mac." of *Variety* correctly noted:

"Laboring mightily to disprove the adage that a good film can't be made from a bad script, director Ron Howard torches off more thrilling scenes in *Backdraft* than any Saturday matinee serial ever dared. Visually, pic often is exhilarating, but it's shapeless and dragged down by corny, melodramatic characters and situations." The brawling brothers, the husband-wife arguments, the reblossoming young love, the solving of the crime, and the male camaraderie at the station house are all portrayed in a stale, clichéd manner. Still, the film offered one great plus, the most remarkable portrait of fire ever put on film, thanks to the vivid pyrotechnics of Allen Hall.

As De Niro's character emphatically says, "It's a living thing, Brian. It breathes, it eats, and it hates. The only way to beat it is to think like it [does]. . . . The only way to truly kill it is to love it a little." This notion, the film captures brilliantly: the love/hate relationship of firemen to fire, the degree to which their fire fighting borders on a quirky, kinky romance. The firemen in the film (like the firemen in real life) do not merely rush into a burning building and squirt water everywhere. Instead, they act as a well-trained army, the officer in charge sizing up the enemy's strategy, then hurriedly planning a counterstrategy.

Filmmaker Howard (*Cocoon, Parenthood*) should have trusted his marvelous imagery; instead, he allowed

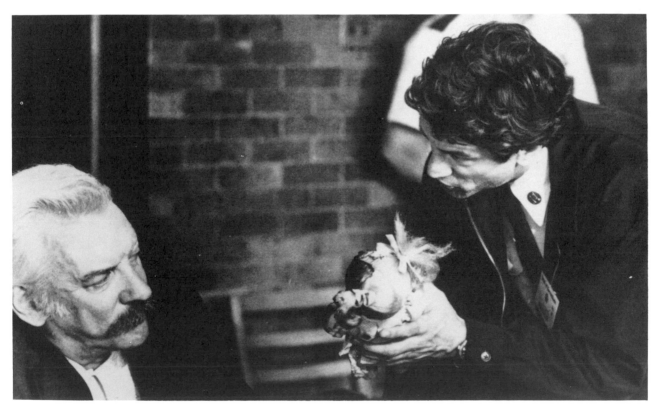

Rimgale confronts a crazed firestarter (Donald Sutherland) in jail, in hopes of picking up some ideas as to the identity of his current quarry.

Director Ron Howard and his team of experts staged the most spectacular
firefighting sequences in movie history.

226

a bombastic score to be added. The pounding, soaring, overpowering New Age quasi-mystical music simplistically attempts to manipulate the viewer's emotions and cheapens the otherwise realistic effect.

Production on the film began in early November 1990, with a sixteen-week schedule. Howard's Imagine Entertainment shot it as part of a twenty-film financing/distribution deal with Paramount, and early on the company slated *Backdraft* as their major release for the following summer. Howard had always perceived the Rimgale role as a key to the film, explaining why he was delighted to sign an actor of De Niro's stature. Before production began, Howard claimed that the character was a "charismatic, very individualistic guy who totally understands fire as an almost mystical, living entity. . . . He can talk about fire like no one else [in the movie] can because he really understands it and how it moves, how unpredictable it can be." Rimgale, then, is not only the resident Columbo of the piece, but also the film's conscience—the single voice that speaks with knowledge and perception. Though it's a supporting part, Bobby gave it as much prefilming preparation as he had his previous leads. While Baldwin, Russell, and Glenn

trained as working firemen, De Niro undertook his customary meticulous research. Learning that his character had been based on a real-life investigator, whose name actually was Donald Rimgale, De Niro traveled to the Windy City and joined the man at work. "I spent one day with him where I took him to watch an autopsy of a fire-murder victim," Rimgale later recalled. "It was rather gruesome, but he didn't flinch at all. It was impressive how he [took the] research so seriously."

Bobby then went to more than twenty-five fire scenes with members of the Chicago Office of Fire Investigation (OFI). Commanding fire marshal Chief Pat Burns later reflected, "The strange thing was that De Niro immersed himself so much into the role that we all started to think of him as just another investigator, not the Hollywood actor Robert De Niro." In fireman-turned-screenwriter George Widen's opinion, it was this hands-on research that brought such arson-oriented detective work—as well as fire fighting—to believable life on-screen: "Fire investigation is like a black art. These guys could walk into a room that the average person would look at and wonder, 'What's the big deal? You know, it's a bunch of burned walls.' [But] the fire

Kurt Russell and William Baldwin as the firefighting McCaffrey brothers.

investigator can go in and tell by the depth of the char on the wall [or] by which side of a light bulb is melted whether [this was a case of] arson or not."

So far as acting was concerned, most critics concentrated their attention on young Baldwin in his first leading role, noting that Bobby offered solid support in an undemanding part that was perhaps unworthy of his talent. Maslin noted that "De Niro has reached the stature of an eminence-for-hire, which means he now speaks lines of dialogue that do not remotely sound like words of his own." A few reviewers were negative: in the *Los Angeles Times,* Kenneth Turan—who felt that the script was so stilted it impacted on the performers—wrote: "Even De Niro's innate naturalism seems awkward and out of place in the film's contrived situations."

Georgia Brown of *The Village Voice* came closest to the truth, noting in passing that "with uncharacteristically quiet style, De Niro plays Rimgale, a smoldering ex-fire-fighter (his back is a relief map of old burns) whose weighty presence makes *Backdraft'*s theme scar tissue. Too bad some speeches he's given are clumsily written and sound as if they were inserted after the fact." Too bad also that the relationship between Rimgale and Ronald was not made the focus of the movie, allowing those old cinematic adversaries De Niro and Sutherland (who had crossed paths once before, in *1900*) to become

true doppelgängers for one another—the good and the bad man who share a basic, instinctual understanding of fire as a spiritual force.

Still, Brown's words ring true. De Niro is quiet here, a tone he has too rarely been allowed to play on-screen. His character is, as critics have noted, both "obsessive" and "intense," but Rimgale is never in danger of breaking out of a quiet mood and exploding into a barely repressed rage—Travis Bickle reconstituted as an arson investigator. Instead, any mild obsessiveness and underlying intensity are just that—quiet, in the best sense—and part of a normal, rather than a neurotic, man's makeup. Rimgale is diligent, smart, and totally professional. He can share Ronald's dark vision of fire, which calls for a complexity within his own mind and soul, yet we never fear that he'll give in to an inner darkness and become a Ronald. He is a highly serious man (though one with a sly sense of humor) who shrewdly, passionately, humbly goes about his work, an offbeat occupation that he happens to be the best at. The actor is totally believable in this very untypical role; those critics who commented that he walked his way through it were not watching closely enough. Though Rimgale was a supporting character, he nonetheless represents a major achievement for Robert De Niro, actor.

Real-life firefighters Cedric Young (second from left) and Kevin Casey (second from right) played roles in the film.

A CRACKER FROM HELL:

Max confronts attorney Sam Bowden (Nick Nolte), the man who was supposed to defend him, but did not.

Cape Fear

(1991)

A Universal release of an Amblin Entertainment/TriBeCa production

CAST:

Robert De Niro (*Max Cady*); Nick Nolte (*Sam Bowden*); Jessica Lange (*Leigh Bowden*); Juliette Lewis (*Danielle Bowden*); Joe Don Baker (*Claude Kersek*); Robert Mitchum (*Lieutenant Elgart*); Gregory Peck (*Lee Heller*); Illeana Douglas (*Lori Davis*); Martin Balsam (*Judge*); Fred Dalton Thompson (*Tom Broadbent*); Zully Montero (*Graciella*).

CREDITS:

Director, Martin Scorsese; producer, Barbara De Fina; executive producers, Kathleen Kennedy and Frank Marshall; screenplay, Wesley Strick, from the original screenplay by James R. Webb, in turn taken from the novel *The Executioners* by John D. MacDonald; photography, Freddie Francis; production designer, Henry Bumstead; costume designer, Rita Ryack; editor, Thelma Schoonmaker; music, Bernard Herrmann—adapted, arranged, and conducted by Elmer Bernstein; running time, 128 minutes; rating: R.

Ordinarily, a contemporary remake of some classic film never has a chance of competing with the perfection of the original, though that problem was not present in the case of *Cape Fear*. The 1962 version, which had been written for the screen with the intention of its being directed by Alfred Hitchcock, was instead realized by J. Lee Thompson (*The Guns of Navarone, Taras Bulba*), a competent if uninspired filmmaker. The first *Cape Fear*, featuring then-reigning superstars Gregory Peck and Robert Mitchum as, respectively, a small-town Southern lawyer and the crazed ex-con who menaces him and his family, proved a huge hit, climaxing with their deadly confrontation on an isolated, storm-racked houseboat. Still, the movie—when viewed today on home video—plays as surprisingly mundane for a supposed "classic."

Pretending to be a drama coach, Max awaits the arrival of unsuspecting Danielle Bowden (Juliette Lewis) in the bowels of her high school.

So the announcement that Robert De Niro would star in the remake (playing the Mitchum role), with frequent collaborator Martin Scorsese directing, certainly suggested the new *Cape Fear* would improve upon the original. Scorsese, as much a heavyweight for our time as Hitchcock once was, is likewise a filmmaker who brings his Catholic background to his art in terms of style, symbolism, and substance. An early decision De Niro and Scorsese made, working with screenwriter Wesley Strick (after Stephen Frears and Donald Westlake, who had fashioned *The Grifters* for producer Scorsese, left this project), was to include one of Hitchcock's favorite Catholic themes: original sin coupled with universal guilt. In Thompson's simplistic film, lawyer Bowden is a totally innocent man who witnessed one of Cady's crazed attacks on a woman, then did his duty by testifying in court. Scorsese's Bowden (Nick Nolte) was Cady's defense attorney, purposefully withholding evidence that might have let his client go free—to attack other women. Therefore, Bowden—less than pure—has largely brought Cady's wrath down upon himself and his family. This approach extends further, to the woman Cady rapes and beats in order to call attention to himself. In the original, she was a stripper (Barrie Chase), someone Bowden did not know until the brutal incident brings them together; in Scorsese's film, she (Illeana Douglas) is Bowden's cast-off mistress (which is why Cady picks her to torment), sleeping with Cady only because Bowden has left her alone and lonely. Though Cady does the beating, Bowden is, by implication, guilty—having indirectly brought about the young woman's plight. In Scorsese—as in Hitchcock—the good, however normal, are far from pure, while the bad, however evil, are something other than motiveless malignancies.

Together, then, De Niro and Scorsese seemed likely to transform the stock suspense-thriller into an important film. Surprisingly, that was not to be the case. As Todd McCarthy noted in *Variety*, "this clearly reps a case of Scorsese taking on an obviously commercial project involving material outside his interests," as compared to the artistic integrity with which he shapes, often originates, his typical projects. McCarthy rightly added that *"Cape Fear* is the most story-driven film he has ever made, as well as the one most rooted in genre." Perhaps this helps explain why *Cape Fear* is in many respects the least impressive of the De Niro/Scorsese collaborations.

The finished film offers evidence of a tug-of-war between Scorsese's gut instinct to create serious, autobiographical art, and his decision to make a commercial studio-style genre film at the request of old friend De Niro and Steven Spielberg, who together brought Marty the material when they realized Steven's commitment to do *Hook* would preclude his directing *Cape Fear.* "He tries to always do something different," Barbara de Fina—Scorsese's wife of six years and the executive producer on the project—claimed on location (Florida sat in for the Carolinas), "but the way it's evolving, [the story is] getting very personal. I see a lot of him in the characters." At the same time, Scorsese sensed that the "hyperreality" of his filmmaking approach might not jell this time around: "How can it blend with thin material?" Which explains why the director's heightened visuals, usually in perfect rapport with his material, seem inappropriate for what is, when you come right down to it, a conventional thriller.

The visual effects call attention to themselves, as if Scorsese desperately—if unconsciously—were driven by a desire to somehow take the viewer's mind (along with his own) off the fact that this project is ultimately nothing more than a genre piece. But the style, however dazzling, seems imposed on the material rather than arising naturally from it. "It gives you a pumped-up, thrill happy ride (assuming you have a stomach for violent pulp)," *Newsweek's* David Ansen wrote, "but it doesn't linger in the mind as Scorsese's richest movies do. It's a swell B movie dressed in haute cinematic couture." That "couture" included the Catholic imagery: Max Cady's recitation of a Mass in Latin as he sinks into a bog. Still, the Southern accents all ring slightly phony, while there's no sense that the director knows and understands the part of the country he's telling us about.

De Niro's Max Cady is flamboyant, to say the least, a highly intelligent psychopath, educated about the law owing to diligent reading while in prison. Max is covered with elaborate tattoos, many religious in nature, with the scales of Truth and Justice along with the biblical phrase "Justice Is Mine!" as if to remind Sam and the world that

Robert De Niro as Max Cady, a psychotic ex-con on a trail of vengeance.

it is Max who has been wronged. "I tried to create a psychopath [while working in close collaboration with De Niro] that was more interesting [than the menacing killing machine of the original]", Strick commented, "[one] who has a real sense about himself being on a religious quest. The vengeance that he's seeking is pure and just and cleansing. Not only for him, but for Sam, too. He absolutely believes that he's Sam's doom, but he's also Sam's redemption. I think Marty sees Cady's point of view. He can let his vision extend to the most black part of his characters."

Some critics were impressed, including *Variety*'s Mc-Carthy: "Quite distinct from Mitchum's more laconic villain, De Niro's Cady is a memorable nasty right up there with Travis Bickle and Jake La Motta. Cacklingly crazy at times, quietly purposeful and logical at others, Cady is a sickie utterly determined in his righteous cause, and De Niro plays him with tremendous relish and is extremely funny in several scenes." J. Hoberman of *The Village Voice* wrote that "De Niro's Cady is less the snake in the Bowden family Eden, more the projection of their unconscious fears. A cross splayed across his back, a Stalin pinup on his cell wall, he's a self-taught nut

Sam and Leigh (Jessica Lange), a modern deeply-troubled couple, try and decide how to handle this terrible threat.

job, as much a mythological beast as a unicorn or yeti. Cady's release from prison is heralded by a drumroll of thunder. He's the return of Bowden's repressed—[reminding] him that Bowden betrayed his trust. Cady is two-bit de Sade with delusions of grandeur. He sees himself as avenging angel. . . . Hair slicked back under a white yachting cap, mouth wrapped around the world's biggest stogie, tattooed torso draped in a flannel aloha shirt, half-camping on his Southern drawl, De Niro is a cracker from hell. . . . The conception is wildly baroque—and most of the time, De Niro is more crazy than menacing. . . . His Max Cady is a riff, and he never lets you forget it." *Newsweek*'s David Ansen insisted that "it is De Niro—his body covered with tattoos and the tackiest wardrobe in the New South—who dominates the film with his lip-smacking, blackly comic, and terrifying portrayal of psychopathic self-righteousness. De Niro's character is a Nietzschean superman disguised as a cigar-smoking Pentecostal sleazebucket. He has the ability to transform himself, like Satan himself, into the shape of his enemy's worst fear or desire. He can outsmart Sam at his own lawyerly games and, in the movie's best, most disturbing (and quietest) scene, seduce Danny (Bowden's fifteen-year-old daughter) by insinuating himself into her divided, rebellious heart. Cady's no longer a realistic figure but a white-trash Wrath of God."

Certainly, Ansen is right about this being the best scene. The Cady-Danielle sequence—which does not exist in the original—is fascinating if only because here (and only here), Scorsese didn't rely on cinematic pyrotechnics to make his point. Rather he relaxed and allowed a restrained camera to capture, in a single long shot, the fascinating drama between Cady, who has entered Danielle's school and slipped into the basement, and Danielle, who has gone there to meet a man she presumes is her new drama coach. Sitting on a theatrical set, Cady playacts the part of the teacher, improvising a performance for the girl who believes herself to be in a real-life situation that calls for her to act (audition) for a teacher. In time, she comes to realize this is the very man who has been terrorizing her family, though by then she has fallen under his hypnotic spell, continuing to act as if she still believed him to be the teacher even while sensing that he is not. The sequence has numerous levels, the most important being the notion that acting takes place in reality as well as in plays, life becoming theater even as theater becomes life—another theme Scorsese shares with Hitchcock. The sequence allows newcomer Lewis and old pro De Niro their best, and least stereotypical, moments. De Niro gets to play a marvelous Machiavellian villain, rather than the over-the-top monster he incarnates in most of this movie—a country-fried Travis Bickle. But those critics who were

Max exacts revenge on former attorney Sam Bowden.

typical 1990s American family: dysfunctional, with the husband and wife on the edge of divorce, their MTV-addicted daughter all but estranged from them both. The image of the modern family is raised but, alas, never developed. Simply, the conventions of the thriller plot do not comfortably allow for the delineation of such issues, which is why they muddle, rather than enrich, the proceedings.

Though Scorsese and De Niro respected the original enough to incorporate its Bernard Herrmann musical score, while casting Peck, Mitchum, and costar Martin Balsam in cameo roles, they clearly fashioned their film in the mold of the man who had originally been scheduled to direct in 1962. A week before the film's release, De Niro told me, "We spent less time reconsidering the *Cape Fear* film from 1962 than we did watching many of

Danielle and her mother cringe in fear as Max traps them on their stormbound boat.

less than enthralled with *Cape Fear* were likewise less than impressed with his performance. *The New Yorker's* Terrence Rafferty wrote: "De Niro's frenetic but thoroughly uninteresting performance is emblematic of the movie's inadequacy. He's covered with tattooed messages and symbols, but he doesn't seem to have a body. We could feel Mitchum's evil in all its slimy physicality; De Niro's is an evil that we merely read."

Certain changes from the original suggested that De Niro, Scorsese, and Strick were initially on the right track. Whereas the menaced threesome in the 1962 version is, understandably, your typical all-American family (devoted husband, loving wife, innocent daughter) of that era (the original *Cape Fear* was made just before the assassination of Jack Kennedy plunged us into the national nightmare from which we've never fully extricated ourselves), the remake features an equally

233

the old Hitchcock classics, which were truly our inspiration here." For a specific example of that generalized idea, I turned to Scorsese. He recalled the early scene in which the lawyer, while enjoying a July Fourth parade with his family, notices Cady staring at them from the other side of the street. This was nothing more than functional at best in Thompson's version; in Scorsese's remake, it is a terrific little moment, as all the other people across the way turn their heads in unison to follow a float as it drifts by, then in unison turn back to look at the next to approach—except Max Cady, who menacingly stares straight ahead at Sam and the family. "What I had in mind there," Scorsese explained, "was that great moment in *Strangers on a Train,* where the hero [Farley Granger] is playing tennis, hitting the ball back and forth. The camera slowly closes in on the crowd watching, and we see everybody's head turning back and forth as they follow the ball's movements—all except the villain [Robert Walker, Sr.], who stares straight ahead."

A wonderful moment, though one that suggests what's wrong with this movie: Scorsese has filmed *Cape Fear* as Hitchcock might do it were he alive and working today, rather than truly doing his own interpretation. Still, some critics saw this as less an homage to Hitchcock than as Scorsese's attempt to make an upscale *Nightmare on Elm Street* film, decked out in art-house mannerisms but introducing mainstream audiences to the essence of Freddy Krueger flicks: "Like Krueger," Ray Greene wrote in *Village View,* "Cady is the past perpe-

trator of horrific crimes (both characters are child-molesting murderers). . . . Krueger and Cady, though ostensibly the villains of their respective films, in actuality are the heroes. Anyone who sat through the explosion of applause that routinely greeted Krueger's first appearance in an *Elm Street* opus knows what that was about."

As always, De Niro prepared meticulously for the part. At a time in preproduction when he was still expecting Robert Redford to join him in the project (in the Sam Bowden part), De Niro turned not to the old movie but to real-life Southern prisoners. His dialect coach, Sam Chwat, would recall, "[Bobby] was trying to determine which one most resembled his concept of Max Cady. He kept coming back to this one guy." Though Chwat did not know the identity of that inmate, he did recall that the convict (apparently tattooless) had committed a "horrible assault" and was "self-possessed, intelligent, judgmental, with a strong air of personal conviction." De Niro noted that Max is "incessant. He just keeps coming and coming. What's terrifying is the idea that you can't stop someone no matter what you do. He's like the Alien or the Terminator." De Niro pumped iron to add muscle to his body, claiming, "I feel if you're going to do certain parts, you really have to commit to them all the way to make them special." There are limits even to that philosophy, though: the tattoos were not real. But the Best Actor Oscar nomination he received was.

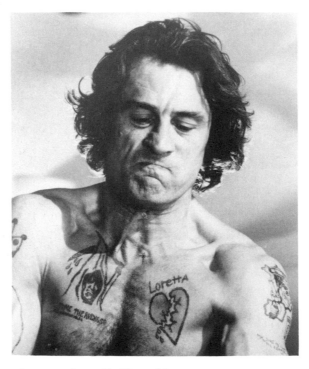

The Tattooed man: De Niro as Max.

THE BIRTH OF TRIBECA:

Robert De Niro and Danny Aiello apparently having great fun with their respective screen mistresses, Jean Smart (left) and Sheryl Lee Ralph. In fact the movie is far more bitter than this shot might suggest.

Mistress

(1992)

A Rainbow/TriBeCa Release

CAST:

Danny Aiello (*Carmine Rasso*); Robert De Niro (*Evan M. Wright*); Martin Landau (*Jack Roth*); Eli Wallach (*George Lieberhoff*); Robert Wuhl (*Marvin Landisman*); Jace Alexander (*Stuart Stratland*); Tuesday Knight (*Peggy*); Laurie Metcalf (*Rachel Landisman*); Sheryl Lee Ralph (*Beverly*); Jean Smart (*Patricia Riley*); Christopher Walken (*Warren Zell*); Ernest Borgnine as himself.

CREDITS:

Director, Barry Primus; producers, Robert De Niro and Meir Teper; screenplay, Barry Primus and J. F. Lawton; photography, Sven Kirsten; production designer, Phil Peters; costume designer, Susan Nininger; editor, Steven Welsberg; music, Galt MacDermot; running time, 109 minutes; rating: R.

With the creation of TriBeCa, his own filmmaking company and film center in New York City, De Niro

moved from pawn to producer, not only acting in other people's projects, but also instigating films he might or might not appear in. He received a "producer" credit on *Thunderheart*, a well-intentioned if uneven combination of murder mystery and message movie about Native Americans that he did not appear in. Then De Niro helped old friend Barry Primus (who played a supporting role in *New York, New York*) finally bring a pet project to realization after years of disappointment.

Stage and film actor Primus had tried developing a short, independent film about actors and came close to finding investors several times. But he and collaborator John Lawton discovered that numerous investors were willing to put up money only with the stipulation that their girlfriends (who desired to be movie stars) be given at least token roles in the picture. Primus and Lawton realized this would necessitate their taking the script in directions that would force them to seriously alter, even

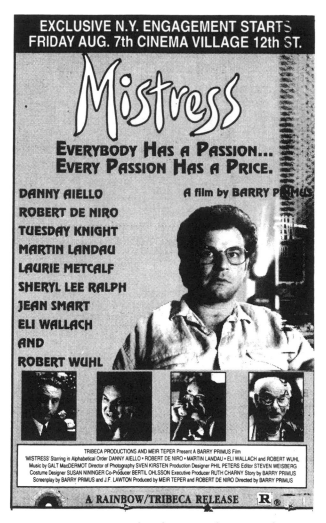

A minimalist ad campaign for a minimalist movie.

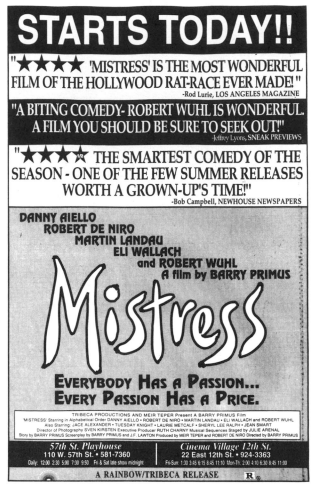

corrupt, the movie they had set out to make (writing in silly roles, and doing so specifically for nontalents).

Primus and Lawton gave up on the little movie and instead wrote *Mistress*, basing it on their experiences. Primus showed the script to a pre-TriBeCa De Niro, who loved it and took it around to power people he knew, but whom Primus could not reach, saying, "Here's another movie somebody should make someday. I don't necessarily want to be in it. I'm not in the producing game, but maybe you'll do it." No one did, fearing the film would not be a moneymaker. Primus made a thirty-two-minute short called *Final Stage* to prove he could direct, while De Niro created the TriBeCa studio, the idea being that he would not churn out more of the usual Hollywood product, but rather produce those little movies that the big boys on the West Coast scoffed at as noncommerical. Almost immediately, he put Primus's *Mistress* on his slate.

Unfortunately, the film followed closely on the heels of Robert Altman's *The Player,* also a criticism of the built-in compromises of commercial moviemaking. *Mistress* was largely written off as a hurried follow-up to *The Player* by people who had no idea just how long Primus had been trying to make his own film. Though an intimate and minor movie compared to Altman's epic, *Mistress* is in fact less pretentious and perhaps even more entertaining in its delineation of the corruption of a project, and the milieu is completely different: it's about fringe filmmaking rather than mainstream movies. Robert Wuhl plays a destitute filmmaker named Landisman (reduced to shooting cooking videos), who receives a call from washed-up producer Roth (Landau). Roth has just come across an opportunity to shoot a movie (any movie), needs a script fast, and recalls that Landisman has one. Landisman is ecstatic, but insists not one word of his manuscript be changed. Gradually, though, he gives in as he meets the moneymen (Danny Aiello, Eli Wallach, and De Niro), each of whom has (in addition to hard cash) his own ideas about how the film could be improved by the addition of a flashy role for his girlfriend. Complicating matters: Wright and Rasso unknowingly share the same mistress (Sheryl Lee Ralph), while Stratland starts sleeping with the blond mistress (Tuesday Knight) of Lieberhoff.

Most critics were hardest on Wuhl, whom they found one-note and off-putting, and kindest to Landau, who made something quite special of his sleazy role. Of De Niro's performance, *Boxoffice* magazine reported: "Since [his] company, TriBeCa Films, produced *Mistress,* it's not surprising to find him appearing in the film; but what is surprising is how singularly uninteresting his performance is. In the past, when De Niro has taken supporting turns, there's been a certain gleefulness in his acting. We remember his performances in *Angel Heart* and as Al Capone in *The Untouchables* as examples of the relish with which he performs when freed of the burden of carrying a film. Here, he is completely lifeless." This summarized the position of those who felt that De Niro—now appearing in several films a year rather than one film every several years—was spreading himself too thin, dissipating his talent. David Hunter of *Village View* found De Niro's performance "broadly drawn, imposing, and transparent." However, *Vogue* noted that Mr. Wright is "played by Robert De Niro with some of the satanic confidence he displayed as the devil in *Angel Heart.*" And Jeff Menell of the *Hollywood Reporter* wrote: "De Niro is just perfect as the implacable Mr. Wright. It is to De Niro's credit that his character doesn't overshadow the proceedings," making clear that even if he had taken a role in the film mainly to help get it financed, he had no intention whatsoever of taking over the film from friend Primus.

De Niro and Lange discuss a scene with director Irwin Winkler.

Night and the City

(1992)

A 20th Century-Fox release of a TriBeCa/Penta Entertainment production

CAST:

Robert De Niro (*Harry Fabian*); Jessica Lange (*Helen Nasseros*); Cliff Gorman (*Phil*); Alan King (*Boom Boom Grossman*); Jack Warden (*Al Grossman*); Eli Wallach (*Peck*); Barry Primus (*Tommy Tessler*); Gene Kirkwood (*Rennick*); Regis Philbin as himself.

CREDITS:

Director, Irwin Winkler; producers, Jane Rosenthal and Irwin Winkler; screenplay, Richard Price, based on a script by Jo Eisinger, from a novel by Gerald Kersh; photography, Tak Fujimoto; production designer, Peter Larkin; costume designer, Richard Bruno; editor, David Brenner; music, James Newton Howard; running time, 104 minutes; rating: R.

Though De Niro would fervently deny that there was anything but coincidence in the fact that he was now often seen starring in remakes of old movies, critics and audiences could hardly fail to note that, in short order, he showed up in *We're No Angels, Cape Fear,* and then *Night and the City,* a remake of a little British film noir thriller from 1950 that had starred Richard Widmark as a young hustler desperate to succeed in life. De Niro insisted the old film had never been one of his favorites, while director Winkler told me that one of the French filmmakers who had seen Winkler's recent *Guilty by Suspicion* at Cannes suggested that Winkler ought to do a film noir next, and that *Night and the City* would be a good choice. Without any great knowledge of the original (which has a cult following and is modestly interesting without being any great shakes), Winkler and De Niro apparently proceeded to do just that.

Kenneth Turan of the *Los Angeles Times* dubbed the result "film noir lite. A movie that wants to be hard-hitting and gritty but lacks the stomach for the job, it meanders—what should be a lean and focused narrative and ends up a letdown . . . like an athlete who has all the tools but can't function in competition." Most critics agreed, and the movie did disappointing business when released in the fall of 1992, even though there was scant competition for the adult audience the film was supposed to have appealed to. One major problem is that Winkler, the rightly respected producer of *Raging Bull* and *Rocky,* has no sense whatsoever of how to direct, merely putting together what he considers a good script with a fine cast; as a director, he remains a producer, failing to draw us inside the film's sleazy little world in a way Martin Scorsese might have done.

Screenwriter Price changed Harry Fabian from a young man to a middle-aged one, and from a nightclub tout to a low-life lawyer. Fabian (De Niro) hangs out at Boxers bar in New York (though the characters there relate to one another more as the denizens of a London pub might, an awkward shadow of the original), where his only friend, Phil (Cliff Gorman), runs the place. Still, Fabian is having an affair with Phil's dissatisfied wife, Helen (Jessica Lange, playing the role that Googie Withers did in the original; the Gene Tierney female lead from that film was eliminated for the remake). Fabian tries to get Phil to bankroll his bizarre scheme to bring back old-fashioned boxing tournaments, even though boxing in this area is controlled by the dangerous Boom Boom (Alan King). When Fabian decides to befriend Boom Boom's estranged brother (Jack Warden), he's warned by Boom Boom to make sure nothing happens to the old man—who shortly drops dead. Meanwhile, Phil has learned of the relationship between his wife and Fabian and offers to give Fabian the money he desperately needs, all the while planning to renege— and destroy Fabian's dream—at the last moment.

The main problem with the movie is that it's impossible to care about any of these small, sniveling, self-serving characters. Whereas Scorsese somehow managed to make a group of unpleasant people seem significant to his audience in *GoodFellas,* Winkler lacks the ability to make us believe that there's anything we can learn from these lowlives and their shabby dreams, or that any entertainment is to be had in watching them run around in their sad little circles. As Richard Schickel of *Time* noted, "they approach, but never attain, something like tragic status [since] as characters, they are not complicated or resonant enough to sustain that kind of grandeur [so instead] they lurch toward a conclusion that is merely melodramatic—and rather lamely so." Also, writer Richard Price never made clear whether Harry Fabian's dream of a return to the golden age of boxing is a marvelous idea that circumstances (or fate) will not allow him to pull off, or an awful idea that could not be made to work no matter how lucky he became. That is a major distinction, and without a sense of one or the other, the viewer cannot comprehend how to take the film, or the character of Harry Fabian.

Most critics were not kind. Mike Clark of *USA Today* wrote, "De Niro's portrayal half recalls, and not always appropriately, the more unctuous moments of his great tour de force in *King of Comedy,*" pointing out that Bobby had begun repeating himself—something he once cautiously avoided, but that was probably inevitable now that he was knocking off movies at such a rapid rate. J. Hoberman of the *Village Voice* wrote: "A master of fast-paced whining who doesn't seem to join the movie until halfway through, De Niro builds his performance around a succession of bob-and-weave stand-up routines—some blatantly hijacked from other movies. . . . De Niro runs a few variations on Brando's 'contender' speech from *On the Waterfront*"—and this may have been the first time that a comparison between Brando and De Niro was intended negatively! Far

Robert De Niro as Harry Fabian, the enterprising hero.

Harry discusses his schemes and dreams with bartender Phil Nasseros (Cliff Gorman) . . .

. . . and later involves Phil's wife Helen (Jessica Lange).

Harry takes a shot at the big time, enlisting retired prizefighter Al Grossman (Jack Warden) . . .

. . . but soon gets a warning from Al's powerful brother Boom Boom (Alan King).

kinder was David Denby of *New York,* who noted that "De Niro's jiggling, dancing, arm-waving performance is frenetic. Yet there's a sweetness in him that I've never noticed before." And Janet Maslin of the *New York Times* wrote: "De Niro, though sometimes straining to make Harry's antic delivery sound lifelike, creates a full and affecting character." Todd McCarthy of *Variety* added that "De Niro conveys splendidly the drive, naïveté, and edge of desperation that fuel Harry's cease-

less movement, as well as the enthusiasm necessary to convince people to do things against their better judgment."

With his appearance in yet another lesser project from TriBeCa, the onetime superstar who previously appeared in only one movie every several years in order to insure something important and original every time out was now repeating himself in movies that few people bothered to see.

De Niro and Lange, together again for the second time (following *Cape Fear*).

MINOR LEAGUE:

Mad Dog and Glory

(1993)

After Wayne Dobie (De Niro) accidentally saves hoodlum Frank Milo's (Bill Murray) life, the two strike up a one-sided friendship. (photo: Ron Phillips)

A Universal Pictures Release

CAST:

Robert De Niro *(Wayne Dobie)*; Uma Thurman *("Glory")*; Bill Murray *(Frank Milo)*; David Caruso *(Mike)*; Mike Starr *(Harold)*; Tom Towles *(Andrew)*; Kathy Baker *(Lee)*; Derek Anunciation *(Shooter)*; Doug Hara *(Driver)*; Richard Belzer *(M.C.)*; Richard Price *(Detective)*.

CREDITS:

Director, John McNaughton; producers, Barbara de Fina and Martin Scorsese; coproducer, Steven A Jones; executive producer/writer, Richard Price; photography, Robby Müller; production designer, David Chapman; costume designer, Rita Ryack; editors, Craig McKay and Elena Maganini; music, Elmer Bernstein; running time, 97 minutes; rating: R.

As the titular head of TriBeCa, De Niro now had the opportunity to control his own fate as never before; he could pick and choose his roles so as to alter his image,

casting himself to reveal his range as an actor. It's not difficult, then, to understand why he would have wanted to play the part of Wayne Dobie in *Mad Dog and Glory*; despite the title character's nickname (it's ironic), Wayne is a mild-mannered policeman, a softspoken and even timid man—providing a marvelous contrast to De Niro's recent string of nasty types, including the arrogant, ambitious heel in *Night and the City* and the crazed killer in *Cape Fear*.

Unfortunately, the film offered little more than a chance for De Niro to indulge himself in reverse typecasting. The minimalist writing of Richard Price, coupled with the uncertain, awkward, low-key tone of the director John McNaughton *(Henry: Portrait of a Serial Killer)*, conspired to dim the potential of what might have been an offbeat and engaging love story. *Mad Dog* isn't a bad film, by any means, but it is a "little" movie in terms not only of budget, but also of impact. The film might have stimulated the emotions and the intellect; instead, it only allows the audience to consider the characters from a distance, rather than become totally involved with them and their unique, intriguing plight. As with *Mistress,* De Niro appeared to be self-consciously moving out of the major leagues and into the minors.

Wayne is a Chicago police photographer, who snaps realistic shots of murder and mayhem, but would rather be off doing some romantic, aesthetically pleasing art photography. Late one night, he happens upon a robbery in progress at a convenience store, where through accident and circumstance he saves the life of another customer. In time, Wayne realizes the man was none other than Frank Milo, loan shark and gangland member who also likes to perform as a stand-up comic in his club. Gradually, Frank sucks the lonely Wayne into his twilight-world of neon, money, and power.

Calculating, clever, and quietly sinister, Milo sends Wayne a present: the gorgeous "Glory" (Uma Thurman), a virtual slave to Milo. She is expected to sleep with anyone Milo instructs her to, thereby saving the life of her brother, who owes Milo money. Wayne is as repelled by the idea as he is attracted to Glory; he wants to send her back immediately, but relents and lets her stay in his apartment, without sex, for fear she will incur Milo's wrath should she fail to "satisfy" Wayne as ordered. During their week together, however, Wayne and

De Niro as Wayne "Mad Dog" Dobie, an evidence technician in the crime scenes unit of the Chicago police force. (photo: Ron Phillips)

Milo, wondering how his new friend feels about a thank-you gift, plays Wayne a visit at the police station. (photo: Ron Phillips)

243

Glory fall in love. So when Milo stops by to pick up his possession, he discovers that Wayne will, for once in his life, stand up and say "No!"

Thurman, impressing as a beauty with talent much as the young Michelle Pfeiffer did a decade earlier, brought a radiance to her part that lit up the screen, salvaging this otherwise middling, unsatisfying film. Murray, in his first "serious" role since the disastrous *The Razor's Edge* in 1984, seemed stiff and self-conscious, a situation which never occurs in his more conventional comic work, like *Groundhog Day*. De Niro was fine, if less than truly compelling, as Wayne, through this clearly seemed a case of choosing the part over the picture.

Price, who once described himself to this author as "a New York Jewish wiseguy writer," opted for edgy comedy-drama, in which unexpected gags punctuate the serious story. His main characters are certainly unstereotypical, with marvelous little quirks that really do make them seem unique individuals rather than movieland cliches. The supporting roles, however, are all broad and Runyonesque, funny-gangsters drawn in a humor-approach, each with an immediately identifiable quirk that dictates every gesture and word. This might have worked in the hands of a more experienced and self-assured director. But as Mike Clark of *USA Today* reported, "McNaughton, a daring choice, directs in anti-sitcom style, which means he fails to punch up laugh-lines either out of choice or an inability to do so. Accordingly, occasional guffaws are the deadpan, left-field kind—very much a product of McNaughton's inclination toward long, cold, stationary-camera takes."

Certainly, the movie does not hit home the way De Niro's earlier, more conventional but also more satisfying buddy-buddy flick, *Midnight Run*, did. Still, *Mad Dog and Glory* did have its defenders, chief among them Vincent Canby, whose *New York Times* review insisted: "The great satisfaction . . . is watching De Niro and Murray play against type with such invigorating ease. Each is the other's straight man, a relationship that is hilariously set up in the initial encounter. . . . After playing a long line of larger-than-life characters, Mr. De Niro has a ball as the self-effacing [Wayne]. . . . De Niro, who put on a dangerous number of pounds to play Jake La Motta in *Raging Bull*, gives the impression of having grown shorter for his role here. . . . Not since *The King of Comedy* has De Niro had such richly comic material to work with." In *Variety*, Todd McCarthy concurred: "Robert De Niro delivers some of his best work in years."

The gift turns out to be one week with Milo's girl Glory (Uma Thurman), to whom the initially uncomfortable and uninterested Wayne soon finds himself attracted. (photo: Ron Phillips)

BACK IN THE BIGTIME:

Smooth-talking, colorful Dwight Hansen (De Niro) makes a home with Caroline Wolff (Ellen Barkin) and her son Toby (Leonardo DiCaprio). (photo: Takashi Seida)

This Boy's Life

(1993)

A Warner Brothers Release

CAST:

Robert De Niro (*Dwight Hansen*); Ellen Barkin (*Caroline Wolff*); Leonardo DiCaprio (*Toby Wolff*); Johan Blechman (*Arthur Gayle*); Eliza Dushku (*Pearl*); Chris Cooper (*Roy*); Carla Gugino (*Norma*); Zack Ansley (*Skipper*).

CREDITS:

Director, Michael Caton-Jones; producer, Art Linson, executive producers, Peter Guber and Jon Peters; screenplay, Robert Getchell, from Tobias Wolff's book; cinematography, David Watkin; production design, Stephen J. Lineweaver; editor, Jim Clark; music, Carter Burwell; running time, 115 minutes; rating: R.

De Niro leaped back into the big leagues resoundingly with *This Boy's Life,* his most auspicious film in several years. Though he once again played what was (despite top-billing) a supportive role, this time around it was in a highly-touted literary adaptation; understandably, the Warner release received much advance publicity for its artistic ambitiousness. This film did not receive any scathing reviews from significant critics, instead dividing them between enthusiastic and lukewarm critiques, the latter hailing largely from those who compared the film unfavorably with Tobias Wolff's rightly acclaimed book. On the other hand, critics unfamiliar with Wolff's memoir tended to take the film on its own merits and shower it with compliments.

Like the book, the film (which contains a considerable amount of narration lifted directly from Wolff, read aloud on the soundtrack by eighteen-year old actor Leonardo DiCaprio, who plays Wolff as a teenager) is less the traditional autobiographical novel—with names changed to protect the guilty—than a vivid reminiscence of an abused child's reality. Set in 1957, it tells the story of young Toby and his mother Caroline (Ellen Barkin) as they hurry away from her latest abusive-lover in Florida, eventually traveling to Seattle where they hope to start a new life. Once there, though, Toby falls in with some rough kids and becomes a typical 1950s juvenile delinquent, smoking, swearing, and stealing.

All this changes when Caroline meets Dwight (De Niro), whose archly conservative crewcut conflicts with the flamboyant, defiant pompadour Toby has cultivated. Sensing early on that Toby takes him for a square, the hard-edged man decides to solve everyone's problems by breaking Toby's spirit, something Toby resists, resulting in a tense battle-of-the-wills between them. What begins as a psychological war eventually resolves itself in physical conflict as the two engage in the most vivid father-son fight since John Wayne and Montgomery Clift had at each other at the finale of Howard Hawks's *Red River* in 1948.

This Boy's Life was initiated by Sony Pictures Entertainment chairman Peter Guber, who in 1989 was in charge of Guber-Peters Productions on the Warners lot. He bought the screen rights to Wolff's book; shortly thereafter, screenwriter Robert Getchell contacted Guber, expressing his own enthusiasm for the piece and offering to write the film version. Eventually, Guber and Warners parted ways, at which point Art Linson assumed the producer's position. Linson okayed Getchell after a brief meeting, then turned the writer loose to approach the adaptation however he wished. Getchell took what was an anecdotal, incidental piece of writing and added a stronger sense of storyline, beefing up the narration in hopes of providing the role with the kind of "motor" or "throughline" that a mass-market movie needs.

At this point, Linson approached frequent collaborator De Niro about playing the role of Dwight. Bobby read—in fact, studied—the book, then set off to visit Tobias Wolff, now a Syracuse University creative writing professor. Wolff recalls that De Niro showed up with an immense notebook under his arm: "It was incredible. The notebook was filled with two hundred observations about [Dwight]. De Niro would ask me about the tiniest details: What did he wear when he came out of the bathroom? A towel around his waist? Did he wear a bathrobe? Did he walk around the house naked? Did he war scivvies and a T-shirt? He compiles details like a scholar. He wanted to know everything."

Scottish-born director Michael Caton-Jones recalls: "Bob must've tried on two-hundred jackets before deciding what he'd wear in a scene, all because he saw the clothing as a statement of his character's makeup." De Niro was particularly intrigued by Wolff's descriptions of the way in which Dwight lights cigarettes in an unnecessarily involved, almost ritualistic manner, employing the

action as some sort of secret ceremony. Yet however many times De Niro read the book, he could not manage to fully understand just how he ought to play these scenes, asking Wolff to demonstrate his stepfather's action from memory. Wolff found an old Zippo lighter and performed the ritual, but De Niro still wasn't satisfied. "He had me borrow a camcorder," Wolff recalls, "and videotape myself doing it over and over. And damn it, when I went out to watch him filming, if he didn't stop in the middle of the street, take out the lighter, and—wham!—open it perfectly with one hand."

Typical of the more reserved criticism were the comments of Todd McCarthy in *Variety*, who tagged this as "a nicely acted but excessively bland coming-of-age memoir" that "provides only limited insight into a familiar situation. Result is less compelling and emotionally wrenching than it means to be." In a similar vein, Vincent Canby of the *New York Times* also felt that the whole of the film was considerably less impressive than the sum of its parts, complaining that the beautifully mounted recreation of 1950s lifestyles ironically hampered, rather than helped, the overall impact: "It's as if Michael Caton-Jones (*Scandal, Memphis Belle*) wanted to make a comedy on the nostalgic order of *American Graffiti*. *This Boy's Life* is so steeped in period detail (music, cars, television shows, hair styles) that Toby and Caroline's sad, bumbling search for freedom seems secondary to the decor [and] get in the way of Toby's personal story, which is simultaneously more melancholy and funnier than the movie is able to acknowledge." It's worth noting that the script was fashioned by Robert Getchell, who previously wrote *Alice Doesn't Live Here Anymore* for frequent De Niro collaborator Martin Scorsese; considering this story's superficially similar single mother/lost son relationship, Getchell fell into the past/pat storytelling patterns he employed for *Alice*, rather than finding a new approach to represent Wolff's unique piece.

Despite their criticisms, however, both reviewers found De Niro's performance highly impressive. McCarthy wrote that "[he] brings forth a rough charm and ferocious power to Dwight, making him the intimidating, bullheaded figure he needs to be," while Canby claimed that "*This Boy's Life* is dominated by the big, sometimes gloriously off-the-wall performance of Robert De Niro, who enters the film late but gives it a coherence it otherwise lacks." On the other hand, Mike Clark of *USA Today* noted that the "chief limitation is [the film's] viewing of De Niro's 'Dwight' character exclusively through Toby's eyes. It tends to make him one-dimensional, despite the actor's heartiest efforts." Of course, one-dimensionality is an impossibility; the worst that anyone can logically claim is that De Niro's

Dwight is two, rather than three, dimensional. However, it's impossible to take any critic seriously when he manages to misspell the author's name throughout his review, Clark referring to "Tobias Woolf's [sic] phooey-on-the-50s memoir" and insisting that the script was "Woolf-faithful" [sic].

At any rate, as for rave reviews from legitimate reviewers, David Ansen of *Newsweek* ironically took what Canby had criticized as a minus, lauding it as a plus. Calling the film a "stunning adaptation," Ansen insisted that "the beauty of *This Boy's Life* is in the details: this meticulously observed story gets the look of the late '50s down pat and, more important, captures the dissonance between the era's ideals of nuclear-family life and the painfully deracinated reality of young Toby Wolff's life. . . . This is well-crafted Hollywood filmmaking in full bloom—moving, smart and made with passion."

Dwight certainly provided De Niro with yet another challenging, complex, singular characterization: A man who is impeccably dressed and groomed, at first appearing to be the perfect father-and-husband figure for people so desperately in need of one. Dwight treats the Boy Scout oath as if it were akin to the salute to the Flag and the Ten Commandments wrapped up in one (hence,

A jubilant Dwight Hansen brings flowers to Caroline. (photo: Takashi Seida)

Toby gets a lesson in the manly art of self-defense from stepdad Dwight Hansen. (photo: Takashi Seida)

the film's ironic title); Dwight believes in truth, justice, and the American way. But there is madness rumbling just beneath the facade of health and fitness, as Dwight is a living caricature of all these qualities, grotesquely reflecting them as in a twisted funhouse mirror. In his own self-deluding way (he is a thief and compulsive liar), Dwight is a more abusive than Huck Finn's horrendous Pap, who at least made no bones about being a prime example of redneck white trash. Ansen wrote that "De Niro, always at his best in volatile parts, finds a kind of monstrous comedy in the role."

Owen Gleiberman of *Entertainment Weekly* did not agree, arguing that in "the role of colorfully dysfunctional father figure," the esteemed actor failed. "It has become clear that Robert De Niro doesn't really ignite as an actor unless he's playing psychopaths or thugs. Dwight Hansen, the raging disciplinarian at the center of *This Boy's Life*, would seem to be a role ideally suited to his gift for emotionally brutal extremes. . . .But for

This Boy's Life to work as ominous domestic drama, it's essential that we see Dwight as flesh-and-blood monster. De Niro, unfortunately, just seems to be reveling in the chance to play another viciously demented freak, like *Cape Fear*'s Max Cady. As Dwight, he mimics people with fey sarcasm, does his patented 'mean' look (turning down the corners of his mouth in fury) . . . though De Niro is physically commanding—he makes the threat of violence scarily omnipresent—there are no shades to his hollow, exhibitionist performance. His Dwight is like Jake LaMotta without the wounded core."

As this book goes to press, Robert De Niro is in post-production on *A Bronx Tale*, in which he stars and also makes his directorial debut. The film is based on the popular one-man show by New York playwright Chazz Palminteri. *A Bronx Tale* is the latest project from TriBeCa, the production company De Niro founded in 1988 with Jane Rosenthal to capitalize on his beloved

Dwight attempts to make his stepson Toby accept his way of doing things. (photo: Takashi Seida)

New York City's diverse creative and cultural resources.

Mr. De Niro also has been overseeing *TriBeCa,* an anthology series that began in March 1993 on the Fox TV network which tells weekly stories about the varied denizens—struggling artists, working stiffs, street people—of New York City's TriBeCa area. Other recent TriBeCa feature-film productions include *Thunderheart* and *The Night We Never Met.* In addition, Mr. De Niro signed in spring 1993 to play the role of the monster (originally intended for France's Gerard Depardieu, who passed on the project) in *Mary Shelley's Frankenstein,* to be produced by Francis Ford Coppola and directed by Kenneth Branagh (*Henry V*), who will also play the part of Dr. Frankenstein.

Robert De Niro as Dwight Hansen. (photo: Takashi Seida)

In the early 1960s, Lorenzo enjoys a warm relationship with his son (Francis Capra), sharing a mutual love of baseball . . .

A Bronx Tale

(1993)

A Savoy Release of a Tribeca Production

CAST:

Robert De Niro (*Lorenzo Anello*); Chazz Palminteri (*Sonny*); Lillo Brancato (*Calogero, age 17*); Francis Capra (*Calogero, age 9*); Taral Hicks (*Jane*); Katherine Narducci (*Rosina*); Clem Caserta (*Jimmy Whispers*); Alfred Sauchelli Jr. (*Bobby Bars*); Joe Pesci (cameo appearance as *Carmine*).

CREDITS:

Producers, Jane Rosenthal, John Kilik, Robert De Niro; director, De Niro; screenplay, Chazz Palminteri, from his play; cinematographer, Reynaldo Villalobos; editors, David Ray, R. Q. Lovett; music, Jeffrey Kimball, Butch Barbella; production design, Wynn Thomas; art direction, Chris Shriver; costumes, Rita Ryack; running time, 122 minutes; rating: R.

One night in 1989, Robert De Niro headed for the 91st Street Playhouse to catch a show he'd heard about, and which—owing to its theme of a young boy's moral education in a 1960s Italian American neighborhood—had piqued his personal interest. Like other theatergoers, De Niro was spellbound by actor-writer Chazz Palminteri's one-man show, relating a quasiautobiographical tale. Standing alone onstage, Palminteri created all the key characters: the youth, his father, a local mafioso, and other briefly suggested denizens of the corner of 187th Street and Belmont Avenue. East Coast native Palminteri had created the bittersweet memory piece while living in Los Angeles, where he searched

. . . though in the late sixties, things grow strained when the now-
rebellious teenager Lillo Brancato begins idolizing the local mob boss.

for parts in movies and episodic TV. Frustrated, *A Bronx Tale* was his last-ditch means of putting himself onstage when no outside offers were forthcoming. The play, which originally premiered at L.A.'s Theatre West, had been an immediate hit, leading to an invitation to bring the show to New York, where it eventually came to De Niro's attention.

Understandably the well-written roles of the boy's dad, Lorenzo, and the mafioso, Sonny, made De Niro consider this a possible screen vehicle for himself; it would be difficult to believe he didn't briefly think of optioning it as the long-awaited vehicle for himself and Al Pacino, though fans of the two stars would have to wait two more years to see them together—in *Heat*. De Niro eventually became far more interested in directing the piece. Most of his fellow heavyweights—Dustin Hoffman, Warren Beatty, Robert Redford, Jack Nicholson, Paul Newman, even De Niro's predecessor Marlon Brando—had all long since tried, with varying degrees of success or failure, their hands behind the camera.

"I really wanted to write something of my own," De Niro admitted at the Toronto Film Festival of Festivals, "but this was something I could do something with, it was the closest thing to that." At age fifty, he was entering that middle-aged period in which some actors repeat and recycle earlier performances. But a try at directing offered an opportunity for artistic revitalization.

"I really wanted to direct," he told interviewer George Perry, "from my early twenties. I wish I had directed earlier. What happens is that the years go by before you know it. Now I want to do it on a more consistent basis, but the project has to be right." Something inside him said that *Bronx Tale* was right, so he approached Palminteri directly: "I told Chazz, if you give it to a studio they'll pay you well, but there's no guarantee you'll do the part. Give it to me, and I'll guarantee it. I know what this picture is and how to do it, and I don't want anybody in my way."

Though Palminteri, still at heart more an actor than a writer, feared being cut out of the performance end, he did grasp that the very nature of the film medium would limit him to a single role, no matter who directed or what company produced. Initially Universal had planned to finance the film. Executives offered $250,000 for the script, with the understanding that he would then take a hike; recalling that nearly twenty years earlier, the young Sylvester Stallone had turned thumbs down on an offer to buy his *Rocky* script as a vehicle for Burt Reynolds, he said no. With the financial backing of old friend Peter Gatien (who would eventually be listed as executive producer of the film version), he staged it again in New York, where it came to De Niro's attention. Universal was particularly keen once De Niro made clear he would be involved, though un-

251

A director's tale: Robert De Niro guides young actor Lillo Brancato (top) and Taral Hicks (bottom) in *A Bronx Tale*.

derstandably the studio would agree to allow him to learn by doing as a director only if he would also agree to play one of the leading roles.

When De Niro accepted this arrangement, Palminteri eventually saw Universal's offer skyrocket to $1.5 million, with Palminteri now allowed to adapt his own play for the screen and, as an actor, receive second billing to De Niro. De Niro initially agreed to Universal's offer of $12 million to cover the entire film. Ordinarily a first-time director works with a crew of "guerrilla filmmakers": young talents, eager to play a part on any project, however humble. De Niro, however, wanted to bolster his directorial debut with the finest technicians in the business. Reportedly he suggested that old friend Michael Balhaus, the respected cinematographer of *GoodFellas,* do the honors on *Bronx Tale* at a fraction of his usual price—for the love of art and out of respect for and friendship with De Niro. The idealistic De Niro was reportedly crushed when Balhaus made clear he would not be interested in such an arrangement. Basically De Niro wanted to make a little movie employing the people who ordinarily make big movies. When he approached Universal a second time, explaining his film would now cost more than $20 million, they considered the fact that Spike Lee had recently brought his New York movie *Do the Right Thing* in for less than $7 million, and decided to eat their initial $1.5 million investment, pulling the plug.

At that point, De Niro's own Tribeca Productions, in conjunction with the venerable Price Entertainment, took on the responsibility of making *Bronx Tale* happen. The newly formed Savoy Pictures helped with the financing, with the understanding that they would distribute the film domestically as their premiere release, content in the knowledge that such a prestige product would set the tone they wanted for their emerging company. Additional financing came from Italy's Penta Entertainment (previously a partner in Tribeca's *Night and the City*), which would distribute the film internationally. The film was scheduled to begin production in August 1992, with a summer and early fall shoot. Plans halted when De Niro broke his foot; in September filming finally commenced, breaking briefly at Christmastime, then continuing for several additional weeks of interiors. An unexpected blizzard, as well as assorted other annoyances, caused the budget to rise to $22 million, in excess of what had originally been planned but, considering the complications, far from out of control.

Ideally the movie was to have been shot in the Bronx, though De Niro soon realized it would be necessary, for financial reasons, to do the location work in Queens, on a section of 30th Street, where it would be easier to return boarded-up buildings to their 1960s condition.

Other than himself, Palminteri, and Joe Pesci (in a cameo near the film's conclusion), De Niro decided to go the route pioneered by the Italian neorealists of the late 1940s, employing unknowns without acting experience for all other parts. "A year before we started shooting," De Niro told the press assembled at Toronto, "I said I wanted to find real people. I did not want to be using an actor, or some precocious young kid who has done too many commercials. I wanted people who were genuine, as genuine as I could get." When the film was released, most critics had only praise for De Niro's work with his cast, in particular the two youngsters who portray Calogero at ages nine and seventeen.

De Niro dedicated the film to his own father, a painter who had passed away in May of 1993, four months before the film's release. Fittingly, the movie emerged as a tribute to the institution of fatherhood, as well as (despite the vivid specifics of the story and setting) a statement of universal regret on the part of maturing children who realize, often too late, that they never properly appreciated their own fathers. For the drama, Palminteri drew on his own childhood memory of a man being shot down in the street during a seemingly minor argument over a parking space; he then refused to testify for police against the shooter. In the film, Sonny, the embodiment of the earlier mobster, befriends Calogero, admiring his loyalty, attempting to become his mentor, and offering to find him financially rewarding jobs. He means to provide the boy with an "in" to the area's Mafia elite.

This does not sit well with Calogero's father, Lorenzo, an impeccably honest, hard-working bus driver (symbolizing every Italian-American who ever resented the stereotypical view that all such ethnics are connected to the Mob). Lorenzo has the guts to stand up to Sonny and demand that the Mafioso keep away from his boy; Sonny has enough respect for or fear of Lorenzo to follow that order, at least in part, though Calogero initially resents this, wishing his own dull dad were more like the flamboyant, fascinating Sonny. Rather than gild the lily by making their story an obvious morality play, Palminteri and De Niro gave their story appreciated shades of gray. The kind, decent father Lorenzo turns out to be a closet racist, while the violent gangster Sonny has the most liberal, enlightened attitudes about mixing of the races.

Reviews were generally kind, citing *Bronx Tale* as a satisfying if less than spectacular directorial debut. "An impressive first feature," Brian D. Johnson wrote in *Maclean's,* "an energetic coming-of-age story that tempers neighborhood nostalgia with urban realism." *Newsweek's* David Ansen concurred, hailing this as "a deliciously well-observed memory piece [that neatly]

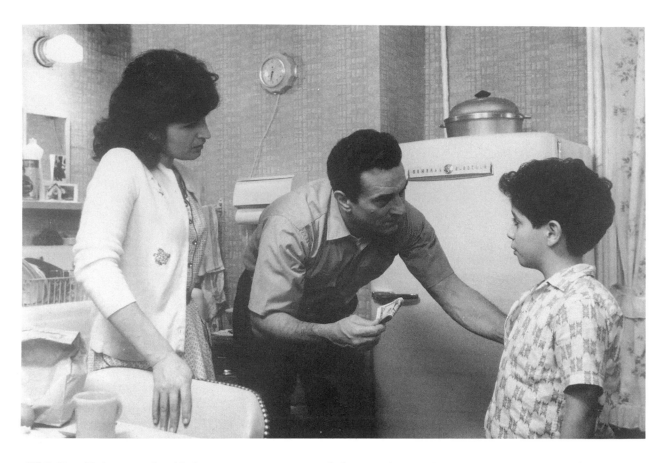

While Mom (Katherine Narducci) looks on, Lorenzo attempts to make his son realize not all Italian Americans are connected to the Mafia, and that to take money from a gangster is to corrupt oneself, however young.

views the radical social changes of the '60s through the prism of a patriarchal society frozen in its ways." Though most actors wish they didn't also have to appear in their directorial debuts (but are unable to wrangle financing unless they do), De Niro won fine notices for his performance as well: "De Niro has cast himself in the script's least showy role," *Variety* reported, "as the responsible, upright man amidst a carnival of flashy hoods, but he delivers some great scenes."

Too many critics, however, simply assumed that the film was influenced by De Niro's longtime collaboration with Scorsese. Janet Maslin of the *New York Times* fell into precisely this trap, completing her complimentary review by claiming that "This film can be seen as a natural offshoot of the work Mr. De Niro has done . . . with Martin Scorsese, whose influence is everywhere." Unfortunately she did not go on to explain, and perhaps couldn't. In fact, Scorsese's influence was in evidence nowhere, other than that both directors made movies about growing up in an Italian neighborhood, understandable considering that this was their common heritage. But Scorsese's films are, in terms of tone and

The mob boss Sonny (Chazz Palminteri, right) and Lorenzo almost come to blows over the little boy's loyalties, while another gangster (Clem Caserta) looks on.

Though Lorenzo would like his son to cooperate with the police and finger Sonny for the crime, Calogero refuses to do so.

technique, violent and unconventional, marked by ever wilder editing experiments and increasingly untraditional storytelling stylistics. Noting the difference rather than the similarity, David Denby of *New York* pointed out that "De Niro may not be a demon [with the camera] like his friend Scorsese, but he has humor and warmth of feeling." De Niro's calm, quiet approach to a conventionally unfolding story is the polar opposite of Scorsese's approach to similar material. Brian Johnson pointed out in *Maclean's* that De Niro's film attempted to "deflate the mystique of gangsterism," anything but the intent of Scorsese's films, which—along with Coppola's *Godfather* trilogy—compose the most significant examples of gangster-movie mythmaking since the Warner Brothers classics of the early 1930s.

De Niro, who as an actor for Scorsese collaborated in the process of reincarnating that myth for contemporary audiences, in his own work turned Scorsese's value system inside out. This explains why De Niro chose to play the working man, rather than the gangster role. "It's an American . . . tradition," he admitted about other people's romanticization of gangsters, "almost a folkloric thing," akin to the notion of heroic gunfighters in old westerns like *Shane*. De Niro's own film, wrongly perceived by naive critics as being influenced by Scorsese, constituted a major statement. De Niro's announced cinematically that despite his respect for Scorsese's talents and vision he himself had an entirely different view of their shared boyhood. However brilliantly Scorsese incarnates the myth, De Niro tells us that we—like Calogero—should ultimately reject it.

Which helps us understand De Niro's carefully chosen words on the eve of the film's release: "Marty has his own style," De Niro said, "and when I work with him, I never even concern myself about style. He wants me to do something, and I do it. But . . . he has his own, and I have my own."

A MONSTROUS UNDERTAKING:

Dr. Frankenstein (Kenneth Branagh) concocts his "Monster," though that term is never once used during the course of the film.

Mary Shelley's Frankenstein

(1994)

A TriStar Pictures Release

CAST:

Robert De Niro (*The Creature*); Kenneth Branagh (*Victor*); Helena Bonham Carter (*Elizabeth*); Tom Hulce (*Henry*); Aidan Quinn (*Walton*); Ian Holm (*Father Frankenstein*); John Cleese (*Prof. Waldman*); Cherie Lunghi (*Victor's Mother*); Robert Hardy (*Krempe*); Richard Briers (*Grandfather*).

CREDITS:

Producers, Francis Ford Coppola, James V. Hart, John Veitch; director, Kenneth Branagh; screenplay, Steph Lady, Frank Darabont; cinematography, Roger Pratt; editor, Andrew Marcus; music, Patrick Doyle; production design, Tim Harvey; art direction, John Fenner, Desmond Crowe; costumes, James Acheson; creature makeup and effects, Daniel Parker; running time, 123 minutes; rating, R.

By the time De Niro signed on to play the creature in *Mary Shelley's Frankenstein,* the project had already survived a series of major upheavals. The movie was originally to have been directed by Francis Coppola, who had just completed his critically acclaimed, commercially successful horror opus, *Bram Stoker's Dracula;* the two films, back to back, would have seemed fitting companion pieces, and considering Coppola's impact on De Niro's early career thanks to *Godfather II,* a reunion between actor and director was long overdue. But De Niro had not yet been approached (perhaps, if he had already been on board, Coppola might

257

My eyes abhorred you: the Creature (Robert De Niro) peers out at the master who has just created him.

have directed after all) when Francis made the decision to assemble the film under his Zoetrope production banner but leave the directing chores to someone else. Meanwhile, the public domain work was being considered for adaptation elsewhere: Jon Peters's Entertainment company was planning a contemporary redux of *Frankenstein* for Columbia, while Warner Brothers executives were trying to lure director Tim Burton and star Arnold Schwarzenegger for their proposed and certainly eccentric take on the tale.

Eventually both of those projects fell by the wayside, though Turner TV did produce a modest but effective film with Patrick Bergen as the misguided doctor and Randy Quaid as his creation. Still, it was Coppola's film—the title suggesting from the outset that this version would be more faithful to the book than had any previous movie incarnation—that attracted the most attention, especially when Kenneth Branagh agreed to direct as well as play the doctor. Coming off a pair of highly lauded Shakespearean adaptations (*Henry V* and *Much Ado About Nothing*), Branagh seemed perfect to bring prestige to the project, dispelling any notion that this would be a simple, superficial B-movie scarefest. Branagh, who was approached by Coppola while involved with a stage production of *Hamlet,* noted that

"I will visit you on your wedding night!"; the Creature holds true to his vengeful promise to Dr. Frankenstein and attacks Elizabeth (Helena Bonham Carter) in her bed.

When treated decently, the Creature responds by reacting decently, as is the case when he experiences warmth at a peasant's pigsty.

Dr. Frankenstein would be a complimentary role to play next, "the other side of that particular coin (since) Hamlet's whole journey is a preparation for death, and dealing with death is what Hamlet obsesses over," whereas Frankenstein is obsessed with life, and in fact immortality.

Branagh made it clear that, as a director, he would respect the story's undeniable elements of horror, but perhaps owing to his classical background, he was far more interested in the romance and the tragedy inherent in Mary Shelley's 1818 fairytale-for-adults.

Branagh attempted to persuade Gerard Depardieu, France's large and lumbering star (as well as De Niro's costar in *1900*), to portray the monster, assuring the "serious" actor he would not be expected to do anything bordering on camp; Branagh's heavyweight ambitions called for a total rethinking of not only the story but in particular the monster role. The famed makeup, so long associated with the part as played by Universal's legendary horror actors of the 1930s and forties including Boris Karloff, Bela Lugosi, Lon Chaney, and Glenn Strange, would be entirely eliminated. Indeed, that makeup had been the inspiration of special effects genius Jack Pierce, yet had nothing whatsoever to do with the "thing" as Mary Shelley conceived him. Branagh

Dr. Frankenstein makes ready to confront his "child" for the first time.

made clear that the word *monster* would not appear anywhere in the film, just as the term *mafia* was never once used in *The Godfather;* just as *The Godfather* emerged as a nongenre movie about gangsters, so would *Mary Shelley's Frankenstein* avoid the trappings of the traditional horror picture, redeeming the tale (essentially, a combination of gothic romance and cautionary fable) from the limitations of genre, offering instead *Frankenstein* as Merchant and Ivory might do it.

Still, Depardieu could not be convinced, so De Niro was approached, and after careful consideration decided the role was worth the considerable danger inherent in any attempt to redo a legendary part. But anyone who feared the classically trained English director-star might clash with America's most acclaimed proponent of the Method since Marlon Brando was wrong; they expressed mutual respect and liking. "One of the things I think people find exciting about watching Robert De Niro," Branagh explained, "is that you know he's going to take risks and you never know quite what he's going to be like. He was up to speed from take one. There was nothing you couldn't use. He didn't [need to] warm up. When he came on, he was *on,* and I wanted to catch that. So I'd always put two or three cameras on him and keep them running." Though Branagh hails from a theater tradition emphasizing preparation, while De Niro comes from one that calls out for improvisation, the two managed to find a happy medium. "We would try a scene one way and then another, a little this and a little that. We collaborated. He has great instincts that way." De Niro returned the compliment: "He understands how actors talk. But then actors can usually get very good performances from other actors, and even nonactors. There are too many directors who really know little or nothing about acting. If you're working with someone who doesn't respect what you are doing, then you have nothing."

Once shooting commenced at England's Shepperton

260

Studios on October 25, 1993, it was necessary for De Niro to spend a full five hours having his makeup carefully applied every day during his involvement with the six-week shoot. By this time, Branagh had decided it was his good fortune not to have won Depardieu over, as that performer's tall, hulking frame would have invited comparisons to Karloff which—be they positive or negative—were precisely what everyone wanted to avoid. "We've had the big, lurching monsters as well as all the humor that can be had out of that. I wanted somebody who could give an impression of massivity and bulk, but who would be able to do those extremes—someone who could be frightening, but also agile. Someone who wouldn't be intimidated by Karloff and all the rest, who wouldn't let the makeup dominate, but who'd act *inside*. Someone who'd be simple at times and very enraged at times—a great actor who would go through all the subtleties and extremes of the part and who you could never be sure of."

The script by Steph Lady and Frank Darabont is one of only two (the other being Hammer's 1970 *The Horror of Frankenstein*) to include Shelley's framing device: A seagoing explorer named Walton, his vessel trapped in the ice of the Arctic in 1794, unexpectedly comes across a delirious Frankenstein, who then recounts his tail even as the creature stalks about nearby. Shelley's Walton is, like Frankenstein himself, a dreamer who hopes to go where no man has gone before—one phys-

ically, the other scientifically—and who, after hearing Frankenstein's terrible fate, decides to learn from another man's mistake, turn around, and set sail for home while there is still time. He—the reader's surrogate—has been moved by the awfulness of events which began when Victor Frankenstein's mother died during the birth of his younger brother.

Following that ordeal, Victor idealistically if naively vowed to eliminate the very idea of death from the world, hoping to perform a great good for mankind. He failed to realize that he suffered from what Greek tragedians called hubris, treading on moral territory where no man ought to go. Frankenstein left his isolated home in the Alps, bidding farewell to the adopted sister he had come to love in a borderline-incest relationship, so as to study in Ingolstadt, where he and his new friend Henry fell under the influence of the eccentric Professor Waldman.

Surviving the plague that threatened those around them, the two began robbing graves, assembling a creature out of the pieces (including the deceased Waldman's brain), nurturing this creation in amniotic fluid. But when the creature finally came fully to life, the doctor found himself unable to look upon it and attempted to destroy his own "child." Lost and lonely, the thing roamed the countryside, killing some wayfarers while learning to love others, depending on their treatment of him. As in Shelley's original, De Niro's creature here fi-

As in James Whale's warmly remembered classic *Bride of Frankenstein*, the Creature is befriended by a blind peasant (Richard Briers) who does not react to the ugly face, but to a good heart and a warm soul.

nally stalks Dr. Frankenstein's own home, murdering first his little brother, then his new bride Elizabeth on her wedding night. Here, Branagh and his collaborators took their only major diversion from the book, having Dr. Frankenstein reanimate his bride, the zombie-Elizabeth then having to choose between the doctor and his creature, whom she now—as an undead thing herself—feels more comfortable with.

Brian Lowry of *Variety* spoke for most critics when he complained that, much like the character he played here, "Branagh seems to overreach himself" by adopting "an almost operatic level that's too feverish for his own good," causing the movie to "spin wildly out of control, unable to strike the delicate balance needed between pathos, romance and horror." That lack of balance is at the heart of the film's failure, as this is a movie that fails to convey an understanding of its target audience. In comparison, Coppola's *Dracula* of a year earlier managed to communicate the literary qualities of its source while still paying off those who had come to see a rousingly good vampire flick. *Frankenstein,* on the other hand, is too polite and pretentious for the audience that arrives at the theater searching for a monster movie; nonetheless, it is too rough and violent for the *Masterpiece Theater* crowd its classier elements play to.

The elegant costumes and sumptuous production designs all but called out for understatement in storytelling, though Patrick Doyle's overblown music provided an unhappy counterpart for Branagh's camera; whereas in *Henry V* he employed simple setups and let the story tell itself, here he had it furiously on the move at almost every moment, as if to compensate by swift, relentless movement (to keep the MTV crowd from getting bored) for the sedate settings and stilted dialogue (a bone to the upscale older crowd). But the results bordered on cinematic schizophrenia: *Frankenstein* came off like an arthouse movie, mistakenly assigned to a director of rock videos. According to Anthony Lane of *The New Yorker,* the film "manages to be both hysterical and tedious—an impossible combination, you might think, but Branagh pulls it off. He wields the camera like a nine-year-old brandishing a Christmas present." Brian D. Johnson of *Maclean's* saw the final results as a sorry marriage between "Old Gothic theatricality with (modern) Hollywood overkill."

If anyone seemed able to break the Karloff mold, it was De Niro. The only question was whether Branagh had the directorial ability to successfully coax the right performance out of him.

Anticipation ran high. "Curiosity about Robert De Niro's performance will almost certainly fuel box office," Lowry insisted in *Variety,* "yet the prospect of one

of the screen's greatest actors in such a notorious role doesn't live up to expectations. Despite the hoopla, De Niro's creature doesn't even approach the terror factor of his role in *Cape Fear,* while failing to inspire the empathy that even Boris Karloff—bolts and all—engendered. De Niro's makeup doesn't help matters, appearing grotesque but not particularly jarring. One can see too much of De Niro behind those scars, never really letting the actor lose himself within the character." For Lowry, and other critics as well, this was the key fault with De Niro's characterization: He and Branagh failed to make the choice between literally hiding the actor-star under makeup that would render him unrecognizable, and the other extreme of playing the creature as nearly human, in which De Niro the actor would be visible throughout. The latter approach, incidentally, worked beautifully in an early 1970s TV version (penned by the estimable Christopher Isher-

wood) called *Frankenstein: The True Story*, in which handsome Michael Sarrazin played the Creature.

The midway approach devised by De Niro and Branagh must have seemed, during preparation, like the perfect solution. But many critics not only found him wanting in comparison to Karloff's classic performance, but once again saw this as an opportunity to deal with De Niro in relationship to the actor he had, two decades earlier, replaced in the *Godfather* saga, setting up a comparison that was perhaps unwanted but inevitable. "As the monster," Richard Schickel noted in *Time*, "Robert De Niro looks like an aging Marlon Brando with his head stitched together. And De Niro acts like [later] Brando too—fake intellectual mumblings and unsuccessfully suppressed rage. His creature is somewhere between Shelley's monster, who quoted Milton and Goethe, and Boris Karloff's, who was a pre-literate child." If De Niro resembled anything, it was

Kenneth Branagh directing *Mary Shelley's Frankenstein*, deemphasizing the horror elements in favor of Gothic romance.

Brando in Coppola's *Apocalypse, Now,* one of the first of those roles (following critically acclaimed work in both *The Godfather* and *Last Tango in Paris*) that caused devoted followers of Brando's work to wonder if perhaps he was now giving a lazy, self-conscious performance.

In the early 1970s, De Niro was the New Brando: a young actor who brought to the screen (and to Don Corleone) an intensity coupled with the same organic energy that marked the young Brando's work. Those qualities were notably missing from Brando's distracted, disappointing later work. In the 1990s, was De Niro about to follow suit? In *Maclean's,* Johnson took the comparison in another direction: "De Niro . . . gives an intriguing performance—what we see of him. But, as his character acquires speech, it is hard to take him seriously; the Creature sounds like Robert De Niro doing an impression of Marlon Brando in *The Godfather* through the world's most hideous Halloween mask"; even those who appreciate Johnson's lighthearted take on the part might wish he'd referred to the questionable Brando performance in Coppola's *Apocalypse, Now* rather than Brando's final piece of beautiful work in Coppola's *The Godfather.*

Understandably, the only major critic who defended De Niro's performance was David Denby, who also stood alone in praising the picture. Whereas others complained about the visual and aural hysteria, Denby insisted that Branagh "tells the story *through* hyperbole," purposefully and effectively employing this as "the cinematic equivalent of Mary Shelley's feverish mind—the tenor of literary romanticism at its most ripe and expressive." For Denby, "De Niro's monster is nearly bald, with a strong nose and blackened eye sockets (the eyes are of different colors), and he moves rapidly but unsteadily on legs of different length, darting at times like a nervous animal. Robert De Niro, making amends for his ridiculous excess in *Cape Fear,* consistently underplays. At first, his speech is thick and halting, as if he were still the retired, drunken Jake LaMotta in *Raging Bull.* But as the Monster grows into his capabilities and speaks in rational sentences ('Who are these people of whom I am composed? Do I have a soul?'), De Niro becomes more and more moving." Intriguingly, both critics who liked and critics who didn't like the performance felt the need to describe it in terms of De Niro's earlier performances; his work now formed a cinematic canon, was a part of the popular consciousness, and served as points of reference for both De Niro and other actors as well. He was, in a sense, becoming the prisoner of his own earlier performances, for better or worse.

A romantic love gone wrong: Though Ace showers cash and presents on the money-hungry Ginger (Sharon Stone), she never forgets an earlier love affair with her pimp.

Casino

(1995)

A Universal Release

CAST:

Robert De Niro (*Sam "Ace" Rothstein*); Sharon Stone (*Ginger McKenna*); Joe Pesci (*Nicky Santoro*); James Woods (*Lester Diamond*); Don Rickles (*Billy Sherbert*); Alan King (*Andy Stone*); Kevin Pollak (*Philip Green*); L. Q. Jones (*Pat Webb*); Dick Smothers (*Senator*); Frank Vincent (*Frank Marino*); Melissa Prophet (*Jennifer Santoro*); Oscar Goodman, Frankie Avalon, Steve Allen, Jayne Meadows, and Jerry Vale playing themselves.

CREDITS:

Producer, Barbara De Fina; director, Martin Scorsese; screenplay, Scorsese, Nicholas Pileggi, from a book by Pileggi; cinematography, Robert Richardson; editor, Thelma Schoen-maker; production design, Dante Ferretti; art director, Jack G. Taylor Jr.; set design, Steven Schwartz, Daniel Ross; costumes, Rita Ryack, John Dunn; running time, 177 minutes; rating, R.

On the eve of *Casino's* late-November release at the outset of the 1995 holiday movie season, screenwriter Nicholas Pileggi boasted to the press that in some fifteen years, film historians as well as anyone in the general public who truly cares about movies would "discuss the great Scorsese Trilogy as though *everybody* knows" of its importance. Like Francis Ford Coppola's more-or-less concurrent *Godfather* trilogy or John Ford's famed cavalry trilogy from the late 1940s and early fifties,

Various portraits of Robert De Niro as Sam "Ace" Rothstein, as he surveys his little kingdom in varied moods of control, contemplation, and humor.

In Las Vegas, Ace is joined by his old pal, the trigger-happy Nicky Santoro.

Casino would doubtless be acknowledged as an ambitious multi-movie epic from an undisputed master. To a degree, that seemed a safe bet; in 1973 Scorsese had established himself with *Mean Streets* as a young turk to be watched closely, becoming a modern master over the following decade and a half before returning to essentially the same subject, though from a more mature point of view, in *GoodFellas*. *Casino* would serve as the fitting conclusion to his ongoing vision of organized crime as a harsh metaphor for the quality (or lack thereof) of life in modern America.

Casino was intended as the last of a series of concentric cinematic circles, continually rippling out in scope and ambition while always remaining true to the central vision as expressed in the first film. *Mean Streets* had taken place in a self-contained demimonde, Little Italy; *GoodFellas* stretched the perimeters of the director's physical and philosophic geography, allowing its mean-spirited but fascinating characters an extension into the immediate surrounding universe of New York and New Jersey; now, *Casino* would make clear that organized crime had also spread into the mainstream, touching places as far away as the Southwest. This—coupled with Scorsese's ever more distanced and adult perspective on

Martin Scorsese on the set with Robert De Niro. For their eighth collaboration, De Niro once again put his own artistic vision (effectively expressed in *A Bronx Tale*) aside in order to provide the gifted Scorsese with what he needed to bring an ongoing vision to life onscreen.

266

Martin Scorsese directs Sharon Stone as Ginger; most critics thought she outshone both De Niro and Pesci, perhaps because her fine work was fresh and unexpected, while they had done similar parts before.

his characters and their activities—would allow him, Pileggi, and collaborating star De Niro a sense of closure. Following *Casino,* the filmmaker would be free to concentrate on period pieces (he had already adapted the important novels *Last Temptation of Christ* and *Age of Innocence,* the former awkwardly and the latter successfully).

Pileggi had begun working on the story shortly after wrapping *GoodFellas,* his original intention to write a book. During five years of research on the project, he shared his concept with Scorsese, who became so intrigued that he wanted to make a film version simultaneous with the writing of the book, rather than waiting until after publication. Pileggi noticed that while he was writing the script, Marty was "writing the music, he's writing the shots, the visuals, the tone. He was writing a movie as I was writing a script. . . . He would have notations for music on cards, he would draw pictures on cards of scenes. He was seeing the movie in its totality in his head. He's the same little kid who sat home and used to draw these religious movies on the telephone-book edges. He makes them in his head. It's quite amazing."

But, as had been the case with Coppola's *Godfather III,* there was a critical blight on the impressive project. It received respectable reviews but was considered inferior to its predecessors. *Casino* was termed a fascinating failure, a work with endless examples of stylistic brilliance and technical wizardy that nonetheless did not completely satisfy an audience. *The New Yorker*'s Terrence Rafferty spoke for many critics when, in the midst of a review filled with qualified respect for the filmmaker's skills and impressive ambitions, he concluded that "Scorsese certainly hasn't forgotten how to make a movie; what he appears to have forgotten is *why.*"

Casino opens with what appears to be the death of its central character, Sam "Ace" Rothstein (De Niro), blown into near-oblivion by a car bomb. As Ace flies through the air (literally and, thanks to effective slow-motion and special effects, symbolically), he sets into motion a voice-over narration that will continue throughout the film, explaining how he first came to Las Vegas as well as the whys and wherefores of a grand dream gone sour. This was the era when the mob still controlled Vegas, after Bugsy Siegel had literally created the town as a jaded Disneyland for decadent adults in search of an escape valve.

Though Ace and the other key players were based on actual characters, Scorsese, Pileggi, and De Niro all agreed that the names should be fictionalized to remove their work from the limits of docudrama; this key decision allowed them to reveal details about how Vegas operated during its gangster days without being enslaved by specific facts. Scorsese and his collaborators could impose their vision on the material without being accused, as was the case with Oliver Stone in *JFK* and *Nixon,* of playing fast and loose with the reputations of real people.

According to Scorsese's version of the events, the man here called Ace was dispatched from Kansas City to Vegas in the early 1970s as a result of a liaison forged between the mob and the Teamsters union, their pension fund being the key source for money used to build various casinos. A quiet Jewish gambler, Ace is soon joined by tough little Nicky Santori (Pesci), the occasionally charming thug who can physically enforce Ace's softly spoken orders on the street. With Philip Green (Kevin Pollak), a seemingly "clean" spokesman ostensibly in charge of the operation that Ace actually runs, the casinos are soon sending suitcases full of hard cash back to the bosses in the Midwest, with everyone from bigwig local politicians to the parking attendants grabbing his chunk of change along the way. But not everyone is welcome to a share in the riches: Numberless grifters, who show up with plans to take the casinos, are violently dispatched, in graphic onscreen depictions. (The film narrowly avoided an NC-17 rating only when Scorsese agreed to trim a sequence in which a man's head is crushed in a vise until his eyes pop out.)

The virtual Eden of the casino (filmed at the Riviera, here called the Tangiers) comes to a harsh, ugly end in large part owing to Ace's own personal Eve, Ginger McKenna, the hard-edged hooker whom he marries. She, however, cannot get over her sleazy pimp boyfriend (James Woods). Sinking ever deeper into alcoholism as a result of his absence, Ginger finally falls into the arms of Nicky, becoming his lover, thereby destroying the Camelot-like existence at the casino by bedding her own Arthur's First Knight. The sharp irony in Scorsese's conception, however, is that here we have a Launcelot who is considerably less attractive than the King; a greater irony still is that the slimy, sullen Lester Diamond seems so unworthy of Ginger, the kind of repulsive man whose very touch should make her cringe. On the other hand, De Niro—in his turquoise shoes and bright yet strangely tasteful suits—had not appeared so handsome and glamorous onscreen since *The Last Tycoon,* in which he also played a softspoken Jewish entrepreneur.

Indeed, one of the movie's marvelous contrasts grows out of the extremes of De Niro's character: Ace can be as harsh as Don Corleone in *The Godfather* when dealing with gangsters and grifters, though he is an absolute pussycat when alone with his wife, tolerating her affair for as long as he possibly can, never raising a hand to her even after it has become unbearable. Ace is an un-

expectedly enlightened man in the privacy of his home, however coldblooded an operator he has to be at work. As with Travis Bickle in *Taxi Driver,* De Niro and Scorsese presented a marvelous dichotomy, two sharply divergent sides coexisting within a single believably realized person.

Ginger—who, incidentally, turned out to be anything but an unsympathetic villainess—is not the only reason the kingdom crumbles. Nicky becomes greedy, taking more than he has a right to while exacting such violence on perceived enemies that even the mob back East begins to worry about his gross excesses. Ace makes the mistake of standing up to a local power broker (L.Q. Jones), refusing to rehire the man's nephew (Drive-In film critic Joe Bob Briggs) after catching the geeky youth fixing a game for friends. Clearly, Ace and Nicky each suffer from hubris. And to display that flaw automatically brings on one's fate: The mob will reckon with Nicky, just as those locals will have their revenge when

Joe Pesci (right) huddles with Scorsese; Pesci's main concern was that he not merely repeat his role from the earlier *GoodFellas,* which had won him an Oscar.

Ace becomes vulnerable owing to a seemingly small mistake, failing to pick up a proper gaming license.

Clearly Scorsese was trying for a full tragic dimension here. According to Peter Travers of *Rolling Stone*, "Scorsese plays it as Shakespearean tragedy with Ace as an Othello so driven by jealousy and pride that he loses his wife and his fiefdom"; "Pride goeth before the fall," David Ansen wrote in *Newsweek*, "in the testament according to Scorsese and writer Nicholas Pileggi. Their ambitious epic wants to be both a definitive anthropological chronicle of the inner workings of Mafia-run Vegas and a personal tragedy. In the story of the overreaching Rothstein and Santoro . . . we're meant to see a fall of Shakespearean proportions." But for most critics, Ansen included, the tragic impact did not play properly.

The first hour of an unwieldy three-hour-plus running time is overloaded with information about the mob's Vegas system. This made *Casino* fascinating on

the level of documentary, yet none of the characters were properly developed, nor were their relationships made comprehensible, leading to a lack of compassion for them. After the first hour, the information flow began to gradually diminish, and the audience was then expected to watch the film on a different level entirely, accepting all the earlier detail as backdrop while getting into the story. But it was too little, too late; other than Sharon Stone's dazzling turn as Ginger, the other characters remained virtual ciphers. In earlier pictures, Scorsese and De Niro compelled us to sympathize with characters unworthy of that emotion; here, it is difficult to feel anything for anyone—a serious liability, especially in such a long film.

Ansen complained that "De Niro faces a problem: 'Ace' Rothstein, a former bookie and gambling expert, has the soul of an accountant. For all De Niro's weight, there's no way he can make this guy a tragic figure, and it seems a little screwy to try." But Ansen was quick to let De Niro off the hook, blaming Scorsese and Pileggi instead: "It's not the actors' fault that no one is able to break through the film's gorgeous but chilly surface. You watch *Casino* with respect and appreciation, reveling in its documentary sense of detail. Filled with brilliant journalism, *Casino* leaves you hungry for drama." Other critics, who noticed the film's flaws but wrote them off as minor missteps in a masterpiece, lauded the actor's work. Todd McCarthy of *Variety*, after praising the picture as "an extraordinary piece of filmmaking," went on to proclaim that "De Niro's perf touches a number of bases from his past, not only his outings for Scorsese but his reserved, businesslike, highly controlled Monroe Stahr in *The Last Tycoon*." Still, even such a bravura notice contained the seeds of criticism; as the screen's contemporary man of a thousand faces, had De Niro at last reached a point at which he was unable to come up with anything entirely new, now reduced to reviving performances he'd offered in earlier pictures?

"De Niro," Travers wrote, "badly miscast as the repressed Jewish outsider in a mob world, takes the eye-of-the-storm tack he tried as the Jewish film executive in *The Last Tycoon*. He simmers quietly, wearing 52 eye-bruising suits, ranging in color from salmon to pistachio, that are louder than he is." Not everyone agreed; in *The Wall Street Journal*, Joseph Morgenstern argued that "No single performance in Mr. De Niro's long career can match this one for ineffable authority. It's as if he had never heard of Robert De Niro; all his mannerisms have fallen away. He has even reduced his famous impassivity—gimlet stare, mouth turned down ever so slightly at the corners—to an absence of response, as opposed to a subtle display of unresponsiveness." What the above reviews—one positive, one negative—share is the notion that it was now impossible to review a De Niro performance without taking into account (for better or worse) the considerable body of work that preceded it.

Though Richard Schickel of *Time* praised in passing "the controlled rage of De Niro's playing" and Tom Gliatto of *People* marveled that "*Casino* is worth seeing for De Niro's powerful performance alone," it's notable that numerous critics didn't even mention De Niro's acting. That at first seems strange, considering his reputation as one of America's leading cinema actors, but the critics had a legitimate rationale. *Casino* was not the kind of film that offered its performers (other than Stone) a

Sharon Stone as Ginger, the playgirl who turns a wiseguy into a romantic hero; the role won Stone a Golden Globe Award and her first Oscar nomination for Best Actress.

chance to shine. The acting was, as in such European masterpieces as Fellini's *8 1/2*, relegated to an element in the texture of the director's sharply realized world, much like the costumes, set designs, and music. The acting was properly contained within a true auteur's personal vision, a quasibiblical worldview that defines money as the root of all evil.

"A money machine" is how Ace initially describes Vegas, and the phrase—all but thrown away in the film's context—is in fact significant. The effectively edited TV advertisements for *Casino* were played against the old rock 'n' roll standard "Money (That's What I Want)"; money is in fact not only a key metaphor here but, beyond that, the overriding concern of Scorsese's trilogy. In many respects, it is the essence of his entire body of work, though particularly in his collaborations with De Niro. When asked about the violence in *GoodFellas,* Scorsese played down this element of mob behavior, insisting that to understand the picture, a viewer had to grasp his point that violence was only a means to an end: "The film is about money. Throughout, you constantly hear them talking about who owes who how much. It's very important, because that's what they're really in business for. The violence is not the main thing—it's just a way to consolidate power and money." *Casino* takes that theme to the limit: During the opening half hour, we see more images of money onscreen than we do of the three central characters. Money is counted, collated, channeled; it is skimmed, stolen, and stored away for future use. Money is the goal of the American Dream, the false god of the capitalist state to which every character enslaves himself and for which he sacrifices others. Very often, though, each forgets why he or she wanted the money in the first place, while still pursuing it with either manic excitement or sullen obsession; characters living in the lap of luxury are ready to kill for more money than they can possibly spend.

Other key themes from earlier Scorsese–De Niro collaborations are also in evidence. *Casino* is a movie about betrayal and the abiding sense of loss when one realizes a friend will betray for hard, cold cash; "Money doesn't mean anything without trust," Ace says, mouthing the movie's message. Like most other Scorsese–De Niro heroes—particularly Jimmy Doyle and Jake LaMotta—Ace is a closet romantic, falling in love with a woman at first sight, enamored of her image though unable to accept the real flesh-and-blood person who exists beneath her shimmering surface. It's worth mentioning, though, that this notion—fully developed elsewhere—is merely suggested in *Casino.* Devoid of the rich dramatic rendering in earlier works, this led to the impression that Scorsese and De Niro had walked to the same well once too often.

Though true romantics, the nature of the De Niro–Scorsese heroes is anything but sexual; as Caryn James noted in the *New York Times*, "Like the wise guys of *Mean Streets* and *GoodFellas*, Ace puts sex and women in their own tidy compartment, like a good meal to indulge in from time to time." She might also have added *Raging Bull*, the most extreme expression among De Niro's films of such an attitude.

For his eighth collaboration with Scorsese, De Niro committed to *Casino* well before he'd seen the script, even before Scorsese and Pileggi had started working on it. As De Niro stated the week before the movie's release, "I'm very fortunate. I speak to other actors who say, 'I wish I had somebody I could work with all the time, could always rely on and go back to . . .' It's considered that your work is special, and I like that. I know that if he says it, it's going to be what he says. I also support him as a director. I'll do whatever he wants, [much the same] way he would do whatever I want, even if he feels it's not right."

TOGETHER AGAIN, FOR THE FIRST TIME:

McCauley and Shiherlis engage in one of the remarkably planned and perfectly executed robberies for which they are famous.

Heat

(1995)

A Warner Bros. Release

CAST:

Robert De Niro (*Neil McCauley*); Al Pacino (*Vincent Hanna*); Val Kilmer (*Chris*); Jon Voight (*Nate*); Tom Sizemore (*Cheritto*); Diane Venora (*Justine*); Amy Brenneman (*Eady*); Ashley Judd (*Charlene*); Wes Studi (*Casals*); Mykelti Williamson (*Drucker*); Tom Noonan (*Kelson*).

CREDITS:

Producer, director, writer, Michael Mann; coproducer, Art Linson; cinematography, Dante Spinotti; editors, Dov Hoenig, Pasquale Buba, William Goldenberg, Tom Rolf;

music, Elliott Goldenthal, Budd Carr; production design, Neil Spisak; art direction, Marjorie Stone McShirley; set design, Robert Fectman, Steven Schwartz, Paul Sonski; costumes, Deborah L. Scott; stunt coordinator, Joel Kramer; running time, 172 minutes; rating: R.

Toward the end of the 1995 Academy Awards ceremony, yet another pair of actors stepped to the podium and announced the winner of an Oscar. Only this time, the crowd hushed and took note: Robert De Niro and Al Pacino, who ordinarily didn't take time out from their work as the nation's most famous "serious" actors

Al Pacino as detective Vincent Hanna, whose life is as emotionally
messy as McCauley's is controlled and rational.

273

for the task of trading scripted gags at an awards show, had proceeded to do precisely that. Pacino received his own long-overdue Best Actor Oscar just the year before; De Niro had for some time owned both a Best Supporting and a Best Actor statuette. But winning an Oscar is one thing; presenting one, quite another. While neither seemed terribly comfortable doing the Hollywood celebrity bit, kidding each other and their audience, they not only acknowledged one of that year's winners but also set into motion the long train of hype for an upcoming film. It would be another nine months before their highly anticipated joint venture would reach the screen, yet this televised global moment helped crystallize the excited anticipation that fans had felt during the past twenty years.

Though De Niro achieved fame by assuming (from Marlon Brando) the young Don Corleone in the second *Godfather* film, with Pacino cast again as his son Michael (already a star, thanks to the first one), they played no scenes together, though they did share top billing, since Vito and Michael were viewed at different points in time in the sequel. So *Heat* promised to offer something very special: Allowing them to share a scene, it would feature De Niro and Pacino, together again, but for the first time. Everyone who cares about and follows contemporary films knew that there was mutual artistic respect and personal liking between the two, such warm feelings tempered by a certain competitiveness.

The two had, after all, been constantly mentioned for the same choice roles over the preceding two decades. "Get me Pacino or De Niro," more than one producer demanded of his underlings. Together they constituted an event. It was as if Marlon Brando and Montgomery Clift—who, as the leading Method actors of the 1950s, likewise vied for the same parts a generation earlier—had agreed to do a film in which their extreme similarities, as well as their fascinating differences, would be the unstated but all-important subtext. But other than *The Young Lions*, in which they shared star billing yet occupied separate dramatic sections of the story, Marlon and Monty didn't play a single scene together onscreen—and the loss is ours. Happily, Bob and Al did, under the guidance of Michael Mann, who had established himself as a consummate stylist via TV's *Miami Vice* and *Crime Story*, and the motion pictures *Thief* and *The Last of the Mohicans*.

Heat begins with a magnificent teaser, an intricately involved robbery that neatly set up both the filmmaker's technical prowess at presenting urban action and his Camus-like vision of criminal activity as an existential act. (The same style and theme had earlier been introduced in Mann's *Thief*.) Employing the logical strategy

of a master military man, neat and nattily dressed Neil McCauley, abetted by his cohorts, takes an armored truck in the middle of downtown L.A., grabbing a huge payroll. A recent recruit to the gang, however, goes kill crazy and shoots three of the guards, which repels McCauley, who has no desire to inflict unnecessary pain on his fellow man, any more than he is adverse to perpetrating acts of violence when he believes them necessary. As a career criminal, McCauley approaches each job as rationally as possible. He's offended, disgusted even, by sudden emotional outbursts. He has a cool, detached approach to his particular branch of criminality and likes to avoid messy emotions in his personal as well as professional life.

No sooner is the crime committed than homicide detective Vincent Hanna is on the job. Though Hanna looks a little bit like McCauley, and from a distance could be mistaken for him, the two men couldn't be further apart in orientation. Hanna is something of a slob, a burn-out who has gone through two previous wives and is about to lose his third and current one. Like McCauley, Hanna is dedicated to his craft to the point of being a workaholic, and performs it well, even excellently. Small clues even a smart cop might have missed soon send Hanna on the trail of McCauley. But while he's an absolute pro, Hanna is messy and overly emotional; he puts so much effort and energy into solving crimes that when he gets home to Justine and his suicidal stepdaughter, there's nothing left to give. On the other hand, McCauley—who plans to pull off one last great heist, then slip away to someplace warm like New Zealand—is contrastingly on the verge of falling in love with Eady, a shy young bookstore clerk.

The film contrasts their lives, Hanna's chaotic and out of control, McCauley's subdued and subtle. Yet Hanna must employ reason to crack this case, just as McCauley must allow himself a romantic involvement, at least once before he dies, even if it gets in the way of his last great work of art, the perfect crime. This dramatic situation allowed Pacino and De Niro to demonstrate the key differences that distinguish the two actors who, both Italian American and both associated with contemporary crime films, are sometimes thought of as variations on a single theme. However Pacino, like his character, tends toward a larger-than-life approach to parts, building his big speeches by starting small, then exploding toward the end, unleashing great volcanoes of emotion and, at times, bordering on pure ham. De Niro, on the other hand, has always been at his best when acting in an implosive fashion, bringing a speech down as far as he can until, by the end of a sequence, he's on the verge of disappearing into himself.

This contrast in styles reached its zenith in *Heat*

McCauley in action.

As Chris Shiherlis, Val Kilmer offered an in-depth portrait of a young
man caught in a difficult situation, helping to draw the film in
"serious" directions and far beyond its urban-action orientation.

when the two finally played a scene together, and the long awaited moment was not a disappointment. The meeting occurs midway through the movie; Mann's instincts were right to deal with it at that point, rather than forcing the viewer to hold on until the final reel, the filmmaker perhaps then finding nothing for them to do that was worthy of all the anticipation. Hanna manipulates his prey into meeting him for a cup of coffee, at which time the two let slip all sorts of secrets they would never reveal to anyone else—not Hanna to his fellow cops or McCauley to his co-criminals—about who they are, where they've been and are going next and, most important, why they are the way they are.

Mann knew from the outset that, considering the casting, more was riding on this one than even the usual colossal budget for a large-scale urban action flick. He also understood that this was a genre Pacino and De Niro had always left to the likes of Sylvester Stallone. *Heat* had to be not only a perfect example of the urban action thriller (like the first *Die Hard* film) but, beyond that, a movie that transcended the genre entirely, to make it worthy of its stars. *Heat* had to provide all the expected explosions, so that an audience attracted to such stuff would not leave unsatisfied. But it had to like-

wise play to the upscale clientele that would see the names De Niro and Pacino and expect in-depth human drama. In the eyes of most critics, Mann succeeded beyond anyone's wildest expectations.

"*Heat* occupies an exalted position among the countless contemporary crime films," Todd McCarthy announced in *Variety*. "Stunningly made and incisively acted by a large and terrific cast, Michael Mann's ambitious study of the relativity of good and evil stands apart from other films of its type by virtue of its extraordinarily rich characterizations and its thoughtful, deeply melancholy take on modern life . . . only occasionally has there been this kind of grand, even philosophical, view [in the context of a crime film] that serves to paint a bigger picture of society at large." In *Newsweek*, David Ansen hailed this as "A genre movie with epic ambitions. . . . Mann's not interested in good and evil . . . but in behavior; the choices people make, the internal pressures that can cause the best laid plans to go awry."

Naturally, the critics felt a need to comment on the screen meeting of De Niro and Pacino. "A terrific scene," McCarthy wrote, "the first ever between these two great actors, in which they exchange confidences about their extreme, abnormal lives and warn each

McCauley finds himself becoming emotional for the first time in his life when he meets a shy bookstore clerk (Amy Brenneman), realizing he's attracted (perhaps fatally) to another human being.

other that, if forced to, they'll take the other down." Without the film ever turning pretentious, the two characters—and the actors playing them—became what Joseph Conrad termed "secret sharers"; as McCarthy put it, "Playing opposite sides of the same coin, Pacino and De Niro are undiluted pleasures to watch." David Denby of *New York* also noted that the moment the two come together for their cataclysmic scene, the audience automatically becomes aware of the actors as actors, and their uneasy career-long relationship, in a way unnoticed up to that point: "The mental duel between hunter and quarry—redoubled by the implicit rivalry between Pacino and De Niro—holds the picture together. Mann demythologizes his two figures without making them any less frightening or heroic. . . . At one point, they pause in their furious activities and meet over coffee, exchanging views with ironic politeness, like two rival bankers or novelists. Mann has created a mythic moment . . . but he purposely underdramatizes the meeting, not wanting to do anything obvious, and the double meanings catch up to us slowly. These are two killer actors who despite all their differences in technique have come together."

Only Owen Gleiberman of *Entertainment Weekly*, the single major critic who damned the film with faint praise, voiced any objections: "Pacino is still doing his spasmodic overacting from *Scent of a Woman*—you know, that thing where he speaks quietly and then SHOUTS! a random word or two REAL LOUD! De Niro gives a physically commanding performance, but here, as in *Casino*, he's playing an ice-minded humanoid. Mann's most perverse decision was to cast these two legends and then keep them apart from each other. Halfway through, they finally get an extended dialogue in a coffee shop . . . and you can feel their joy in performing. We're not watching McCauley and Hanna anymore; we're watching De Niro and Pacino trying to out-insinuate each other. For a few minutes, *Heat* truly has some."

From the coffee shop scene on, the film resembles a film noir, concentrating on the themes of loyalty and betrayal among crooks who, following the big robbery, gradually turn on one another under pressure. Val Kilmer as Chris, the young gang member who cannot give up his unfaithful wife, stands out among the many perfectly realized characters who impress us as flesh-and-blood people rather than the usual array of stock movie heavies.

Mann then throws a beautiful bone to action film aficionados with a stunningly staged sequence at Los Angeles Airport. About that scene, in particular the horribly loud sounds of planes threatening to drown out the words of the two stars, Richard Shickel claimed in *Time* that it is not merely cinematic pyrotechnics but a part of the near-nihilistic view and "Mann's point. Throughout the movie, he has given us a vision of Los Angeles that goes beyond the usual sheen-and-scuzz contrasts it amuses most directors to observe. His L.A. is a void, a blankness, something like an empty movie screen—or an empty modern soul—waiting to be filled up with that most hypnotic of abstractions, violent action." The immense empty soul of the ruined American cityscape has been the canvas of some of the most important films of the past quarter century. That unpleasant but important vision of modern life has been prevalent since the late 1960s. Much of the significance of Robert De Niro's career is that he has brilliantly played many of the modern neurotics who attempt to survive in this nihilistic nightmare of a world.

279

On the field with his hero, Gil (De Niro) gets a taste of what it's like to be Bobby Rayburn (Wesley Snipes). (Courtesy TriStar/Mandalay Entertainments, photo: Linda R. Chen)

The Fan

(1996)

TriStar Pictures

CAST:

Robert De Niro (*Gil Renard*); Wesley Snipes (*Bobby Rayburn*); Ellen Barkin (*Jewel Stern*); John Leguizamo (*Manny*); Benicio Del Toro (*Juan Primo*); Patti D'Arbanville-Quinn (*Ellen Renard*).

CREDITS:

Director, Tony Scott; producer, Wendy Finerman; screenplay, Phoef Sutton from the novel by Peter Abrahams; cinematography, Dariusz Wolski; production design, Ida Random; costumes, Rita Ryack and Daniel Orlandi; editors, Christian Wagner and Claire Simpson; music, Hans Zimmer; running time, 105 minutes; rating: R.

As we go to press, De Niro's latest film, *The Fan,* has just been released with the expectation that it will be a summer blockbuster. De Niro's character, Gil Renard, might be considered a darker version of his earlier Rupert Pupkin, that adoring fan who idolized, stalked, and kidnapped a TV talk-show host out of frustration concerning his own total anonymity. But if that black comedy seems, in retrospect, a mere tip of the iceberg that began to emerge in the early eighties, *The Fan* readjusts the situation for the mid-nineties, when the general tone of life itself in America—as well as such fan stalking—has become increasingly ugly, cruel, and nasty. So now, the once harmless Rupert Pupkin has been transformed into something far more dangerous, on the order of Max Cady from *Cape Fear,* a king of horror rather than comedy.

The target of this fan is a baseball star, Bobby Rayburn (Wesley Snipes), who is adored by millions the world over. When the stadium lights blaze, men and women screech their intense appreciation of his talents. Gil reaches a point at which he cannot separate his own life from that of Bobby; since Gil can't achieve anything of value in his own mediocre life, he takes the notion of being a fan to the ultimate and vicariously lives out fantasies of glory through Bobby's successes on the diamond. When Bobby's career begins to take a downward spiral, Gil feels personally betrayed and begins to formulate a grotesque plot to return his idol to his former glory. When Gil learns that Bobby's career slump may be a result of an ongoing rivalry with Juan Primo (Del Toro), a San Francisco Giants teammate whose position Bobby has usurped, Gil starts considering murder as a possible way of returning Bobby to eminence.

The stalking of such sports luminaries as Monica Seles caused the filmmakers to believe that a statement ought to be made about the dangerous intimacy that people feel with popular athletes. Whereas Rupert Pupkin basked in reflected light and fantasized in private, Gil is more arrogant and aggressive, like the times, angrily insisting on recognition; he is the anonymous face-in-the-crowd who can explode at any moment, in some ways like Travis Bickle in *Taxi Driver,* and yet another variation on a theme that De Niro has returned to at various junctures in his career. Everyone involved with the project agreed that the film would have its intended effect only if the audience sympathized with Gil as a pathetic example of the emerging unemployed blue-collar workers who are filled with aggressive emotions owing to a system they feel has failed them, and who are desperately searching for something to add meaning to their lives.

Director Scott said:

> Bob does a tremendous amount of research for his roles and was very conscious of making the role unique. He examines every possibility. We spent several days interviewing to and talking to knife salesmen [Gil's day job], so that in the end, we knew everything about their lives, their children, the ties they wore, the cars they drove.

ABOUT THE AUTHOR:

DOUGLAS BRODE teaches the Film Directors course at the Newhouse School of Communications at Syracuse University and is the Coordinator of the Cinema Studies Program at Onondaga College. He has worked as a radio announcer, TV talk show host, film critic, and regional theater actor. His books include the college text *Crossroads to the Cinema* and, for Citadel Press, *Films of the Fifties, Films of the Sixties, The Films of Dustin Hoffman, Woody Allen: His Films and Career, The Films of Jack Nicholson, Lost Films of the Fifties, Films of the Eighties, The Films of Woody Allen, The Films of Steven Spielberg,* and *Money, Women, and Guns: Crime Films From Bonnie and Clyde to the Present.* His articles have appeared in such popular magazines as *Rolling Stone* and *TV Guide,* as well as more esoteric journals such as *Cinéaste* and *Television Quarterly.* His play *Heartbreaker* has been professionally produced, and his original screenplay *Midnight Blue,* starring Dean Stockwell and Harry Dean Stanton, was filmed in 1995 by the Motion Picture Corporation of America.

Sleepers (1996)
Marvin's room (1996)
Copland (1997)
Wag the dog (1997)
Jackie Brown (1997)
Great Expectations (1998)
Ronin (1998)
Analyze this (1999)
Flawless (2000)
Men of Honor (2000)
Meet the Parents (2001)
The Adventures of Rocky and Bullwinkle (2001)
15 Minutes (2001)